Love Misdirection

Two people. Two personal tragedies. Can an outrageous lie bring them together?

A quirky romantic comedy

Mari Jane Law

FUCHSIA

Copyright © 2024 Mari Jane Law

First edition 25 September 2024

The right of Mari Jane Law to be identified as the Author of this Work has been asserted by her in accordance with the Copyright, Designs and Patents Act, 1988.

All rights reserved. No part of this book may be reproduced in any form, or by any electronic or mechanical means – except for the inclusion of brief quotations in articles or reviews – without written permission from the author and publisher.

This novel is a work of fiction. All characters and events in this publication, other than those clearly in the public domain, are fictitious, and any resemblance to actual persons, living or dead, is purely coincidental.

Published by Fuchsia Publishing

ISBN: 9798336202434

Cover design: www.publishingbuddy.co.uk

Trigger Warnings

Themes in this book include loss of pregnancy, childlessness from past cancer and serious childhood issues. If you are affected by any issues in this book, in the UK you can get help from:

NAPAC (the National Association for People Abused in Childhood): https://napac.org.uk

The Samaritans: whatever you're going through, a Samaritan will face it with you.

 https://www.samaritans.org

BuddyHelp: connects you to trained active listeners to listen, support, and be there for you https://buddyhelp.org

The Love & Mishaps Quirky Romantic Comedy Standalone Series

Book 1: *Love & Pollination*

Shortlisted for Choc Lit's 2019 Search for a Star competition

Book 2: *Love in the Cupboard*

Readers' Favorite International Book Awards 2023, Silver Medal (Fiction: Humor/Comedy)

The Wishing Shelf Book Awards 2023, Bronze Medal (Fiction: Adult)

Book 3: *Love & Misdirection*

For more information, go to: www.marijanelaw.com

Dedication

For everyone touched by the issues in the story. May you all find your own happy endings, whatever they might look like.

Acknowledgements

I'm grateful to family and friends, Cambridge Writers, members of our romance writers' group, The Romantic Novelists' Association's New Writers' Scheme, and The Wishing Shelf Book Awards' beta readers for all the support and encouragement I've been given in writing this book. Also, thanks to Paul Burridge who designed a great cover and set up the formatting; Anjolaoluwa, Nigerian sensitivity reader and Lisa Woodford, proofreader. Any remaining errors are mine.

Mari Jane Law, November 2024

Prologue

August

A movement on the security monitor caught Harmony Payne's attention as she sat in the office, working at her desk. She stiffened as a dark figure carrying something bulky was skirting around the edge of the large, circular flower bed in front of Pinkerton Hall.

It was almost midnight and the lovely Pinkerton Hall children were in bed. Had all the outside doors been locked?

The figure, dressed and masked in black, faltered, perhaps having made out the light from the edges of the lowered blinds. When the head angled higher, the covered face appeared to be looking straight at Harmony through the lens of the camera. She found it impossible to move. But it was ridiculous to think the person could see her. How could they even know she was here?

She hadn't planned to be working on admin at this hour, but her top-floor apartment was stifling. Although she'd left the windows open wide all day, there was no breeze to cool the space down. Her heart thumped uncomfortably. Was she safe with the office windows open? No staff would be on the ground floor at this time of night... Her stomach churned.

When the figure moved again, it hurried towards the main entrance, the light-coloured footwear crunching on the gravel. The intercom bell sounded. Before she could react, the dark shape charged back towards the road, empty-handed. Small stones sprayed from beneath the runner's footwear.

What was in the package that had been left? Going by the recent news headlines, a bomb came briefly to mind. But this was sleepy Westbridge.

Could the visitor be an arsonist? Would she need the fire extinguisher from the hallway?

Perhaps they were a burglar? But they didn't bring things, they carried them away.

Why press the call button?

Why dress to blend in with the night, furtively approach the Hall and then run away?

She raised the blind and one of the sash windows further. A pillar obscured the view of the front step, but when she inhaled deeply, there was no smell of smoke, only the scent of flowers.

Was that a hedgehog she could hear? Two hedgehogs snuffling at each other? But then the tone and quality of the sound changed and she thought of an injured cat. If so, why bring it here? Pinkerton Hall was a children's home, not a pet clinic.

The wail became louder. *Was that a baby crying?*

When she opened the main door, Harmony found a large cardboard box, with "Walkers Crisps Ready Salted" written on the side, at the top of the steps. There was a tiny, kicking, wailing baby inside. Blood pounded in Harmony's ears. What if she'd gone to bed like everyone else? What if she'd not seen the intruder, heard the bell? What if the baby had *died*?

Carefully, she took the box to the office and peered into the container more closely. The beautiful little baby, in a yellow all-in-one, had light-brown skin, brown eyes and wisps of black hair, and was loosely wrapped in an unevenly knitted striped blanket. When Harmony picked the baby up, she held the soft blanket against the child's back in case a sudden temperature change might cause a chill in the fragile body.

After she gently kissed the velvet cheek, she rested the

tiny body against her chest, the sweet scent suggesting he or she had been well cared for. The cries diminished into pitiful, hiccupping sobs.

With one hand, she called the police, her trembling fingers misdialling twice. On their instruction, she checked the box for a note. There was none. The officer at the end of the phone said to check the blanket.

Cautiously, Harmony laid the baby on the soft seat of an armchair, shielding the edge with her body, and examined the blanket. The crying renewed. Harmony held a little hand in hers while flicking her eyes back to the only thing the child had come with. At first, Harmony thought there was nothing to discover. But when she turned the blanket over, with roughly formed black thread, the bottom edge revealed the word *Patience*. So the mother had named her.

Harmony's throat swelled and tears began to fall onto her cheeks. It was an effort to say the name to the officer who'd stayed on the line.

Why had the mother left Patience here? Or had someone else left her? Was the mother in trouble? How awful it must be for her, to be in a situation where she'd had to give up her child like this.

When the call to the police had ended, Harmony restored the baby to her arms. The crying was reduced to whimpers. Harmony shushed and reassured while stroking the baby's back and kissing her forehead. The jerky rise and fall of the child's chest gradually settled into a smoother breathing cycle.

It was hard to speak coherently when Harmony phoned Candy, the live-in manager. Candy lived in the adjoining apartment to Harmony's on the top floor of the Hall, so she'd reach the office ahead of the police and ambulance.

The baby, Patience, was so small, so defenceless. Longing welled up inside Harmony. It had taken years to accept what had happened, to come to terms with her life and what she expected from it—or rather, didn't expect from it. But here, in her arms, was an abandoned baby. A door that had been locked for so long swung open and a dreadful hope began to grow. Somewhere out there was a mother who couldn't bring up her own child but had instead sought a better life for her daughter.

Harmony's heart beat faster. *Could she keep Patience and bring her up as her own?*

1

Late October

While singing *My Favourite Things* from *The Sound of Music*, Harmony dressed a happy Patience in the bedroom of her apartment for a trip to a baby group in Bristol. No one would have guessed this contented baby was the same as the colicky child who wouldn't settle for hours the night before, her knees rising as she bawled from pain. Halfway through the song, she cooed in cute accompaniment raising Harmony's hopes she'd grow up to be a music lover too — but more confident than Harmony had been.

Although in the past she'd managed to perform in concerts on stage, she'd been acting a part — and had fallen apart in the end. Being herself in the rest of the world, outside of the role of a concert pianist, was so much harder and always had been.

She felt secure in Pinkerton Hall, perhaps because she was so familiar with the place, had been instrumental in setting up the children's home, the first to move in. But outside this oasis of comfort, she was more like a nervous kitten than a proud lion.

Now, as she drove along the country roads of Westbridge towards the bustle of Bristol city centre, her heart was drumming quietly, like the soft touch of drumsticks on a snare drum — tap, tap, tap. She would cope...

In joining the weekly baby group, she was doing the right thing, wasn't she? Her life was so consumed by her passion for children, she didn't have a single friend outside of work, which made it impossible for Patience, if she were to become Harmony's adopted child, to have friends.

Not far from the café on Whiteladies Road in Clifton, Harmony nabbed a parking place. The October wind was biting cold when she joined Patience in the back to take her from her car seat. The baby's wide, trusting eyes watched her. Like her skin, they'd become a richer, deeper brown, and Harmony's heart brimmed over with love, sending a delicious warmth around her body from tip to toe.

Gently, she nuzzled Patience's nose and kissed her delicate cheek. The baby waved her arms, softly cooing, and gave a delightful smile when Harmony chuckled. As she stroked the baby's temple, tiny fingers inside yellow mittens connected with hers.

'I love you so, so much. But you need your mummy, don't you?' And, if she wasn't discovered, and no more suitable adoptive parent was found, Harmony hoped the local authority would change her role from foster mum to adoptive mum. She imagined registering the child at a nursery, proudly giving the name Patience Payne...

When Annie Swannie, the 45-year-old social worker for many of the Hall's children, had been looking for a foster carer for Patience, Harmony would have begged on her knees to be that person. But as she was already approved to work with children, and no foster parent of Black heritage had been available, the process to approve her for the role had been straightforward. But the next step, she knew, would likely be far from it.

When the baby was attached around her body in the carrier, she stepped out of the car to put her coat on over her jeans and jumper so the side panels acted as a windbreaker. Patience's shell-pink all-in-one and matching yellow hat and mittens might not be enough to keep her cosy.

Harmony's reflection in the car window showed a mussed-up fringe. Long wisps of hair had escaped the high ponytail, haloing her face as gusts of wind whipped about her. She didn't look forward to combing out the inevitable knots.

As she paid for the parking ticket, her stomach clenched and her nerves zinged. The idea of trying to make new friends terrified her. Ten years ago, her confidence had been at an all-time low. It only pretended to be back in Pinkerton Hall, where she'd essentially buried herself alive.

When she reached the address, she took a deep breath, shut her eyes and pushed the door open. Scents of freshly ground coffee and warm chocolate wafted towards her. As her gaze fell on a counter displaying enticing cakes thick with chocolate and vanilla icing, some brownies, chocolate chip cookies and flapjacks, she was reminded of the café on High Street in Westbridge.

At least ten women with babies sat at various tables and there was still plenty of space for more customers.

The thrum of her heart strengthened. *She could do this, must do this, for Patience.* Although Harmony had developed resilience over the years, ever since the baby had arrived, her insides had turned to slush. *The old wound had reopened.*

When her gaze settled on a breastfeeding woman in the far corner, Harmony's heartbeat stopped for a moment, then it thumped like a hard-hit bass drum. Life had dealt her some tough blows. If things had been different, she would have had a baby to breastfeed. If only the child had had a chance to be born.

It had been a ridiculous idea to come.

As she turned towards the door, her ponytail swinging with the movement, a voice behind her said in a strong West Country accent, 'Hi. I don't remember seeing you here before. Come and join us.'

Facing the room again, Harmony caught the young woman's welcoming smile.

'There's no need to be shy,' the woman said. 'I know it

can be daunting walking into a place full of new people. Is this your first baby?'

Unable to speak, her throat as taut as piano string, Harmony nodded. She registered an impulse to run, but her limbs were just as paralysed as her voice box. Might she find a back door if she followed the sign for the loos once her muscles were under her command again?

'It'll be a culture shock too then,' the young woman continued. 'It opens up a whole new world once you've given birth. I'm Sophie by the way.'

Harmony cleared her throat and licked her dry lips. 'Harmony.' It came out as a croak.

'And your baby's name? How old is…?' Sophie gave a meaningful tilt to her head, indicating she was reluctant to guess the pronoun.

Pricks of tears formed in Harmony's eyes. She was unable to explain the situation. 'Patience… about nine weeks.' Give or take.

Her gaze darted around the room. Should she escape now? The slushy vulnerability that had been switched back on told her she wouldn't cope for much longer without bursting into full flow. But another woman was blocking the main door. Short of shoving her out of the way, she would have to have some form of conversation to get the mum to move.

Sophie touched her arm. 'Are you all right? A touch of the baby blues?'

What to do? Tell the truth and have an emotional outburst? Or… *play along*.

Harmony nodded.

'It does get better. We've all been through some rough patches so we understand. You're in the right place.'

She nodded again.

Although it was warm enough inside the café, she pulled at the panels of her coat as though for protection. But when Sophie said, 'Don't worry about the extra weight, it'll come off soon enough,' it was clear Sophie thought her coat wouldn't do up, even if Patience weren't adding to her bulk.

Harmony hadn't been worrying about any extra weight. She'd gone up a dress size... or two... through comfort eating after... after the things she tried not to think about had happened. But she mustered up a smile. It wasn't Sophie's fault she'd mistaken Harmony's normal appearance for a post-pregnancy body shape.

'Come and meet some other first-timers.'

Sophie led her towards an empty sofa. The woman sitting opposite looked closer to forty than Harmony herself. A younger blond-haired man sat beside the woman.

'Guys, this is Harmony with Patience who's nine weeks old. I'll leave you to get to know one another.' Then Sophie spun on her heel and left to greet another mum.

'Hi. I'm Miranda.'

The woman's short hair was darker than Harmony's russet hair, but the girth of her figure could be a match. The same couldn't be said of their taste in clothing. The red trousers and orange roll-neck sweater clashed with the muted colours Harmony tended to opt for. Miranda probably considered Harmony's old camel wool coat boring compared to her pink, puffy anorak.

Miranda freed a hand from the baby dressed in green sitting on her lap to give a little wave.

Harmony gave a little wave back. 'Hi.' She removed her coat and Patience's yellow hat and mittens.

The man rose to grab her hand across the table. 'I'm Luke.'

With his height and physique, she'd bet he was keen on sports or working out, despite the definition of any upper body muscles being hidden by his thick, grey jumper. His crushing grip felt proof enough.

Until August, she'd thought she'd healed from past wounds, but since the baby's arrival, she'd been living on tenterhooks. She glanced towards the loos and the possible escape route but then reconsidered and settled herself on the sofa. She must learn not to overreact.

It was strange, sitting with the only couple here while she was on her own. 'So, you're new too?'

'Yes,' he said. 'And if you hadn't arrived, I don't think we'd have had anyone else to talk to.'

'Oh?'

'When I told Luke I was coming here,' Miranda said, 'he insisted on taking time off work to come too.'

'But I don't think I'll come again. It's not congenial enough for me.'

'People have such stereotypes, don't you think?' Miranda asked. 'Wherever we go, we're the odd ones out. But there are plenty of people who've done what we've done; it's not unusual anymore.'

Before Harmony could ask what Miranda meant, he said, 'It's even worse when Gavin's with us.'

'Gavin's the other dad,' Miranda chipped in.

'I'm Daddy and Gavin's Dad,' Luke clarified.

Harmony worried she'd offend them by making a social blunder, but what relationship permutation did the three of them have?

Luckily, Miranda explained. 'Luke's the biological father. Gavin is his husband.'

Luke wiggled his wedding finger to display a gold band. 'Miranda's the mother.'

Harmony had guessed that part. She leaned forward to catch Miranda's words as she shifted closer to the edge of the sofa and lowered her voice to a whisper.

'We were at the same antenatal classes as some of them here; they appeared to change when they found out how I came to have two men with me and had never been in a relationship with either of them. They'd never heard of a turkey baster insemination, and it's as though they just want to socialise with people exactly like them.'

Harmony attempted to absorb the unexpected confidence.

Luke added, 'We're still a family—just not the conventional kind people appear to expect.'

Her heart concertinaed in sympathy; they'd been hurt. 'Of course you are.'

'Let me get you a drink,' he offered. He and Miranda had finished theirs.

'Nothing for me, thanks.' Having a drink might slow her down if she needed to scarper.

'Can we take a peek?' he asked.

'Yes, of course.' Harmony unbuckled the straps of the carrier and soon, Patience was out of her all-in-one, looking curiously out at them.

'She's so sweet,' they chorused.

Luke shuffled to the edge of the sofa. 'Do you mind if I swap sides?'

Harmony shrugged. He came to sit beside her and gently stroked the baby's hand. His expression was so enamoured, she found herself saying, 'Would you like to hold her?'

'May I?'

Harmony passed Patience over, watching as he took hold of the baby.

He smiled into her face before placing her carefully against his shoulder. When he stroked her back, she snuffled and closed her eyes. 'Aw, she's such a cutie.'

Harmony smothered a smile. He was cute himself going gooey-eyed over Patience. Addressing Miranda, Harmony asked, 'How old is your baby?'

'Oscar's just over five months now. How did you find it?'

'From an online search.'

'I meant how did you find the birth.'

How had the birth been?... Long?... Arduous?... Painful?... Would she have to supply details?

'Miranda, you had a hard time of it, didn't you?' Luke said. 'But I was there to hold your hand. You weren't alone.'

'True—and Gavin held my other hand.'

'That's... nice.' Harmony had a mental picture of Miranda on a bed with her legs spread wide and a foot on each of the daddies' hips to give her something to push against when the time was right—she'd seen how it was done on TV, except usually one of the hips belonged to a midwife.

How had Oscar's mum coped with having two non-partner men gawping up her hospital gown, waiting for his head to pop out? Or had the daddies just held her hands while there'd been two midwives in position for the privileged view?

'How did you find it?' Miranda asked again. 'Did you need stitches like me? Did they heal okay?'

Harmony couldn't let the "misunderstanding" go any further. She searched for the right words, the right order in which to say them, a simple explanation of how she'd got herself into this position. But as she opened her mouth to speak, a group of people at a nearby table suddenly got to their feet, chairs squeaking on the floor as they moved backwards.

Miranda's head spun towards the sound.

'Did a whole tray of drinks just get knocked over?' Luke asked softly, probably so those at the next table didn't hear.

Distracted from the question about whether she'd healed from her stitches, Harmony took in the scene. 'Yes, I think so. It certainly looks like it.'

Hearing her answer, Miranda said, 'I'm so glad. Mine took ages.'

Before Harmony could rectify the mix-up about the non-existent stitches from a non-existent birth, Miranda asked, 'Was your partner with you? Did he cope okay?'

Harmony stared.

'Oh, I'm sorry, I shouldn't have presumed...'

Her tongue stuck to the roof of her mouth. 'No... I...' Her companions stayed silent, expecting her to say more, then, amazingly, she found a suitable answer. 'It's complicated.' *It certainly was.*

They nodded their heads understandingly.

'That's too bad,' Luke said.

The situation had become so knotted, it was easiest to let it go. She'd never see them again, and she vowed not to attend any more baby groups until she was told Patience was hers to bring up.

'But you had some support?' Miranda appeared concerned and her tone was sympathetic.

Harmony's mind went blank. Should she invent an urgent need to visit the loo? Incontinence? Double incontinence? All due to a difficult birth, of course, and, hopefully, quite fixable. Because, currently, this conversation seemed quite unfixable.

They waited for an answer.

'My parents live in Italy now, and I don't have many friends.' As soon as she said it, she regretted revealing her unpopularity.

Miranda pulled a sympathetic face. 'That's too bad.'

Harmony should have been honest from the start! But when she'd been talking to Sophie, she'd felt so close to tears. If she explained now... Well, everyone might overhear, especially if her companions raised their voices in surprise. Then, if she needed to go to any baby and toddler groups in the future, she'd likely see people from here. She'd moved to Westbridge to get away from being gossiped about; she didn't want to start something new and go through it all again.

How could she have imagined she had any meaningful experiences to bring to the group when she'd not given birth? Miranda's questions had shown her that.

Patience was snuggled so delightfully against Luke's shoulder, and he appeared so happy to have her, it would have been awkward to ask for the child back. But she'd have to in order to leave.

'Luke,' Miranda said, perhaps having noticed Harmony staring at the baby, 'I think Harmony might like to have Patience back now.'

'Oh, I'm sorry.' He gently placed the baby in Harmony's arms. 'I didn't mean to hog her.' He returned to his seat opposite.

'It's okay. But I was missing her.' And planning their getaway...

'You know, we'd love you to join our group of friends.' Miranda glanced at Luke for confirmation. 'Give me your number so we can keep in touch.' She retrieved her phone from a pocket.

Helplessly, Harmony supplied the requested digits. Soon after, her bag began to vibrate.

'Thanks,' she said feebly, 'I can feel my phone ring.' She'd add the number to her address book later.

'Whereabouts do you live?' Luke asked.

If she answered, revealing she didn't live in Bristol, they might consider it was too much of an effort to remain in contact... 'Westbridge.'

'*Westbridge?*' He sat taller. 'One of our friends lives there. She's having a get-together on Saturday.'

'I'll give her a call,' Miranda said. 'I'm sure she'd be delighted for you and Patience to come.'

A lump of lead formed at the bottom of Harmony's stomach. 'Er, thanks...'

She'd make an excuse not to go. Her discovery of the baby had been in the local paper. There was no way anyone in her home town would have forgotten that drama, even if Bristol had moved on... Slowly, Harmony dressed Patience in her all-in-one again and settled her into the carrier.

'Are you breastfeeding?' Miranda asked. 'I managed to but it was difficult at first.'

Surreptitiously, Harmony eased herself slightly forward on the sofa. 'I'm... not... I can't.' At least that was true.

A little bit further, buttock by buttock...

'I've read some women don't produce enough milk,' Luke said.

'He's read all the pregnancy magazines he could lay his hands on,' Miranda said. 'Same as when Perdita was pregnant.'

The room began to spin. Harmony clutched the arm of the sofa. '*Perdita?*'

'Our friend in Westbridge,' Luke said.

Her chest wall stiffened, making it hard to breathe. Although they'd never been introduced, Perdita would connect Harmony's name to Pinkerton Hall. She'd know Patience was the abandoned baby. Enough media exposure had been created in trying to find the mother.

'Er, can you leave me out of the meet-up? Things have been a bit difficult...' She reached the very edge of the sofa.

'Perdita's lovely. You'll like her,' Luke assured.

'All our friends are nice.'

'That is the point of friends,' he said quietly.

'I'll get her to call you,' Miranda said.

'Please, let me think about it before you contact her.'

Escape. It was all Harmony could think of. Before her pounding heart blasted free of her chest.

What if Social Worker Annie knew Perdita and found out Harmony had, to all intents and purposes, lied? Would it affect her suitability to adopt the child?

The passage to the street door was clear. She deleted incontinence from the menu of excuses, put back on Patience's hat and mittens and rose from the sofa.

'I've just realised,' she said in a rushed, apologetic way, swiftly putting on her coat. 'I forgot to lock my car... Sorry.' With a quick wave, she hurried out.

When she reached the grey Astra, she checked for witnesses before pressing the unlock symbol on her car key fob. The flashing lights as the car unlocked would have been a dead giveaway.

During the drive back to Westbridge, she felt sure Luke and Miranda would mention her to Perdita, even in her absence. The snare drum was back but with a full orchestra playing Maurice Ravel's *Boléro*. The piece had never sounded as menacing as it did now, like a slow but inexorable advance of foot soldiers marching together in time.

Harmony would come clean and see whether she and Patience would still be welcome at the get-together. It had been nearly ten years since Harmony had run away from her problems. Ten long years of having had the freedom to lick her wounds and hide away. As John Donne had said, *No man is an island*... Hiding away was like stepping out of life; if she were to keep Patience, Harmony needed to be brave and step right back in.

2

Harmony drove through the wide entrance to the early nineteenth-century Hall's impressive approach. On the left was the large Dower House, which was almost ready to be lived in; she just had to complete furnishing it. Thanks to Lady Pinkerton's generosity, it would be Harmony's home during her lifetime.

A long time ago, Lady Pinkerton—the last of the Westbridge Pinkertons—had let the Hall to the council to run as a care home for the elderly to recoup wealth lost through the post-war repairs. While Harmony had been working as a live-in companion/carer to Lady Pinkerton in the Dower House, the council had given notice to end the rental agreement of the Hall due to spiralling costs. Then Lilian Pinkerton had paid for work to be carried out to comply with children's home regulations and had supported Harmony's studies, enabling her to have a career caring for children. Sadly, Lady Pinkerton had not remained alive long enough to witness her plans, and Harmony's dreams, come to fruition.

As she parked outside Pinkerton Hall's side entrance, the snare drum, with the rest of the orchestra, was playing a crescendo.

With the baby against her chest, she made the few steps to the entrance, the key fob at the ready. Slamming the heavy oak door behind her, she leaned against it in relief.

The orchestra abruptly stopped. She was home, safe... for now.

Candy, the Hall's manager, reached the bottom step of the stairs, which led to the boys' wing. She brushed aside the short, twisted curls that were parted in the centre of her forehead and spoke in her rich Jamaican accent. 'Are you all right?'

'Fine.'

Candy stepped closer. 'You don't look all right.'

So her fixed smile hadn't passed Candy's casual appraisal. Sweat prickled Harmony's scalp and her shoes were glued to the floor. 'Actually, I think I might be having a heart attack.' But she was only thirty-six.

Although grateful the vital organ was still nestled in the confines of her chest, it oughtn't be pounding as though seeking an escape. When she thought of Annie again, the hairs on her skin rippled.

Candy approached, concern wrinkling her brow. She took hold of Harmony's wrist while checking her watch. 'Do you feel dizzy?'

'Mm.'

'Do you feel sick?'

'Mm.'

'I'm not surprised. You're hyperventilating.' Candy dropped Harmony's wrist. 'Give me Patience.'

'I'll be all right soon.'

Candy shook her head. 'Let's chat about what's upset you. In the front library.' When Harmony didn't move, her tone became stern. 'Now!'

Harmony blinked. Being on the board of trustees, she was effectively the manager's boss—and was the front library that catered for the younger kids more private than the office or had Candy been thinking of comfort rather than privacy?

As the glue on the soles of Harmony's shoes dissolved, her legs suddenly found the power to move again, and she discovered it wasn't such a difficult journey after all.

When she was settled in a plush leather armchair, Candy said to wait while she made her a mug of tea. 'I'll also fetch Patience's feed.'

Harmony had lined the bottles up in the staff fridge every morning since the baby's arrival. She made to stand; she should be getting Patience's milk.

Candy waved her down. 'Relax. I was worried you were doing too much. What with the baby and still doing some work here.'

Harmony removed her and Patience's outer clothing and sat cuddling the baby.

When the manager returned with a mug of tea and a bottle of formula milk, she said, 'I'll feed her while we chat.'

Candy's hard gaze always affected the children and, with it aimed at her, Harmony understood why they did exactly what she asked. As the manager gathered Patience in her arms, it was as though a part of Harmony was being stripped away like she imagined a marsupial deprived of its joey might feel.

'Share the burden.' When Candy stroked the nipple of the bottle against Patience's lips, the baby opened her mouth and began to suck with healthy determination.

Harmony took in a deep breath. 'You know you said I needed to get out more? Make some friends?'

'Yes. You need to have a separate life outside these walls or you risk burning out.'

'Well, I took your advice.'

'That's good.' Regarding her closely, Candy added doubtfully, 'Isn't it?'

'No. It's bad. Very bad.'

'How can having friends be bad? Where did you go?'

Unable to meet her gaze, Harmony mumbled, 'A baby group.'

Candy stared. 'Full of mums who've had babies?'

'There was one dad... I changed my mind and was about to leave. But I was told there were lots of newcomers and that there was no need to be shy.'

'You're not shy,' Candy said.

'Not here, no. But there, I felt shy. Very shy.'

'So, what happened then?'

'I sat with a woman who gave her birth story. So...'

Candy gaped. 'You made out you'd given birth to Patience?'

In a tiny, little girl's voice, Harmony admitted, 'I might have. By accident.'

'Don't the people you met know who you are?'

'I went to Bristol.'

'So, you won't see them again.'

Tears sprang from her eyes. 'They've got my number and are going to call me about a get-together. Right here. In Westbridge. Perdita might have already been told my name.'

'Perdita?'

Harmony's chest felt like it had shrunk and she fought for breath again.

'Perdita knows all about the Pinkerton Hall children,' Candy said. 'Some have babysat for her—remember that summer party she had?'

'I really do... think... I'm having a heart attack.'

'It's not a heart attack,' Candy said. 'Have you had panic attacks before?'

'*What?* No!'

'Well, now's your first. I'm not surprised by the lack of sleep. I'll take Patience tonight. Even paid foster carers need a break from time to time.'

'That's not fair on you,' Harmony reasoned.

'I insist.'

Tiredness must have contributed to the rash decisions she'd made earlier; she was no good if she didn't get the rest she needed.

'All right. Thanks, and I'll call the person I met today and explain everything. But if I adopted Patience, then it would become true... mostly.' Patience appeared to be of mixed Black ethnicity. 'By her appearance, I could...

perhaps... have been her biological mother...'

When Candy's eyes widened, Harmony added quickly, 'There aren't many approved Black adoptive parents are there?'

'Less than five per cent.'

'So Patience might have a long wait for a couple she can visually identify with.' Without knowing where Patience's ethnicity originally hailed from, Harmony could never discover the languages her family spoke or their customs, diet, beliefs and values. 'In the Dower House, I could give her a stable home life, and we've got a diverse mix of children here. That would count, wouldn't it? If no more suitable parent was found?'

'Patience was placed with you as an emergency,' Candy said. 'Annie's got time to find a more suitable permanent placement.'

'Guidelines allow adopters from other cultural and ethnic backgrounds—'

'True, and if we were speaking of an older child, mixing with all the children here with diverse backgrounds would definitely count.' Candy's steady gaze was serious. 'But babies under six months are the most sought after and can get two parents—and, most likely, in Patience's case, of Black ethnicity. You'd be a last resort if the local authority allowed you to adopt Patience.'

Harmony squared her shoulders. 'Then I can be a last resort. A safety net in case Patience doesn't get what she truly needs.'

'Why not wait to have your own children?'

She dug her nails into her hand to protect against the emotional thorn that had resurfaced. 'I'm not going to have a child of my own.'

'Don't be so pessimistic. You don't know that for sure.'

But Harmony did know it for sure, and it had nothing to do with pessimism. 'I've had a hysterectomy.'

The teat of the bottle popped out of the baby's mouth as Candy's hand jerked in surprise. 'Oh, you poor dear.'

Gently, she offered the teat back and the sucking resumed.

'When I came to Westbridge, I wanted the past to stay in the past, and so I didn't tell anyone. It was over. My cancer was over.'

The manager's head shot up, her tight strands of curls giving a brief swish. 'You had cancer? Are you all right now?'

'Mm. I'm fine.'

'That's good. But you mustn't get stuck on Patience.'

'Too late.' That plane had taken off the moment Harmony had set eyes on the baby. 'And I can only bear losing her if I believe she's going to a better place, with the ideal adoptive parents.'

3

James Traffurth stood alone in the Edwardian three-bedroom terraced house in Montpelier, not far from Bristol city centre. He recalled Felicia's excitement the day they'd moved in about twelve years ago.

'Isn't it wonderful?' With outstretched arms, she'd jigged around the empty living room, her flat shoes thumping the bare floorboards, her shoulder-length blonde hair catching the sun streaming through the window.

'It is wonderful.' He'd laughed as he'd put out his arms to steady her, mindful of her well-advanced baby bump.

They'd stretched themselves to the limit to buy the house. Their forever home, Felicia had called it. It would break her heart if she knew he was selling it now. But with only his salary coming in…

Completion was set for midday. The new owners from London would collect the keys from the local estate agents when they'd finished up in Ealing. He wondered if they appreciated how hard it was at times to find a place to park on the narrow streets of Bristol.

James had taken the day off for the move. At breakfast that morning, his eleven-year-old son Tim had repeated his wish for a day off too.

Tim stuck his chin out. 'I don't see why I have to go to school. My things are being moved as well.'

'Don't you think you've missed too much school

already?'

Priya, Felicia's old school friend, was going to drop Tim off to save James from coming back to Bristol.

'Just say it,' Tim shouted. 'You don't want me around!'

'Now, that's not true. I love you. How could you think that?' Tim was all he had left... 'I'm doing my best to see you're educated. I've had enough phone calls over your unofficial absences. I know you're hurting—we both are—but I'm trying to act in your best interests.' Then, before he could stop himself, James stupidly added, 'Mum would have wanted you at school too.'

Tim's expression froze. He stood up and grabbed his school bag. 'Mum would have wanted us all here, to work together as a family.'

James's throat swelled. He'd always been able to confer with Felicia over how to handle the boys. 'Mum's not here now. So it's down to me—'

'Don't I know it!' Tim made for the front of the house and, before James had a chance to say more, his surviving son slammed the door behind him.

James fought back tears. He'd made the right legal call but the wrong call for their relationship. He should have ignored his head and listened to his heart, to Tim. Perhaps in the countryside, in Westbridge, surrounded by the vast Pinkerton estate, he and Tim could learn to talk comfortably to each other again...

Wandering around the echoing rooms, James checked he'd done a thorough job of filling the removal boxes. He'd ensured the shrubs and flowers in the garden had remained watered during the hot summer months to keep them from perishing, and they were still thriving. Hopefully, the newcomers would tend to Felicia's plants well.

Although he'd advertised the furniture he wished to sell online, he'd initially only had two takers. One for his younger son's desk with drawers. The other, the cot that he'd hoped one day would be assembled for the third time—if Felicia had changed her mind about having another child.

James had lowered prices until he was offering the remainder for free.

Over the last week, Tim had come home from school to another empty area yawning at him. The gap from the missing sofa had made the most impact downstairs, but it was too large to fit into the new place. James and Tim would have to manage with an easy chair each for now. The small bookcase, coffee table and TV would take up the rest of the area in the cottage's compact living room.

James had kept Georgie's room shut as neither he nor Tim needed to see it devoid of furniture. Georgie's personal items, with Felicia's, had gone over a year ago.

But James had optimistically kept many cookery books and a scarf Felicia had worn that held the floral fragrance of her perfume. Actually, he'd kept her scent bottle too. He'd sometimes sprayed some Issey Miyake's L'Eau D'Issey onto the scarf so he could fall asleep in the pretence she still lay in bed beside him. When the eau de toilette bottle was empty, he'd decided it was time he let Felicia go, and he hadn't bought a replacement.

A new start was what he and Tim needed, where only Saul—Felicia's school friend—and his wife Perdita, knew them. Ongoing sympathy had become ingrained pity by do-gooders with their kind words, softened voices and pasta bakes.

James had attempted to recreate some of the meals Felicia had featured regularly in their diet. But Tim had picked at the ratatouille served with fresh basil leaves, 'Ew, the aubergine's too chewy', wrinkled his nose at the vegetable tagine, 'The carrots are soggy!', and spat out the chicken, spinach and chickpea curry, 'Dad, the rice is hard, and it tastes horrible!'.

Worst of all came the repeated cries of, 'This isn't how Mum used to make it!'

James's deficient culinary skills were not down to a mindset of believing it was a woman's job to do the cooking; he hadn't avoided the art altogether. But what husband would get behind a hob every night if his partner was a kitchen fairy dietitian who loved to create delicious and nutritious dishes?

His and Tim's new life in Westbridge was going to be good; it needed to be, *had* to be. There had to be more to the effort he was making than having off-road parking.

The rumble of the engine and the squeak of the brakes told him the removal people had arrived.

Later, when James locked up for the last time, he brushed away a tear. He and Felicia had been so happy moving in. But the family of four they'd become had been reduced to a family of two. Financial problems aside, he and Tim must leave the reminders of the past if they'd any hope of moving on.

4

Shame drove Harmony to come clean the moment she could make the call to Miranda in her bedroom, in private, while Patience was snuggled on Harmony's chest.

The phone was answered after two rings. 'Miranda?'

'Harmony?'

'Yes. Hello. I... it was lovely meeting you today. But there's something I have to tell you, and it can't wait.'

'Oh?'

'I've done something very idiotic, and I'm terribly sorry.'

'What did you do?'

'I led you to believe I gave birth to Patience. But she's not mine. I... I just wanted to make some friends.'

So you borrowed a baby?

'I'm her foster mum—although I'd love to adopt her if no suitable couple is found. At the café, with all the mums and babies, I was overwhelmed so I went along with everyone's assumptions. Then you asked me whether I'd had stitches and if they'd healed, but I was replying to Luke about the table with the spilt drinks. It got so complicated, I couldn't find the words to get out of the muddle I'd made.'

'Oh... Well, I haven't contacted Perdita yet. You asked me to wait so you could think about it.'

Harmony closed her eyes in relief. 'Thank goodness. Can you explain to Luke and say I'm sorry? I realise this probably means I'll have to go without your friendship, but—'

'Hey,' Miranda said sharply, 'what do you mean, go without my friendship?'

'I haven't exactly behaved sensibly.'

Miranda laughed. 'I wasn't exactly sensible when I chased Luke across Perdita's lawn at a summer party to ask him to have a baby with me.'

'Wow.'

'I'd heard he wanted a woman to share a child with him… I'll explain to Luke and pass your number to Perdita. She need never know about the misunderstanding. I… I don't have many friends either and, to be honest, I still feel a bit like an outsider. Luke and Gavin have known Perdita and the others for years. I'm the newcomer.'

Miranda was too kind. 'I don't think—'

'Let me sort it out and get you invited.'

It was better than Harmony could have imagined. 'Thanks, that's very generous of you.'

'I'll contact her now.' Miranda hung up.

A little while later, Harmony received a text message from an unknown number.

Hi. I'm Perdita. Miranda's passed on your number. I'd love it if you and Patience could join us…

The details followed. With huge relief, Harmony replied: *Thank you so much. It's very kind of you.*

You're very welcome. I've wanted to meet you for ages.

In a much lighter frame of mind, Harmony took the baby downstairs to the office. She popped Patience in the pram, passed her the tiny, soft doll toy she loved—more than the soft teddy Harmony had also bought her—and placed the blanket from her mother lightly over her. It was almost time for the scheduled interview for finding a new domestic. Harmony glanced at the CCTV monitor.

A removal van had come to a halt outside the cottage opposite, which used to be part of the Pinkerton estate. It had been sold to pay for repairs after the Second World War.

Without the money, the Hall would have been demolished—like many other requisitioned country homes—as the grounds had been used for battle training and the bomb blasts had blown out the windows. In recent years, the cottage had been used as a holiday let, but the landlord had sold up.

While she watched the driver and his mate get out of the removal van, a red, low-slung Porsche came into view. At first, she thought the fancy car was connected to the cottage but when it turned into the Hall's approach, she scotched that notion. The vehicle stopped outside the main entrance. A young woman wearing challenging heels and a light-grey, tailored suit emerged from the sporty-looking car, her blonde hair arranged in a fancy chignon.

There was only one person expected. It wasn't until the intercom bell sounded and a posh, child-like voice said, 'Saskia Walker-Pearson here,' that Harmony believed it was her. Usually, applicants turned up to interviews for the post of domestic in fairly smart-casual clothes and never in more than a modest car if they came in one at all.

Wishing she'd not been dazzled by Saskia's neat handwriting and impeccable grammar, Harmony went to meet her eighteen-year-old interviewee.

Generally, when people first entered Pinkerton Hall, they looked around in awe at the grand scale of architecture, even though the fine decorative detail had been destroyed. But Saskia breezed in without a need to take in her surroundings. Perhaps it was quite plain compared to what she was accustomed to. Lady Pinkerton had told Harmony that the majority of the original panelling and carvings had been ripped out and used as firewood by the British Army.

After the introductions, they sat in the office, Saskia with her knees to one side and one ankle tucked under the other.

Harmony angled the pram so she and Patience could see each other. 'I'm taking care of a baby, so I apologise if she starts to cry.'

'I don't mind babies,' Saskia said. 'I used to be one.'

Harmony blinked. 'Er... so, could you tell me why you would like to work at Pinkerton Hall?'

'Grandfather says I have to learn the value of money.'

Harmony took in Saskia's earnest expression, her beautiful, well-defined, sky-blue eyes. 'Oh?'

'He's made Mummy stop my allowance. Unless I can keep a job for at least six months, I won't get it back.'

The use of "Mummy", "Grandfather" and the mention of an allowance placed Saskia in a much higher social class than the Hall's current employees. Her appeal as a suitable candidate for working—and fitting in—with the domestic team just kept plummeting.

Harmony admonished herself for being judgemental. She must be fair, give the woman a chance. 'Why do you think you're suited to being a domestic?'

'A domestic what?'

Appraising her to check she wasn't taking the mick, Harmony said, 'Someone who undertakes domestic tasks like—'

'Oh, yes,' Saskia enthused. 'I set Mummy's hair for her—I'm as good as her hairdresser now. I do her nails and put Mummy's letters on the table for Jenkins to post. Oh, and I give her advice on whether her shoes and bag go with an outfit—'

Harmony rubbed her temple. 'That's not the kind of domestic I meant. Cleaning: toilets, bathrooms, kitchens, floors. Dusting. Vacuuming. Sorting out the laundry. Changing beds. Have you ever done any of those tasks?'

'We have help to do that...'

'So, if you've never done it before, how do you think you would cope with the demands of the job?'

'Me? Do all that?'

'Did you read the advertisement?'

'Grandfather did. He said it was best if you explained what I'd have to do when I saw you. He said a lot of children are looked after here. Is it a home for orphans?'

Gently, Harmony said, 'It's a home for children who have not been suitably provided for in any other way. They aren't necessarily orphans.'

She imagined Saskia having had a charmed, protected life.

Saskia's fingers plucked at the material of her skirt. 'You know, I thought I would be working in an office.' Her gaze took in the piles of papers and folders that lay across the desks. 'I'm good at tidying up.'

'Candy—the manager— and I do the tidying in here. Do you have any other questions?'

Harmony suspected that if it weren't for "Grandfather", Saskia would have ditched the interview and hightailed it by now.

'How much would my salary be?'

Harmony mentioned the amount, doing her best to keep her impatience in check; Saskia should have read the advert.

Her dainty red lips parted. 'Per *hour*? Oh... When would I have to start?'

'If you were to be offered the job, we'd need to wait for your enhanced DBS check to come through. Child protection.' Although, if chaperoned the whole time, she could start immediately.

Inhaling audibly, and her eyes wide in protest, she said, 'But Daddy was cleared of all of that. None of us saw anything like what... what was said. Later he took it back and the police left us alone. Mummy said he was after some money. It's all over now, and no one speaks of it anymore.'

Used to hearing all manner of things, Harmony kept her expression bland. So Saskia hadn't been completely shielded from some of the grimmer aspects of life after all. Although Harmony's heart went out to the younger woman, she did have an obligation to pick the most suitable applicant.

Standing up, she said, 'Well, I'll let you know if you're successful in due course.'

Saskia rose to her feet. 'Thank you. It was a pleasure to meet you.'

'And you.' Harmony was unsure of how much of a lie that had been. 'If you aren't successful—I wish you the best in finding a job somewhere else.'

They shook hands.

Saskia's downcast face showed she knew the job would not be hers.

5

After the young woman had left, Harmony changed and fed Patience. As she was winding the baby for the second time that feed, the phone jingled and Patience burped.

'Hello, Pinkerton Hall. Harmony Payne speaking.'

'Good afternoon. My name is Roderick Walker. I understand that you interviewed my granddaughter, Saskia, for the post of domestic earlier.'

Harmony's stomach made a sharp descent. 'That's right.'

'I am calling to enquire as to whether Saskia has been successful in securing the position.' Roderick Walker's voice was deep and strong. His accent was well-polished yet not standoffish. She rather liked it.

'Due to issues of confidentiality—'

'I surmise that you are not going to offer her employment.'

'Erm...'

'I can quite understand. I would certainly not hire my granddaughter to work on my estate.'

Bridling, she asked, 'So why did you think I should?'

'I've heard great things about your place. How you can turn children around; Saskia needs to understand what work is about.'

'There must be something she's more suited to than becoming a domestic, and she's no longer a child.'

'Spending family money is the only occupation to which she is currently suited. I referred to your work with children as it is doubtful that Saskia's brain appreciates that responsibility comes with being an adult. The manner in which she has been acquainting herself with the finest possessions money can buy augurs ill for the future. So I would be extremely grateful if you were to offer her the job.'

'Saskia would probably make more work for others than lessen it.'

'How about if I pay her wages? Then she could work alongside someone who could show her the ropes. Keep her on track.'

'I don't think Saskia would fit in with the ethos of the place or—'

'I'll pay Saskia's wage *and* the wage of the domestic you need to hire. For six months. By then, we'll know whether she can cut it. Also... I'll give a generous donation if you manage to keep her for the full six months and sort her out.'

Harmony felt an urge to throttle the handset. *'Sort her out?'*

Roderick's voice boomed into her ear. 'Get Saskia to understand the value of money. What it means to work and be proud of her achievements instead of her reflection in the mirror. I have every faith in you. I've been following the progress of the Hall since it became a children's home. You've done very well.'

'Thank you.'

'Will you take Saskia on?'

She wasn't sure. 'What would Saskia do after the six months? Go back to her current lifestyle, whatever that is?' If so, it wouldn't be worth the effort.

'I am hoping that, by the time you've worked your magic on her, she will want to stay working.'

'As a domestic?'

'She is not exactly the sharpest tool in the box. Probably one of the bluntest. Amazing how so little sinks into that head of hers. Her private education was a complete waste of money.'

An irrational urge to stick up for Saskia overcame Harmony. 'Her application form was—'

'I wrote it.'

'*You*—?'

'Yes. Please could you do for her what money and family could not? Make her a useful member of society— and be happy doing it. I would be tremendously in your debt.'

Saskia had appeared incredibly vulnerable when the subject of her father's—and therefore the family's—ordeal had come up. Deep inside, she might not be at all happy. The family being questioned by police, "Grandfather's" disapproval, withholding of funds, failing with her education, being brought up to be a society girl and not much else.

Harmony found herself agreeing to Roderick Walker's generous terms.

Resigned, she called Saskia's mobile to offer her the job and invite her back for a tour of the Hall.

She arrived half an hour later and gave Harmony a broad smile. 'I'm so pleased you've offered me the job. Thank you. I felt sure you were going to say no. But Grandfather told me to have more faith in myself, and he was right, wasn't he?'

'Your grandfather is a very wise man.'

'He is, isn't he?' Saskia beamed.

Harmony placed Patience in the carrier so she could easily take her around with her.

After showing Saskia the primary and secondary school-age kids' libraries, they went into the massive kitchen. Seven boisterous children, having milk and biscuits in an adjoining area, could be seen through a large hatch.

'Gosh, you do have a lot of children here.'

'There are a further eight who attend secondary

school. They have their drink and snacks a bit later. Their care and accommodation are separate, but we do have joint activities and meals too.'

Then Harmony showed her the laundry room used for items not cleaned by the commercial firm that picked up sheets and towels. 'Can you wash clothes and iron?'

Saskia gulped.

'Maggie, the person you'll be shadowing, can point out where all the linen and cleaning equipment cupboards are. We have lifts for the wheeled laundry bins.' Harmony sometimes used it for Patience if she was asleep in her pram.

After showing Saskia the staff locker room and giving her a key to a unit, they went to the two living rooms and then to the dining room. The stage at the far end was home to a grand piano and a drum kit.

'The children are encouraged to join in with our orchestra, even if it's just playing the triangles, bells or tambourines. A music teacher visits each week—and we also have a coach for the choir.' Harmony pointed. 'Through that door is what has always been called the print room, where we now keep many of the instruments and sheet music. I'll show you.'

There was no remaining evidence of the prints with which the Pinkerton family had seen fit to decorate the walls, which had been stripped, plastered and painted over.

'You need to be very careful when you clean in here,' Harmony said.

'Mummy wanted me to learn to play the clarinet. But blowing it made me feel dizzy. Do you play anything?'

'I learned to play the piano but other people teach the kids if they want to play an instrument.'

She recalled the final public performance she'd given with The Avon & Somerset Symphony Orchestra. It had been her first time back after her fiancé had left her waiting at the altar. Her mum had been at home nursing a painful wrist, awaiting surgery and, although her dad had still been with the orchestra, he'd been chatting to other violinists during the interval. Harmony had been a sitting duck when a recently hired flautist, Léonie Escoffier, had approached her to say how sorry she was to hear the marriage hadn't gone ahead and how it must be especially hard after her other troubles.

'What other troubles?'

Léonie had lowered her voice. 'My aunt had cancer, and she couldn't have children either.'

All through the first half of her performance of Ludwig van Beethoven's *Piano Concerto in D Major*, the conversation with Léonie had intruded in Harmony's mind, together with flashbacks to her fiancé, David. Her notes had become uneven and her fingers had slipped until, finally, she'd stopped playing. *The whole orchestra knew everything there was to know about her; her past was used for gossip.* She'd run off the stage in tears and had never played in public again.

Her Fazioli baby grand had gone into storage when she'd gone to work for Lady Pinkerton and the family home had been sold so her parents could live in Italy, teaching music. When Lady Pinkerton had discovered that Harmony had been a professional musician, she'd offered to make room for the instrument in the Dower House where they'd been living.

For a long time, Harmony had ignored the Fazioli. But, after a while, she'd been able to play when she'd been alone and, later, to Lady Pinkerton.

Now, because of Patience, Harmony had started to play lullabies on the grand piano in the dining room.

She smiled at Saskia to indicate they must move on and led her to the sensory room. She switched on the power. 'We always take off our shoes before we go in.'

Saskia stepped out of her heels. 'Gosh, it's so pretty.' She touched the bubble tube and gazed at the coloured shapes projected onto the walls and ceiling.

'It helps people relax.' Harmony pressed a couple of switches on the control panel. The room went dark and stars appeared. Soft music played. 'It's helpful when the kids get upset—some of them have challenging behaviours and all have had some kind of trauma—but it's especially effective for those on the autism spectrum.'

She was thinking of Robbie, who could have spectacular meltdowns. Although he was intellectually beyond his peers' capabilities, emotionally, he was still quite immature. His family had been unable to manage him, and his outbursts had affected his younger siblings. With trained support and set routines, the improvement in him had been dramatic. Now, funding had been finally approved for him to board weekdays at an out-of-area special school during term time from January.

'It would be great to have a room like this,' Saskia whispered.

'The kids love it. The red light above the door outside shows it's occupied, but sometimes the kids forget to flick the switch. The mirror on that wall...' Harmony pointed. '... is a viewing window. But there's a complete blind spot underneath so it's best to go by the lighting to determine whether the room's in use—with the main lights off, you can see the patterns of the sensory lights. If someone's in here, please come back later to clean.'

On the first floor, Harmony said, 'The boys and girls sleep in opposite wings. We separate the ages too. There are some rooms on this floor for staff on shift to use. On the second floor, we have larger staff accommodation—Candy, the manager, and I live there. Maggie can show you around the apartments after you start. They're included in the rota.' When flesh puckered between Saskia's eyes, Harmony added, 'The cleaning timetable.'

Down on the ground floor again, she showed Saskia the entertainment areas. One room contained a pool table, a table tennis table, games consoles and board games—plus a powerful music centre with karaoke. The other was the playroom for the younger children.

Saskia's gaze was wistful as she approached a farm set.

'These animals are so cute.' She bent as though to pick one up and then suddenly straightened as if remembering herself. 'I was thinking how nice it must be—for the children.'

They were in the staircase hallway again when a breathless, shiny-eyed Robbie hurried towards Harmony, one hand holding a small plastic container and the other hand cupped over the top. 'Can you find out what I've caught?'

'Let's get the book out and see.' She turned to Saskia, 'It's kept in the front library.'

When they entered, Candy was listening to a boy read while sharing a massive bean bag.

Harmony found the insect book and laid it open on the table. It couldn't be much longer before the boy had identified all the insects in the immediate area.

It would be good for the newest employee to get stuck in and start to get to know the children. 'Robbie, would you like to show Saskia your bug? Then she can help us find the right picture in the book.'

Saskia put out her hands to take the container from Robbie. But instead of passing it to her, he tipped the creature into her palms. Screeching, she flung up her arms.

The bug, whatever it had been, flew into the air and vanished.

The door intercom bell rang.

6

The blood-freezing shriek wouldn't have been out of place in a TV murder mystery. If James had heard it a couple of seconds earlier, he'd have postponed calling on their new neighbour, despite the need for his son to make new friends. The apparent commotion inside the gargantuan Hall could back up the homicide theory. He exchanged an uncertain glance with Tim, who was shifting from foot to foot.

The heavy door was opened by a woman with a heart-shaped face, tawny eyes, long russet hair held up with a scrunchie and a curvy, attractive figure. She was almost a head shorter than him, possibly in her mid-thirties. A baby was nestled against her chest in a sling.

As she swept her fringe away from her beautiful eyes, she smiled. 'Hello? Can I help you?' She glanced between James and Tim.

Through another open door to the space behind her, there was pandemonium.

Someone was wailing, 'I can't stand bugs. I can't, really, I can't,' while someone with a Jamaican accent replied, 'I know, I know,' and a deep voice said, 'Saskia, come and have a cup of tea.'

The owner of the Jamaican voice came into view. She might have been in her late forties and wore her black hair in short strands of twisted curls. 'Robbie,' she said, 'let's take a break in the sensory room.'

James's attention returned to the woman who'd opened the door, children pressing against her, jostling for an improved view. She put her arms around those next to her in such a loving, motherly way that his heart was drawn to her.

Surely the children were too close in age for her to be the mother of all of them? And—by the range of complexions—they couldn't all have had the same father. There were a few adults around so perhaps it was a family get-together or a party. Or the kids were cousins or had friends around and they didn't all live there. If the kids had all been older, he'd have suspected it could be a children's home, despite the lack of signage outside. But he knew from a school classmate who'd been in the care system that babies and young children were either fostered or adopted. She couldn't be fostering or adopting so many with a baby to look after—even if it were hers—surely?

'Hi,' James said. 'We've just moved in across the road. A friend told me children were living here, and I wondered if there might be someone my son's age. He's starting at Westbridge Primary when half-term ends.'

The woman gave a warm, engaging smile. 'Oh, do come in.' Addressing the children, she said, 'Come on kids, give our new neighbours some room.'

So they *did* all live there. Well, the place was big enough to house several families. Or perhaps it was a blended family?

The children shuffled further into the building to make way.

He motioned to Tim to wipe his shoes on the mat as they went inside. Beyond the porch, there was a vast rectangular hallway. James beckoned his son to follow.

'I'm James Traffurth and this is Tim.'

A door slammed and there were more voices. Some teenagers came into view from a corridor and ran up the stairs. It sounded like two girls were having a spat. A couple of younger kids broke away and followed the din.

The woman who'd opened the door to them extended her arm. 'I'm Harmony Payne. Pleased to meet you.'

This place was the least harmonious home he'd been in, but Harmony—what a lovely name!—remained surprisingly serene. He accepted her hand and gave it a brief shake. But then he realised he'd been holding it far too long because he'd found it difficult to tear his gaze away from her beautiful face, hoping to catch another engaging smile.

With a rosy hue on her cheeks, she said to the remaining children, 'Everyone, say hi to James and Tim.'

A cacophony of 'Hi's sounded.

He wanted to ask how many children lived there. Instead, he said, 'Hi,' too and nudged Tim to do the same.

Typical Tim, he merely grunted.

Turning the nearest children around, she said, 'Kids, get on with what you're meant to be doing. Off you go.'

James wondered how many of them were hers. To see so many children in one home when he hadn't been able to keep both of his kids alive tore at his heart.

'It's quieter in the library.' Harmony gestured towards a nearby door. 'Let's go there. The children can get lively. Once they've eaten, they'll be much more settled. Like babies with full tummies.'

Talking of babies, wouldn't it be polite to enquire after her latest addition to the family? 'How old's your baby?'

She appeared to falter for a moment. 'About nine weeks. But she's not mine.'

Then whose? Perhaps she'd help him understand the numbers. 'From the little I know of the area, it appears to be a great place to bring up children.'

'It is a great place. How old are you, Tim?'

'Eleven.'

It was a surly, impolite rendition of the word, but she didn't appear to mind. When she beamed at Tim, the deep softening of her face was... endearing.

'He'll be going to secondary school next September,' James said.

'If you wait here, I'll look for the two who'll be in his class. I won't be long.' She left the room, closing the door behind her.

He took the opportunity to browse the library shelves. The room provided a rich reading and reference experience. A book was lying open on a table. Who was the budding entomologist?

Tim scrabbled backwards on the carpeted floor, an open graphic novel close by. 'Aargh!'

'What is it?'

'I don't know.' He sounded scared. 'It's a black thing. Beetle, I think.'

Was that why the insect book was out? Because the place had pests? The theory tied in with the commotion earlier.

'Where is it?' James crouched beside Tim who pointed towards a dark corner underneath the shelving.

'It was running in that direction.'

Crawling forward, James held his head low. 'I can't see it.' He grabbed his phone from his pocket and aimed light from the torch app into the space. When his hand moved so he could illuminate the darkest point, he spotted it. But not for long. The creature moved fast. *'It's a cockroach!'*

'A cockr—?'

There was the sound of approaching voices. 'Shh.' The door opened as he was scrambling to his feet.

'Is something the matter?' Harmony asked.

Brushing down his trousers, he smiled benignly. 'No. No. Not at all. Tim thought he'd seen a spider.'

'It wasn't a—' Tim began.

'Hush,' James said. 'Say hello to...?'

Two boys were standing next to Harmony.

'This is Patrik.' She indicated a blond boy with curly hair who appeared underfed. 'And this is Anil.' He was a chunky lad with black hair.

If they were both her children, they'd have had to have been born at opposite ends of the academic year. 'Tim's birthday was in September,' he said. 'He's already eleven.'

'I'll be eleven in August,' Patrik said.

'My birthday's in May,' Anil said.

So she couldn't be mum to both of them.

'And we're best friends,' Anil added.

'But we don't mind being friends with Tim too,' Patrik said.

Was the place a commune?

'Would you like some tea and biscuits? Cake? Squash?' She regarded James expectantly.

He thought of the cockroach. 'No.' It came out badly and a flicker of hurt crossed her eyes. 'I... I wouldn't dream of troubling you when you have your hands full.'

He didn't want Tim or himself to catch a stomach bug as a consequence of being too polite to refuse a drink.

'Well, do sit down.' She took one of the armchairs, undoing the buckles of the baby carrier. 'Boys, why don't you show Tim the games room?'

She turned to James as the boys left. 'There's quite a bit there to keep them occupied.' The baby, a bonny-looking child, was in her arms. Every so often, she stroked the baby's cheek. 'So, you've just moved here?'

'Yes. From Bristol. I thought Westbridge might be a better place to bring up Tim.'

And to escape the silence. Georgie had only been six when he'd... well, he'd loudly role-played with his toys or watched cartoons on the TV with the volume uncomfortably high. Felicia used to sing along to songs while she bustled about. Tim used to play the drums but hadn't touched them since Felicia and Georgie had gone.

James hoped that one day, Tim would play again—as well as make good friends from families who cared about their children enough to teach them the difference between right and wrong and the value of a good education. Friends who didn't lead him astray, get him into vaping and truancy again. Maybe James could find someone special to help fill his agonising loneliness.

His thoughts stilled when Harmony replied, 'I agree. Westbridge is a good town to move to. Plenty of open spaces, fresh air...'

'Do Patrik and Anil go to the after-school club?'

'No. All the primary school kids come back here. Will Tim be going?'

'Yes. I'll pick him up after work.'

'He could come back with the kids. If they get on all right, of course.'

'Thank you. That's kind of you, but I'll see how things go.' He didn't want to offend the lovely woman. But he and Tim needed to get a sense of the area, the school and the other pupils who went there too. Besides, the appearance of the cockroach was a concern. James had inspected enough premises to know that where there was one, there were often many more.

She nodded equably. 'Well, if he's lonely at all, he's very welcome to pop around. It must be hard being an only child. Or has he got siblings?'

The reference to an "only child" stung. 'Thank you and, er, it's just Tim.' He wanted to change the attention from them to her. 'What about you—do you have siblings?' Did they live there too? Perhaps the children *were* all cousins.

'Just one. A sister... Melody.' Her brisk tone suggested she didn't want to talk about her.

He wondered what the problem was and what was with their parents naming their daughters Harmony and Melody?

Harmony must have noticed his frown as she explained, 'Our parents are professional musicians. That's how they met. They live in Italy now, have done for years.'

It must be very tough for her without their support. With so many kids to take care of—and she hadn't mentioned any partner to help. 'Was this the family home?'

She frowned. 'No... I'm sorry, didn't your friend tell you this is a council-funded children's home?'

Recalling Saul's words: *There were sure to be some kids in Tim's year in the home opposite,* James shook his head.

'Although income from the Pinkerton Hall estate allows us to give the children extras to make it special. The manager, Candy, and I live here.'

'The sign outside only says Pinkerton Hall…' What did that mean about her relationship status?

'Not putting a sign up is deliberate, to protect the children. Everyone who needs to know knows… usually. I'm sorry, if I'd realised—' Her expression became thoughtful, perhaps replaying their meeting and conversations. She'd guess what had been going through his mind and hoped it wouldn't put a barrier between them.

'I thought young children and babies are fostered?'

'Usually, yes. But there's a great shortage of foster families and we have the capacity to take in emergency cases of primary-aged children. We don't accept babies but—and I can tell you as it's been in the media—Patience was abandoned on our doorstep. I offered to foster her as there had been no more suitable foster carer available and I… well… Anyway, we do our best to make it a real home for them all, however long they stay.'

'Yes, I believe that.' He wondered what she'd struggled to say about the baby.

She blushed. 'Well, thank you…'

Harmony appeared very caring, a great mother figure. But unease settled in James's stomach. Troubled Tim was making friends with troubled children, and they lived in an environment where at least one cockroach was running free.

'I hope Tim likes Westbridge,' she said.

'The area does look great. How many—'

'Children are here?' she said.

'Yes.'

'At the moment, sixteen with Patience. But it's a fluid thing. Kids come and go; some stay long-term… Westbridge is a very friendly place. What is it that you do?'

He fixed her with a flinty stare. 'I'm an Environmental Health Officer.'

Appearing confused, probably from not knowing what she'd done to warrant his hard tone and stony gaze, she turned crimson. He felt unkind and wretched, but the presence of a cockroach was serious.

'Well, thank you for your help with Tim,' he said. 'I think it's time he and I get stuck into unpacking.'

A veil had come down over what had been an open expression. 'I'll find him,' she said and left the room.

James winced. He'd hurt her feelings.

As James and Tim crossed the road to go home, Tim became animated for the first time since the tragedy.

'Can *we* have a visitor book?'

Harmony had asked them to fill in the large sign-in and sign-out book on the shelf by the main entrance next to a pot of pens.

'Pinkerton Hall's a children's home run by staff.'

'I know. Patrik told me.'

'You don't need a visitor's book when you're a family, like us.' They used to have many people call around but now they would be the ones calling on others. The cottage wasn't set up for entertaining. 'The staff at the Hall need to know who's in the place in case of an emergency. They use the book to check everyone's accounted for. It's a legal requirement.'

James unlocked the front door and stepped back to let his son inside first.

Tim appeared to have given up on the idea of having a visitor's book as he said, 'They've got a pool table and a table tennis table, and I've never seen so many games.'

'I'm glad you had such a good time.'

James hoped Patrick and Anil were decent kids. That they all were, despite whatever difficulty had brought them to the Hall. If not, what was he to do to keep his son from getting into trouble too?

Then there was the cockroach problem. How could one have found its way into the library if hygiene standards had been kept to?

James was torn. Report the roach and antagonise—causing further hurt—the first woman he'd truly looked at since he'd been with Felicia? Or go back, help her find it?

But if an infestation was discovered later, his office would find out that, instead of reporting it, he'd helped to cover it up. He could lose his job or worse... And then where would he and Tim be? And what about the Hall's children being put at risk for longer if he covered up what might not be an isolated appearance of the roach?

It was clear they'd known about the roach from Saskia screaming about bugs and the insect book being out. Much as it pained him, James had a responsibility to public health—and he couldn't risk his livelihood and freedom for the sake of a stranger, no matter how lovely she was.

If the sighting turned out to be a one-off, he'd do his best to make things right with Harmony. Be ready to help out with whatever she needed.

7

With Patience in the pram, Harmony was beginning to despair over the lost bug's recapture. It scuttled away at high speed every time the light from her, Candy's or Robbie's torches picked it out. One blink and it had disappeared. Eventually, by blocking escape routes with hard-backed picture books, the creature was scooped into Robbie's container.

'Make sure the lid's on,' Harmony said.

'Can you tell me what it is now?' Robbie asked.

Candy took the lidded container to the still-open book.

As lack of sleep was taking its toll, Harmony flopped into an armchair and closed her eyes.

'Goodness!' Candy exclaimed.

'What is it? What is it?' Robbie asked.

Harmony opened only one eye, hoping soon to be able to close it again.

'Goodness.'

She opened the other eye and found Candy staring at her.

The alarm in Candy's expression churned Harmony's stomach. 'What's up?'

Robbie jumped up and down as though bouncing on an imaginary pogo stick. 'What is it?'

'It's a cockroach,' Candy whispered.

'*What?*' Harmony was on her toes in a flash to compare

the real-life insect with the photograph in the book. 'Eek.'

'It's all right, we found it.'

'But it's a *cockroach*.' Horrified, she stared back at Candy.

'We'll clean the floor, and the books. Job done.'

'No... James... He was in here with Tim. They found something. James mentioned a spider, but Tim was about to say something different when his dad shut him up. It must have been the roach.'

Why hadn't James told her, helped them catch the creature? His silence suggested he had something else in mind. Something that wasn't at all neighbourly. Although unsure at first, once they'd begun chatting, she'd gotten to like him. But after that hard look, as he'd revealed his occupation, she'd reversed her opinion. Of course it was important not to have an infestation, but she could have explained the situation.

When he'd turned cold and distant, she'd wondered if he'd caught her staring, fascinated by the cowlick in his hair, sweeping the brown strands to one side. How his eyes were so incredibly blue against his perhaps slightly tanned skin. He was the most gorgeous-looking man she'd ever set eyes on.

She'd been convinced he'd suspected her of sizing him up when there was a Mrs Traffurth somewhere in the picture. By the fire in her skin, she must have turned an unattractive shade of beetroot, confirming his suspicions.

But it hadn't been any of that. It had all been about the roach. Or was it both? She hoped she didn't see him any time soon... if at all.

'So?' Candy said. 'What about James?'

'When I asked him what he did for a living, he gave me a very hard, very unkind look.'

Candy slapped her hand down on the table in a show of impatience. '*And?*'

'*He's an Environmental Health Officer.*'

She appeared to deflate faster than a blown-up

balloon, released before tying the end. 'Oh, goodness.'

Oh, goodness indeed. Harmony spoke to Robbie. 'There are rules about certain insects in buildings. Some people are specially trained to make sure that we, and others, stick to those rules. Cockroaches carry dangerous bugs that can fall off when they walk around.'

'How are they dangerous? What do they do?'

'Well, if these tiny bugs get into our food or on our hands that we later put in our mouths, we can get very sick. So we must wash them straight away, with lots of soap and very warm water. I'll get someone to tell Saskia to wash her hands too.'

'You don't need to,' he said. 'I saw her washing them in the cloakroom, but we might need more soap.'

Harmony let out a long breath. "Grandfather" hopefully wouldn't learn of the insect's identity. If the story became known outside the Hall, its reputation might become sullied. The council or Care Quality Commission might become involved. But, from James's demeanour, it was a given that the local environmental health department would pay them a visit at the first opportunity.

'From now on, we'll identify bugs outside,' Harmony said.

Robbie nodded before trotting off to a wash hand basin, and she and Candy followed.

Harmony would take the roach to one of the outbuildings; she was sure she'd need it as evidence of recapture.

When Robbie emerged from the cloakroom, his hands were pink from hot water. 'Do the specially trained people get down on the floor looking for cockroaches like we did?'

'They certainly look carefully in all sorts of places.'

'Wow. Like detectives?'

'I suppose so. Tim's dad is an Environmental Health Officer—which is also known as a Public Health Inspector. Because they go around inspecting things.'

'*Inspector?* That's like a detective too, and they go

inspecting places for cockroaches?'

'As well as other things. Let's keep the library closed until it's cleaned.'

After all evidence of both sittings for the evening meal was cleared away, Harmony grasped the biggest gong mallet from the stand in the staircase hall. She struck the suspended forty-inch Zildjian bronze alloy gong three times, the big wool tip of the beater making contact just below the centre marking. The powerful resonance grew to a pleasing roar. It meant all staff and children must assemble downstairs without delay.

With everyone in the dining room, Harmony stood on the stage and projected her voice. 'We're going to have a special cleaning and tidying blitz of the Hall with you all being split into teams.'

There were sounds of protests and groans.

'As a reward, tomorrow night, we'll watch a great film with lots of yummy snacks.'

The kids cheered.

She would prove to any inspectors the place was far too hygienic to harbour cockroaches.

After an early Saturday morning breakfast, the kids were shepherded to the entertainment rooms.

Just after nine, the main door intercom bell sounded. The CCTV screen showed two men, neither of whom Harmony recognised.

She pressed the talk button. 'Hello?'

'Environmental Health.'

'One moment.'

When she opened the door, Patience strapped around her, she gave a welcoming, confident smile. 'Good morning.'

One of the men was bald, exceptionally tall and slim, as though he'd been stretched. The other was of average height and build, with a mop of brown hair.

'We've come to inspect the premises. We have reason to believe there might be a pest problem.' Inspector Brown Mop made the introductions and they showed their credentials.

She feigned surprise. 'Oh? Why do you think that?'

'We don't divulge sources of information, madam,' Inspector Brown Mop said.

The inspectors donned some disposable gloves and Inspector Stretched said, 'We'd like to start in the library.'

Guessing which library was of interest, she led them straight there.

They moved the chairs, sofa and bean bags and examined the rugs. They crawled around aiming torches under the bookshelves, giving Harmony the unappealing view of their rear ends from all manner of angles.

She'd thought it best to let them scour the place so they could be confident there was no pest. If they'd admitted the reason for their visit, she would have explained. But they'd preferred to play games. Well, she could too.

'Has this room been cleaned recently?' Inspector Stretched asked almost accusingly.

'Yes.' She kept her face deadpan because the battle was not yet won. They would try to find fault somewhere, she was sure.

'We'd like to see where the meat's stored next,' Inspector Stretched said.

She led them to the kitchen area.

The men removed their disposable gloves, chucked them into a pedal bin and found new pairs. They checked the refrigerators and freezers with their thermometer, performed visual checks on all the surfaces and delved into cupboards and drawers.

'This is one of the most—'

'If not *the* most—'

'Cleanest places we've—'

'Ever inspected.'

She hoped the inspectors would repeat what they'd just

said to James.

'Have you ever had any cockroaches in the place?' Inspector Brown Mop asked.

'Yesterday,' she said. 'An insect-obsessed boy found a bug in the garden and brought it in for identification, but it escaped. We recaptured it and have informed the boy that, from now on, all insect finds must be identified outside.'

The men exchanged glances.

'You wouldn't happen to have the cockroach?' Inspector Stretched asked.

She couldn't help a tad of smugness creeping into her tone. 'I do.'

The men exchanged more glances. 'May we see it?'

She led them to the outbuilding with the roach and switched on the light. It illuminated stacks of shelving with a single line of glass jars and a large terrarium. 'This is where Robbie keeps his garden insects.'

The men homed in on the jar containing the cockroach.

'And this is exactly the same one that was in the library yesterday?' Inspector Brown Mop asked.

'Yes.'

Inspector Stretched rocked on his heels. 'Taking the cockroach will lay concerns to rest at a higher level, prove the risk has been eliminated.'

So James was senior to them? She'd have liked to have offered to wrap it, finishing off the gift with a bright red bow. Or an offensive sign.

'I understand.' She'd warned Robbie this might happen. But he'd been far more interested in the inspectors than worrying over losing his find.

'Are any insects kept inside?' Inspector Brown Mop asked once the roach was stashed in his case.

'Some.'

'May we take a look? To check there's nothing else that could pose a danger to health.'

'Yes, of course.'

In Robbie's room, the men peered into the terrarium

housing the stick insects and then at the stinkpot terrapins basking on their rocks under the UV lamp.

'Do any of the other children have pets?' Inspector Stretched asked.

'One of the girls has fish.' Harmony knew more than she'd ever wanted to know about fish and insects. The Hall hadn't yet had an avid bird-watcher join them, but it was only a matter of time. At least Katie's interests were external; she couldn't beam the moon and stars into the Hall through her astronomical telescope.

'May we see some of the other rooms, and bathrooms, for completeness' sake?' Inspector Stretched asked.

Harmony led them to wherever the inspectors indicated and all areas were spotless.

'This boy of yours,' Inspector Stretched said as they made their way out.

'Robbie?'

'Yes. How old is he?'

'Eight.'

'Such a passion for insects. All those posters on his walls.'

'Yes. He reads up on everything he finds—and more.' She was grateful Robbie wasn't an arachnophile—although there was a good chance his interest might broaden into spiders...

'I wonder where he'll end up,' Inspector Brown Mop said.

Inspector Stretched smiled. 'I reckon he'll be an entomologist.'

'Going by the interest he's shown since he's learned about safety with insects,' she said, 'I think Robbie's much more likely to become an Environmental Health Officer.'

8

That afternoon, Harmony made her way downstairs with Patience in the carrier.

Candy spotted them and waited for them to reach the last tread. 'Where are you off to?'

'Perdita's get-together.'

'I think it's best Patience stays here. You'll be seeing the same people you met at the baby group and there might be another misunderstanding.'

'I've already told my friend I'm Patience's foster mum—although I'm hoping to adopt her.'

Candy lowered her voice, 'That's not going to happen. There are so many childless couples—'

Harmony's lungs became tight. 'But not so many childless couples of Black heritage looking to adopt. I might end up being a last resort, even though I'm not from a Black ethnic background and am single.'

Katie, the seventeen-year-old budding astronomer, came by to go upstairs. But Nia, a fourteen-year-old girl with long brown pigtails, quickly came down with her drawing pad and pencil case, saying, 'Harmony wants to adopt Patience but—'

'Nia!' Harmony exclaimed. Out of all the kids in the Hall, Nia had to have the most acute hearing by far.

'I didn't mean to listen. I was trying to get the shading right on the spindles on the stairs.'

Nia aspired to having an artistic career, supplementing school art lessons with ones on social media. Which was an amazing turnaround from the angry, intractable girl who'd joined the Hall two years ago following a string of failed placements.

'You'd make a great mum,' Katie said. 'You love me more than mine.'

Harmony put a tight arm around her. 'I'm truly sorry about your mum.'

Despite promises, every time a younger Katie had been reintroduced to the family home, her mother had reverted to leaving the underaged child alone, including having nights away. No food. No money for the meter. Clothes unwashed. Even now, her mother missed many of the arranged family visits.

'You're like a mum to all of us,' Nia said.

Harmony smiled. 'Thank you.' She sideways hugged them both. They were delightful kids.

Candy waved them away, saying, 'Off you go.'

The children wandered off.

In the office, she said, 'Let me take Patience. Just for the visit to Perdita's.'

Not having Patience with her meant Harmony wouldn't have to explain her situation to anyone else, which, considering what had happened at the baby group, might not be a bad thing.

'Thanks, Candy.'

Harmony had worn flats to walk to Perdita's. As she turned into the gravelled drive, she had an impulse to swivel around and make her way home again, her confidence diving. The tension and butterflies were hard to ignore, but she took a deep breath before striding forward to rap at the door.

It was opened by a stranger who returned to the group she'd been talking to after a perfunctory greeting. Harmony slung her coat across the already over-laden bannister and made her way into a large living room, still carrying a bottle of white wine. As she failed to find Luke and Miranda, a nervous twinge plucked at her heart.

The burst of a child screaming led her to investigate the room opposite.

Underneath the bay window, darkened by foliage, two girls were playing with a train set.

The little girl with blonde pigtails was screaming, 'I had it first. She took it!'

Luke was crouching next to her. 'Is there another train driver in the Duplo box?'

'No!'

'Petal, calm down.'

The other little girl with short dark hair was clutching something close to her chest. 'I want him.'

'You know what happens when kids can't play nicely with something?' Luke said. 'Neither of you get to play with it. Who's played with the driver the longest today?'

The other girl pointed at Petal.

'Then, Petal, it's time to let your friend have a go. You can load and unload the train and later, you can swap back.'

The girls began to play.

He straightened and smiled when he spotted Harmony. 'Hello. Glad you could make it. Petal's my goddaughter. Perdita's her mum.'

'Oh. Hi, Luke, Petal.' Harmony gave a little wave, but Petal only glanced around and then concentrated on the game.

He gestured to where Miranda and a man with black hair—the second daddy?—were sitting. 'Come and join us.'

'I'm so pleased you made it,' Miranda said.

Harmony smiled. 'Me too.'

'This is Gavin, the other daddy,' Luke said.

Harmony extended her hand. 'Hi.'

Gavin stood to shake it. 'Pleased to meet you. Would you like a drink?'

'Not for the moment, thanks. But could you pass this to

Perdita?' She handed the bottle over and took a seat next to Luke.

'Where's Patience?' Miranda asked.

'A colleague's taking care of her.'

Gavin had been studying them with a puckered brow. 'How come you guys know each other?'

'We met at a baby group,' Harmony said, then wished she hadn't as his expression darkened.

'You met Luke and Miranda at a baby group?'

She didn't want him to feel he'd missed out. 'Yes, although it didn't come across as a particularly friendly place.'

He addressed Luke. 'You and Miranda went to a baby group without me?'

'I should have mentioned it.' Luke's shoulders appeared high from tension. 'Sorry.'

'You deliberately didn't tell me.' Gavin flung a hurt glance Luke's way before leaving the room.

'I'm sorry,' Harmony said. 'I'd no idea—'

Miranda scowled at Luke. 'We agreed everyone knows everything in this triple relationship. Well, don't you think you'd better go after him?'

He disappeared through the doorway, his head bowed like a chastened boy.

'I'm sorry—' Harmony began.

'Not your fault. Luke's not playing by the rules. All I need is a breakup between those boys...' Miranda tutted and raised her gaze to the ceiling.

'It must be hard being part of a three-parent family.'

She smiled. 'Sometimes. Although it's a plus having regular breaks. But I do miss Oscar when he's not with me. Now, tell me more about Patience.'

Harmony gave a detailed account, ending with, 'Whoever dropped Patience off charged out of the grounds so probably wasn't a mother who'd recently given birth. The police believed there must have been a vehicle tucked out of view of the cameras.'

'Do you think the father dropped the baby off?'

She nodded. 'I'm wondering if the mother's underage—the police thought so too. But if she doesn't come forward soon, she won't have a say in what happens to her baby.'

Thinking about Patience moving on strained her breaths. Candy had taught her deep breathing—getting tips like that was one of the perks of having a fully-trained nurse on board. In the past, she'd worked at Bristol Royal Hospital for Children.

'Would you need to be married to adopt Patience?' Miranda asked.

'Married is better. Engaged might do to prove the stability of a relationship. However, Patience needs at least one of her new parents to have a Black ethnic background. But if they can't find a suitable couple...'

Miranda stroked Oscar's cheek. 'I'm not in any kind of relationship either. Never have been.' She put her mouth to Harmony's ear. 'I'm still a virgin.'

Harmony's eyes bulged.

'As I told you in the café, it was a turkey baster job.'

'I remember but... *never?*'

'No. You?'

'Yes,' Harmony said. 'I lived with him. We were to be married before he dumped me.'

'Here you are,' a kind voice said. 'Sorry I couldn't say hello earlier.'

Turning, she saw a pretty, younger woman with mousey hair and brown eyes.

'I'm Perdita.'

'Hi. I'm Harmony. Thank you so much for inviting me.'

'It's a pleasure to have you.'

They shook hands.

'My foster child isn't with me—I left her with Candy. I believe you know her?'

'Yes, she found me a couple of girls to babysit when I had a summer party,' Perdita said. 'We're expecting some other newcomers. The vicar and his wife and baby and a friend of my husband's with his son.'

They went into the other reception room so Harmony could meet more people.

'This is Faith,' Miranda said. 'Best friends with Perdita as well as with Luke and Gavin. Her baby's sound asleep in the study with a couple of other little ones.'

Harmony smiled and they shook hands.

Someone ushered in a couple carrying a baby. The man was obviously the expected vicar and his wife had long, dark hair held back with an Alice band. She wore a long, patterned dress that went down almost to her ankles, sensible boots for walking and a chunky-knit cardigan.

Perdita walked towards them. 'It's so nice to see you… Everyone, this is Roxanne and The Reverend…'

Faith gasped.

Harmony turned to look at her.

'… Matthew Codd,' Perdita finished lamely appearing confused.

Faith grabbed Perdita's arm and guided her out of the room.

'Oh, God,' Roxanne moaned.

'What is it?' her husband asked. 'Who is that woman?'

Roxanne bit her lip and her brow furrowed. 'Someone I'd hoped not to bump into again.'

Harmony wondered what Roxanne had done to provoke Faith's reaction and was weighing up whether to introduce herself when voices she recognised came out of nowhere.

Perdita: 'What's wrong?'

Faith: 'Please can you ask her to leave?'

Perdita: 'What's she done?'

Faith: 'She's Roxy. You know, Foxy Roxy—aka Roxanne Miller. The woman who sells personal pleasure equipment, the woman who had an affair with my ex, and that's probably his child. And she cheated on him by picking up married men at service stations.'

Frantically, Roxanne searched for the source of the sound. Harmony couldn't see a baby monitor anywhere either.

'What's going on?' Matthew asked. 'What does she mean?'

'I'll tell you when we get home.' Roxanne turned over the cushions on the sofa.

Her husband frowned. 'I don't understand.'

Her eyes became moist as she stared at the floor, her expression stricken.

Perdita: 'And it was Roxanne who tried to seduce Tom?'

Faith: 'Yes. Invited him to join her at some motel when she found out he was a Catholic priest. That woman's got no boundaries.'

Roxanne must have a thing for clerics, Harmony thought.

Perdita: 'I'd no idea she was Foxy Roxy. I met her at the baby clinic. I've only known her as Roxanne Codd. I'd never do anything to hurt you.'

Faith: 'I know. That's why we're talking in private.'

Roxanne's gaze flicked around the room. 'I've changed.'

She certainly didn't appear dressed for affairs and picking up men at service stations and, as she'd already nabbed a cleric, needn't look for another.

'I'm not that person anymore,' Roxanne told her husband.

The Reverend Matthew Codd stared at his wife as though he didn't recognise her. 'What is personal *pleasure* equipment?'

'I sold the franchise,' Roxanne whispered, her skin pale.

'What franchise?'

A man said, 'I'm putting a stop to this,' and left the room, presumably for the study.

'That's Tom, Faith's husband,' Miranda whispered.

No one spoke.

Tom: 'Everyone in the living room can hear your conversation through the baby monitors.'

Perdita: 'Oh, no.'

Tom: 'Finish your conversation in the kitchen so no more damage is done.'

Faith: 'All right, but you'd best ask The Reverend Matthew Codd to keep an eye on his parishioners and check his wife's not working her way through the lot of them.'

A sob broke from Roxanne. She turned to leave and her husband followed her.

Tom: 'Faith! That's so unkind. It's none of our business now. Leave it.'

Faith: 'You're right. I went too far. I'm sorry.'

The front door soon clicked open and banged softly closed and there were sounds of footsteps on the gravel outside.

Through the window, Harmony saw them wrap their baby up and put their coats on as they walked. She wondered how the conversation would go when they got back home. With Roxanne's apparent life turnaround, she was determined not to judge her. Harmony didn't have the full story and would not condemn a woman she didn't know for a past she appeared to bitterly regret. She understood how soul-destroying public humiliation felt.

'If she's turned over a new leaf...' she said, 'and is now a vicar's wife...'

But no one replied and gradually conversations resumed. A woman entered and someone whispered something to her.

The woman came to reach behind the sofa by Harmony, pulled out a bag and fished out a baby monitor. 'Sorry—I'd gone to the loo. Otherwise, I'd have switched it off.'

'Not your fault,' a man said. 'We put ours on top of the bookcase. We needed to know if the babies woke up—they come first.'

Having two sources of sound explained why it had been

so difficult for Roxanne to find either monitor.

A few minutes later, Faith, Tom and Perdita returned and the room went quiet again.

'Oh, she's gone,' Perdita said.

'I'm sorry,' Faith said. 'Perhaps she has changed… after all, she's married a vicar. It was a shock to see her and my ex's baby. At least, she said it was his…' Faith turned to Perdita. 'I'm so sorry…'

She put her arm around Faith. 'I understand it was a shock—I think we all do.'

A baby began to cry, hesitantly at first but soon built up to a lusty wail. Two people left the room, presumably to discover whose baby had wakened.

A clear image of Patience developed in Harmony's mind. She could detect that precious baby smell, Patience's weight against her chest. Picture her gummy smile, the way she waved her tiny, soft doll with her tiny fingers. Hear her cooing.

Whatever time she had left, Harmony wanted to be there for Patience. She was going home.

9

Harmony abandoned Escape Plan A—leaving through the front door—when she glanced towards the sound of voices from outside the window. James and Tim were approaching the house.

She missed Patience, had recently witnessed the upsetting scene with Roxanne, felt mortified that James had probably noticed how she'd been unable to tear her gaze away when they'd met and was still smarting from the full-on environmental health inspection. She had no idea whether he'd mention the cockroach or make a public quip dissing her or the Hall. If she were to burst into tears, there'd be more drama at Perdita's than a soap's Christmas special. It all amounted to one thing—she wanted to avoid James like a dose of norovirus.

But how could she escape *and* avoid him?

Escape Plan B: find the back door—but might she be trapped in Perdita's garden? Abandon Escape Plan B.

Escape Plan C? Find a place to hide until she could achieve a clear getaway.

'Where's the loo?' Harmony whispered to Miranda.

'There's one off the hall. If that's taken, there's another on the floor above.'

Attempting to take refuge in the downstairs loo was out of the question as, if it was occupied, she'd be stranded in the hallway or kitchen and would be bound to run into

James. *The Great Escape* came to mind, but tunnelling her way out from the ground floor toilet wasn't an option.

Miranda focused on her more carefully. 'Are you all right?'

'I'm fine. I just... I'm missing Patience.'

'Would you like to leave?' Miranda asked.

'I must get to a loo first.' Harmony hastened away.

When she was scooting past the people in the hall, there was a rap at the front door. By the time there were greetings between someone and the newcomers, she was on the flat part of the dog-legged staircase that allowed a 180-degree turn. On the landing, she peered into the room of the first door that was ajar and discovered the bathroom.

After locking herself inside, she sat on the loo seat and focused on her erratic breathing.

There was a gentle tap on the door putting, an instant stop to her air intake.

'Harmony, it's Luke.' His voice was just audible; hopefully no one downstairs would be able to hear it. 'I saw you rush in, and you didn't look too good. Are you all right?'

She didn't think she was. 'It's nothing you can help with.' Unless there was a secret passage out of there, a hidden secret realm she could access at the touch of a loose tile or the facility to safely abseil out of the window.

'Are you ill?'

'Not yet.' How long would her way be barred by wanting to avoid James? She hoped he had a strong bladder and, if he didn't, the downstairs loo would be vacant.

'A trouble told is a trouble halved. I'm a good listener.'

'I've already told it.' Well, some of it.

'Talk to Uncle Luke about it and halve it again. Unless you'd like me to get Miranda?'

Extracting Miranda from a group of people she might be chatting to could create curiosity; others might follow suspecting more help was needed. Harmony didn't want that kind of attention. She slid the bolt back and opened the door a crack to check Luke was alone.

'Will you come downstairs to talk or do I come in here? The alternative is to carry on the conversation on the landing so anyone can listen.'

Well, she certainly didn't want that. She stepped aside, and Luke joined her before she bolted the door again.

'You don't have a baby monitor on you, do you?'

He chuckled. 'I heard about that—and the tail end of the conversation when they came into the kitchen.' He put his arms up. 'I'm clean. No listening device.'

She couldn't help smiling; he was so nice—warm and funny.

'So, what's up? Is it to do with Patience? Miranda told me about the mix-up at the café and about you wanting to keep her.'

Harmony sat back on the loo seat—she may as well take advantage of the bathroom-based therapy session Luke appeared to be offering. 'I would like to keep her, but what's in my best interests isn't in Patience's. So, it's likely I'll have to give her up. I need friends outside of work, but I find it hard to be around babies because I'm sure I'll lose her.'

He smiled kindly. 'I longed for a baby too.'

Perching on the edge of the bath, he leaned towards her, his forearms resting on his knees. His presence was surprisingly reassuring.

'But you've got Oscar now,' she said.

'Yes, although there's the complex situation of Oscar having three parents and two homes. But we're working it out.'

Thinking it would help to distract her from her own cares, she asked, 'Have you made up with Gavin?'

Luke studied his ring finger. 'Yes. For now.'

'How come it's only for now?'

'It's complicated,' he said.

'It usually is.'

'I want to spend more time with Oscar than Gavin does, so I sneaked in extra contact time. I shouldn't have; it's my fault he got upset. I'll just have to learn to accept the situation.' Luke buried his face in his hands. 'The thing is, I miss Oscar so much when I'm not with him.'

Her heart beat in sympathy. She couldn't get enough of Patience either. Her milky breath, the trust she put in Harmony as her head lulled sleepily against her neck, the snuffling noises as she slept, cooing to songs. The way Patience stared into Harmony's eyes when feeding, unknowingly strengthening the connection between them...

'Of course you'd miss Oscar,' she said.

'But not to the extent I feel jealous that Miranda has him most of the time?' As Luke raised his head, his eyes were teary.

She joined him on the edge of the bath and put an arm around him.

He relaxed towards her for a moment. 'Do you want to explain why you're hiding in here?'

'It's my new neighbour, James.'

'What did he do?' Luke chuckled. 'Or was it that he caught *you* doing something?'

She raised her hands. 'Not me this time. One of the Hall's kids lost an insect he'd brought in to identify, and James and his son saw it when they called around to introduce themselves. Instead of telling me, letting me explain and helping us catch it, he reported us—presumably for having a suspected infestation.'

'What a bastard!'

'He happens, would you believe, to be an Environmental Health Officer.'

'Entirely Heartless Oaf more like—of the jobsworth species.'

She giggled. 'We had a full-on inspection this morning, and I can't face him. At least, not right now.'

'Sounds a douchebag. Do you need me to smuggle you out of here? Get a disguise and so on?'

She laughed. 'What would you suggest?'

'Mm... Be a vicar—by wearing Tom's priest garb? Or a cleaner—carry a bucket while hiding behind a mop? Or how about wearing Perdita's apron and shielding your face with a platter as though you're part of a hospitality service? I'm sure Perdita would be game.'

Surprise caught her. 'You'd do all that for me?'

'Of course. A friend in need...'

'Thanks for the offer, but perhaps you could distract him instead, lead him into the kitchen when I make my getaway?'

'Sure.'

'You know, I think he has a problem with the kids at the Hall too.'

'How so?'

'His expression changed when he found out it was a council-run children's home. But I introduced his son Tim to two of the boys. They're great kids—never been in trouble.'

'Have you got young offenders there?'

'Some children can be challenging, especially initially, but we help them through that. There's no active police involvement with any of them at the moment. You should have seen how miserable Tim appeared when he came. His eyes were shining when he left because he'd had such a good time. I don't think James trusts us.' Rather, he didn't trust *her*.

It was unreasonable of her to expect him to—they were strangers, and he was understandably looking out for his son. But she had a loyalty to the Hall kids too.

'Sounds like a *certified* douchebag.'

Although warmed by the support she was getting, she wasn't sure what Luke meant by "certified douchebag" and whether he'd just made it up. 'It's a thing?'

'I believe you can get certified douchebag documents, T-shirts and whatnot.'

Before she could ask where from, someone tried the door handle. She sprang to her feet.

Luke splashed cold water on his face and then blotted it off with one of the towels. 'We'd best get back to the party. Don't worry, you've got me, Gavin, Miranda and Perdita as friends now. In time, you'll get to know more of us.'

A warm fuzziness stole over her.

Luke opened the door a crack. 'Whoever was there has gone.'

They were leaving the bathroom when Luke pulled her into a hug. 'Maybe you'll soon be a mother with a baby to look after.'

Smiling, she returned the brotherly embrace.

Luke walked to the stairs, but Harmony came to an abrupt halt on the landing. James Traffurth must have discreetly withdrawn to the doorway of a bedroom when he'd found the bathroom occupied. He got to his feet from the crouching position after apparently tying his shoelace and was gawping goggle-eyed. He'd witnessed the hug, heard Luke's words—and his sums had most likely added up to five.

Before she could tell James his maths was wrong, and she and Luke hadn't been copulating in the bathroom, he hurried inside and the lock snapped into place. She guessed he hadn't such a strong bladder after all.

'Where will I find this James?' Luke asked as she caught up with him and they made the turn on the stairs.

'He's just gone into the bathroom. He was up there, in a doorway, when we came out. You should have seen the look he gave me.'

Luke laughed. 'Oh... he'd have thought...'

'It's not funny. It's going to make it even harder to face him.' She should have taken Luke up on that offer of disguise.

10

Two weeks after Perdita's get-together, Harmony was in the office dressing Patience in her all-in-one while Candy was busy with some admin. Harmony was going to meet Miranda in the café on High Street.

'How's Saskia shaping up?' she asked.

On Saskia's first day at work, some toilet water had splashed onto her. She'd become so hysterical, she'd had to shower and borrow some clothes. Now she had an extra locker for her own clean clothes and towels in case of further mishaps.

Candy raised her gaze to the ceiling. 'Well, she's still turning up.'

Harmony wished she could find a role better suited to Saskia's talents to meet Roderick Walker's six-month challenge.

The newsagent was next to the café. As there was time to browse the magazines, Harmony lifted Patience out of the pram and carried her inside. 'Morning, Ramesh.'

His smile was welcoming.

The sought-after display was along a wall behind the shop window; Harmony scanned the titles. Her eyes bulged. Unbelievably, there was a magazine with the headline: *How to Get a Guy in Ten Days*. She grabbed it with the latest puzzle compendium.

Being engaged might help her adopt Patience if there was no suitable couple available. But, regardless of that, Harmony had no one special to share things with, the good times and the bad. *She wanted love.* Moving into the Dower House by herself was sad. All that space, all those bedrooms, to herself…

When she passed the publications to Ramesh, he said, 'You've got more than ten days to get to know your new neighbour. These things shouldn't be hurried.'

She stiffened. Her and the Entirely Heartless Oaf? No way! 'It's not for me, it's—'

'For a friend?' Ramesh chuckled, shaking his head. 'Harmony, you can't fool me.'

Her face burning, she bet he could compare her to someone caught in a shower of red powder at a Hindu Holi festival.

'If you want some help,' he said, 'I could invite you both to dinner. I've been taking note of customers for years and there's been no one as suitable as him.'

Ramesh has been on the lookout for years? 'I think you're barking up the wrong leylandii.'

He giggled. 'If that's how you want to play it… I'll say no more, other than James seems ideal for you. Close to where you work, you like kids—and he's got one who needs a mother—handsome, has a good job…'

She pursed her lips. 'Do you profile all your customers?'

He shrugged. 'I'm a newsagent. Customers talk. New people come in… I ask questions—to be polite of course. I've always felt sad that, despite being a great person, you're on your own. I did wonder but the headline that caught your eye has confirmed it is guys you're interested in.'

Harmony's jaw slackened.

'So now, I give the advice.' He flicked his hand down and smiled. 'Don't worry. I listen and I hear, but I never tell anyone anything.'

'Like you didn't just tell me about my neighbour's attributes.'

'Those are for anyone to see. I wouldn't reveal what's in someone else's heart.'

She didn't want to offend him, and she did want the publications...

He reached out to receive the offered note and passed her the change.

'Have you had—or do you intend to have—a similar conversation with my new neighbour? Because if you do, I'd like to save you the trouble. We've already met, and I don't think either of us is the other's ideal match.'

Apparently undeterred, he grinned. 'Sometimes men need help to see things more clearly.'

Ramesh wasn't hearing the message. 'I'm so not interested in James.' *Not anymore.* 'And I'm sure he isn't the least interested in me.'

'Don't worry, I can be very discreet, very subtle. Harmony, we've known each other for years and built up such an easy friendship. I'm on your side.'

Nevertheless, she felt he was being a little too personal, a little too intrusive. 'Ramesh, James isn't "The One".'

Ramesh's grin widened. 'I'm very sorry, Harmony. I think he is.'

11

As Harmony was wedging the magazine and puzzle book down the side of the pram mattress, a buggy drew up alongside.

It was Roxanne, the vicar's wife, bundled in a beige coat, a stripy, fluffy scarf and a woolly hat.

'Hi. I think we met at Perdita's a while back.'

'Yes, that's right,' Harmony said.

Where did her loyalties lie? But Roxanne had done nothing to her and everyone needed an ally. Although Harmony didn't approve of affairs with attached men, unlike her sister Melody, Roxanne had appeared genuinely contrite.

Roxanne smiled tentatively. 'I don't know your name, but I expect you remember mine.'

Was she short of friends too? 'I'm Harmony. Nice to meet you.' They shook hands and Harmony indicated the baby. 'This is Patience. I'm fostering her.'

'She's cute. This is my son, Joshua.' He was a bonny, contented-looking boy.

Harmony said hello in an enthusiastic tone she used for babies and young children and gave him a big smile. When he gave a gummy grin back, her heart contracted. 'He's gorgeous.' She was due to meet Miranda. What to do to cause the least offence? 'I'm going into the café to meet a friend. Would you like to join us? Or do you have a history with Miranda too?'

'Miranda? Never heard of her.'

Harmony's shoulders relaxed. 'Shall we then? We can leave the pram and buggy in their backyard—there's a gate we can go through.'

'Love to. Thank you, I... need someone to talk to.'

When Miranda entered wearing the Opal Fruits/Starburst ensemble she'd had on when Harmony had first met her, she and Roxanne were having coffee and croissants while Joshua dribbled over a teething biscuit in the highchair. Patience was in Harmony's arms, and she raised one of them to get Miranda's attention, hoping she wouldn't mind Roxanne's presence.

Miranda joined them with a cup of coffee and a chocolate brownie, and sat next to Harmony, who made the introductions.

Glancing at Roxanne, Miranda asked, 'Will it cause a problem with Faith if she finds out I've been socialising with you? I basically live with her. She and Tom have my employer's annexe and are around the main house every day.'

'You live with Faith and Tom?' Roxanne said. 'Does that mean you'd rather I wasn't here?'

Miranda shrugged.

'I don't want to pick sides,' Harmony said, stroking Patience's head. 'Whatever happened in the past has nothing to do with me.' She cut her croissant one-handedly, spread a thick chunk of butter on the flaky pastry and ate from the middle as she always did.

Miranda broke off a piece of the chocolate brownie. 'I guess it's none of my business either.'

'Faith is right to be mad at me,' Roxanne said. 'I did wrong, but I've tried to make amends and live a better life. I'm trying to be a good mother to Joshua but it's not easy.'

'Not easy?' Harmony asked.

'Being a good wife and a good mother doesn't come naturally to me, and I should have been more honest with

Matt from the start. Maybe he should have been more honest with me too.'

'You can be more honest with him now,' Miranda said.

Roxanne took a sip of coffee and then bit into the end of her croissant, apparently deep in thought.

'What's he not been honest about?' Dishonesty between couples always made Harmony curious in the hope she'd be able to better understand David's deceit with her. Why had it had to have been with Melody?

Roxanne looked up as though she'd come to a decision. 'I wouldn't have said anything but... I don't have anyone else to talk to about this...'

'We won't tell,' Harmony said.

'No, we won't,' Miranda agreed.

Roxanne appeared to check the room for overhearing ears and leaned forward. They leaned closer too so that the three heads were almost touching, Harmony shifting to give Patience space.

'He didn't tell me what it would be like, with him,' Roxanne whispered. 'Once we were married, he cooled off. He's showing less and less interest in Joshua and seems to frown upon me if I take up offers of someone babysitting Joshua, so I rarely do... Since Perdita's, he's moved into one of the spare rooms.'

'I'm sorry,' Harmony said.

'He must know he's not the kind of guy I would have normally gone for. But at the time, it seemed the best option for my pregnant self. A new life in a new area with someone dependable. A stable home to bring up a child. I was feeling incredibly vulnerable back then. He was so kind to me, and I loved him for it.'

'I'm so sorry it's not turned out as you hoped,' Harmony murmured. Her life hadn't either.

'How come you married a vicar? This vicar?' Miranda asked.

'I was completely alone. I called a counselling line and was directed to a Christian coffee morning group. It was so unlike me. I suspect the pregnancy hormones morphed me into someone else. But the welcome I received felt good—and I met Matt.'

'Did he know about the baby?' Harmony asked.

'Yes.'

'So, he didn't mind?' How might an available man react to her if she managed to keep Patience? Although the idea of dating again terrified her, she didn't want to spend the rest of her life single.

'As I said, he was very sympathetic,' Roxanne told them. 'His kindness broke me down. He was lonely after his wife died. I told him how much I admired his work, devoting his life to helping others.

'But unless some huge tidal wave takes us safely back out to sea, the marriage will be a wreck in a few weeks. It's virtually on the rocks now. He's not happy with me and—well, suffice it to say, I'm not happy with him anymore. I've been faithful, but he doesn't act like he believes in me or trusts me.'

Miranda ate some more of her brownie. 'Where does Joshua's father fit in?'

'Andy refused to believe the baby was his.'

'And is he?' she asked.

'I can't be sure. I wasn't a one-man kind of girl. Andy refused to do a paternity test.'

'So whose name did you put on the birth certificate?' Harmony asked.

'Father unknown.'

Poor Joshua.

Roxanne's eyes brimmed with tears, light from the window making them shine. 'I can't go on like I am now, I feel so alone, and I'm sorry for burdening you...'

'Don't worry about it,' Harmony told her. 'We all need to share our troubles from time to time.'

Miranda nodded. 'Always happy to listen.'

Roxanne smiled wanly. 'Thanks.'

It was difficult to imagine how she'd done such a

complete turnaround as to marry a vicar, but how could Harmony judge someone for wanting a stable family life for herself and her son? 'I hope things change for the better.'

Miranda agreed and then asked about Pinkerton Hall. After Harmony had described the setup, Miranda said, 'I was brought up with foster families and then at a children's home. Pinkerton Hall sounds so much nicer than where I lived.'

'We do our best.' When Harmony opened her mouth to ask why Miranda hadn't been with her family, the sudden set expression on her face told her the question would not be welcome. So she squeezed Miranda's hand instead.

Roxanne was gawking at Harmony. 'If all the other kids are so much older than Patience, how come you're fostering her?'

As Harmony explained, she stroked slumbering Patience's hand. Then she added, 'I've asked the social worker if I can adopt her, but there doesn't seem to be much chance.' Her eyes began to sting. 'I'm very sensitive about babies at the moment...'

Roxanne reached across the table to pat her wrist. 'I'll be rooting for you.'

Miranda said, 'Me too.'

Harmony gave a feeble smile. 'I felt, when I found Patience, that maybe she'd been left for me. That Fate had given me a gift.'

Roxanne held her gaze and appeared distant as though deep in thought. 'What if you got a partner and later had a baby of your own? Would you love Patience less?'

'I'd love any baby. I can't have children of my own.'

'Oh, I'm so sorry,' they said.

Harmony gave a sad laugh. 'Just to show you how desperate I am, I bought a magazine with an article on how to get a guy in ten days. Being in a committed relationship might help the adoption score. But having a partner might not make any difference, especially if he doesn't have a Black ethnic background.'

Sympathy showed on their faces.

'Don't rush into anything,' Roxanne warned. 'Honestly, it's not worth it.'

Harmony pushed the pram into the empty office. Patience was playing with a row of plastic toys fixed across the frame and didn't fret when Harmony retrieved her magazine and puzzle book.

How to Get a Guy in Ten Days took up a double-page spread. There was an image of a man and a woman laughing together. Below it was an introductory paragraph and columns of numbered advice.

The phone rang. A staff member reported their car had broken down so Harmony needed to find someone to cover the shift. She moved to a computer terminal to check who might be free. The first person she called agreed to fill the breach.

She punched the air, pleased to have such a quick resolution. Then she amended the rota. When she turned to go back to her original chair, she started with a small squeak.

Nia was leaning over the desk, perusing the article.

'Oh! I didn't hear you knock,' Harmony said.

'I did knock. You raised your arm for me to come in.'

'Oh…' Nia must have misunderstood the air punch. Harmony wondered what Nia's reading speed was and how far she'd got… 'Well, how can I help?'

'A few of us are going to Bristol this afternoon, but I left my purse in my school locker. I know it's not pocket money day, but please could I have some money?'

Harmony folded the magazine and put in it a drawer. 'Of course you can.'

After Nia mentioned the desired sum, Harmony took it out of the petty cash box and inserted a note of the transaction. 'I hope you have a lovely time.'

'Thanks.' Nia grinned. 'You too.'

12

It was Monday morning. Having studied the magazine article and tried on clothes she'd not worn in years, Harmony knew she needed a fashion fairy. At Saskia's interview, she'd revealed she helped her mother choose outfits.

'Why are we going to your apartment?' Saskia asked.

'I'd like to understand more about clothes. What things go with what, and which are complete no-nos.'

Harmony led the younger woman into her bedroom where an entire wall had storage space. She popped the baby in the cot and opened the first set of doors. 'Ignore the labels.' There was nothing special about any of the shops she'd bought them in. 'Just tell me what you think.' She steeled herself for a crushing blow.

Saskia couldn't have been warier if she'd found a pile of material poking out of a council litter bin.

'They are clean, you know.'

'I... I'm sure they are.'

'Would you prefer to wear gloves?'

Saskia hesitated but, in the end, shook her head. She stepped forward and, using the tips of her fingers, began to flick through the hangers.

Harmony rubbed one thumb over the other as her apprehension grew. 'What do you think?'

'I'd need to see them on you to know for sure. The fit

has a lot to do with it and whether the colours go with your skin tone and shade of hair and eyes. I'm not sure they all do...'

Harmony shrank inside. 'Would any of them make me look good?'

Saskia appeared apologetic. 'There's no sense of coordination or balance. Your accessories don't go with much. Did you buy them at different times?'

'I, er, just bought things when I saw them... Please, would you come shopping with me—to advise me?'

Saskia's sky-blue eyes were wide with hope. 'Shopping instead of cleaning?'

'Yes. I'll speak to your supervisor.' Harmony checked her watch. 'Meet you downstairs in ten minutes?'

The most amazing smile lit up Saskia's face, displaying two neat rows of perfectly-formed pearl teeth.

Ten minutes later, they were in Harmony's car on the way to Bristol. Patience was in her car seat and a special lightweight, collapsible pram was in the boot.

'I've never been in one of these before,' Saskia said. 'What is it?'

'A Vauxhall Astra.'

'Do you like it?'

'I do.'

'Grandfather says I should buy something more economical. Mummy's paying for the Porsche's insurance and servicing and so on, but he says it builds character to be independent. I'll be able to make better decisions later, he says, when I've learned more about life by standing on my own two feet.'

Was Saskia just switching from the influence of her mother to the influence of her grandfather without developing her own personality and life rules? 'But what do *you* think? What do *you* want to do?'

'I want to make Grandfather proud of me. He talks a lot of sense, I see that now. He's looking out for me, *genuinely* looking out for me.'

'Doesn't your mother?'

Her fingers moved up and down a small stretch of the seat belt. 'Not in the same way. I think she wants me to be like her, but Grandfather says I need to see more of life to make a true choice.'

Harmony paid the Clifton Suspension Bridge toll to cross Avon Gorge. 'How do you like working at the Hall?'

'I hated it at first but it's real life there, isn't it? People care about different things to what I'm used to. It makes me think more.'

'Is that good?'

'I think so,' Saskia said.

'Thank you for agreeing to help me.'

'That's all right. I know you need it, and I like you.'

'Er... thanks. Would you be able to teach me how to make up my face without overdoing it?'

She pointed to her own visage. 'What do you think I do every day?'

It was true; her face appeared lovely, evenly toned with delicate colour in her cheeks. Her eyes were emphasised in an understated way.

'And nails?'

She rolled her eyes. 'I told you at the interview. I can do Mummy's nails as well as style her hair.'

In a dream-like voice, Harmony said, 'Yes, so you did.'

Several exhausting hours later, Saskia helped Harmony take everything to her apartment. She'd bought a jacket, trousers, dresses, shoes, boots, belts, scarves, bags and costume jewellery.

'Grandfather says I'm bad when it comes to spending money so I can't wait to tell him what you're like when you're let loose in a shop.'

'This was a one-off,' Harmony said. 'And now I've seen for myself how good you are at these things, it's given me an idea for tomorrow. I know you're not on shift, but perhaps you could do with the overtime?'

Saskia's mouth opened in protest.

In case this was unfamiliar territory, Harmony said, 'You'd get extra pay.'

It was no surprise that Saskia baulked at the idea of working on a Saturday. But it might lead her in a direction more suited to her talents.

'Do I have to do the cleaning I didn't do today?'

'No. It would be a shopping trip with one of the girls. Would you like to talk it over with Grandfather?'

Her sweet, pink mouth snapped tightly shut. She stayed still for a moment and then nodded. 'I'll let you know tonight.'

The moment Harmony got back down to the office with Patience, the telephone rang.

'Pinkerton Hall, Harmony Payne speaking.'

'Oh, I'm glad I caught you.' The social worker's familiar voice wrenched Harmony's guts.

'Annie?'

'Yes.'

Harmony's heart pumped harder, and she glanced at Candy, who'd looked up from her work.

'We've got an emergency situation,' Annie said, 'and need to place Alfie, a seven-year-old boy, immediately. Can you take him? His care plan's complete—some one-to-one initially as he won't be going to school straight away.'

Harmony's heartbeat slowed. This wasn't about Patience. 'Could you hold for a moment while I check with Candy?'

'Of course.'

Harmony explained the purpose of the call to Candy and, after a brief discussion, she addressed Annie again.

'Candy agrees we can take him. I'm putting you on speaker so she can hear the rest of the call.'

'He's in a state of shock,' Annie said. 'He found his mother in a diabetic coma and, although he managed to call 999, she couldn't be saved. He hasn't spoken since.'

Harmony's view of Candy blurred. 'How terrible. Does he have a father?'

'He's recorded as unknown.'

Alfie was like Roxanne's son: father unknown. Working at the Hall had shown Harmony how lucky she was to have two loving parents—something she'd taken as the norm at school.

'He needs to be kept quiet so that he feels safe,' Annie added, 'and he appears to have regressed—he's more like a younger child. For the past two days, he's been with a foster mother, but there's a family crisis. There's no other foster parent available so the plan is to wait until he can return to the place he'll be coming from.'

Harmony wiped her eyes.

'Can I bring him now?' Annie asked.

'Yes, do. We'd be very happy to have him.'

As soon as the call ended, Candy said, 'The poor boy...'

Harmony nodded, not trusting herself to speak.

'I'll book some agency staff so that I can be with Alfie.'

She blew her nose. 'I'll help too.'

'You won't. You're doing too much already. You should get out or put your feet up when you can.'

The phone had woken Patience, whose whimpers changed to a bawl; she was hungry and needed changing.

A scrawny, tousled, ginger-haired boy arrived with Annie almost an hour later, freckles on pale skin, green eyes wide and red-rimmed. He clutched a limp, grey rabbit with floppy ears. Annie brought in two black holdalls of his things.

As Harmony crouched in front of the boy, she said, 'Hello, Alfie. We're very pleased you're joining us. My name is Harmony.' She gestured towards the manager. 'This is Candy.' She touched the rabbit's paw. 'Who do we have here?'

'Velvet,' Annie said.

'After *The Velveteen Rabbit*?' Harmony asked.

Although Annie shrugged, Alfie's gaze became more

intense.

Candy put out her hand. 'Come with me to the library.'

Alfie made no sign of having heard but grasped the proffered hand and went with her. Standing up, Harmony noticed Annie appeared harassed. But then she usually did, maybe because of her curly, frizzy orange hair.

Annie removed a folder from her bag. 'Can we get the paperwork over with? I've got calls to make and this has eaten into my schedule.'

The busier Annie was, the more she would delay moving Patience on, wouldn't she?

But, after all the admin was complete, Annie raised her head. 'As Patience's mother hasn't been found, I'll be seeking an expedited Placement Order.'

The clutch of dread weakened Harmony's posture, and she steadied herself by resting her arms on the desk. A Placement Order approved a child for adoption and, once a match was approved, the child would be gone.

'If you don't find a suitable match, I'd still love to adopt Patience,' she said.

'It's been noted. But you might yet have a child, and you already have your life filled with children. There are parents who—'

'I can't have children of my own.'

'Harmony, I'd no idea. I'm very sorry to hear that,' Annie said sympathetically. 'I'll be sure to enter it on the system so it's taken into consideration.'

After Annie had left, Harmony pushed the pram into the front library so Patience wouldn't be alone and then went to the kitchen to prepare refreshments.

Back in the front library, Candy was sitting with Alfie on a bean bag, one arm around him, holding him close. She was reading Jane Hissey's *Jolly Tall*, about a mysterious new package arriving in the nursery. It contained a toy giraffe who wanted to make friends with the other toys.

Alfie didn't appear to be paying any attention, but Harmony hoped the sound of Candy's rich voice soothed him. *The Velveteen Rabbit* was upturned on the table, so perhaps it was something his mother had read to him, and he'd found it too sad to look at.

Harmony put the tray of refreshments on the floor by the bean bag. 'I've brought you some milk and chocolate chip cookies.' She held out the beaker of milk to Alfie, but he ignored the offering. 'How about a cookie?' She proffered the plate, but he ignored that too. 'What about Velvet? Would Velvet like something to eat?'

Alfie's knuckles whitened against the toy.

She took a cookie and started to eat it, and Candy took one too. Then Harmony offered the plate again, but he still didn't take a snack so she placed the plate next to the milk.

'I'd love to give you a hug, Alfie,' Harmony said. 'Would that be all right?'

Although he kept his head low, he nodded.

She crouched to put her arm around his shoulder. She wished it could be a magic, healing hug.

13

Roxanne was making lasagne. While layering the meat mixture, béchamel sauce and pasta sheets in a ceramic dish, her remorse weighed heavily in her heart. Selfishness had trumped honesty when she'd kept her past activities—professional and leisure—from Matt. He'd been so kind to her, taken her in, lonely and pregnant. Now their relationship wasn't just gently eroding—it was more like great cliff falls into the sea of conjugal doom. It was all her fault. She knew that.

Was it possible to amend things? Show Matt affection like she used to? But affection seemed to have left town to go on vacation; she wasn't sure it would find its way back. However, whatever she was feeling, he must be feeling a whole lot worse; he'd not signed up for a dishonest wife with a chequered past.

At one time, she believed she'd been in love, seduced by his warm heart and broad smile. But the emotions that had bloomed had since wilted—like a part of Matt's anatomy. In recent weeks, it had seemingly forgotten how to perform, even when she'd approached him, naked under her dressing gown, damp from her shower. She wanted him to forgive her, to see how sorry she was, how she hadn't meant to hurt him by hiding her past.

Once the lasagne was in the oven, she mashed boiled potato with butter, milk and cheese and put it on a high-rimmed plate with the remaining meat mixture and some petit pois. She cleared the toys from Joshua's highchair and sat next to him with his semi-cooled meal.

'See what yummy food Mummy's got for you.'

Joshua waved his arms and legs excitedly and opened his mouth as the first spoonful came his way. She was grateful he wasn't a fussy eater. Sometimes he became distracted and then she'd play an aeroplane game, occasionally flying past his open mouth to make it fun.

'Now, how about some of that egg custard that's left from yesterday?' She'd taken it out of the fridge a while ago so it wouldn't be too cold. 'Would you like to feed yourself?'

She put the deep bowl and a child's spoon within his reach. She'd allowed for half to coat his face and tray, drop onto his clothes and the floor. If she was lucky, it wouldn't get flicked in her direction or decorate the walls. If she came across a splash-patterned dress, she'd buy it.

Once the feeding event was over, she cleaned up Joshua and his surroundings, then set to washing up while he played with a shape and number puzzle.

Studying other mums had been an eye-opener. Roxanne's mother hadn't delighted in her, played with her. So these other public mums were her role models. But she didn't seem to feel how they appeared to feel. Deep inside, she knew she wasn't good enough. Deep inside, she knew she shouldn't have gone ahead with the pregnancy. She often went through the motions of motherhood without being emotionally present. A bit like an automaton.

Matt returned, his thin, black hair windswept and damp. It made his forehead appear even wider than usual, accentuating his receding hairline. Kindness had attracted her to him. Looking at him now, in the recent absence of that kindness, all she could concentrate on was his retreating hair.

'The lasagne's done. I'll serve it up, shall I?' She smiled, trying to focus on his blue eyes, willing the lines on either side to crinkle with joy at seeing her like they used to.

Matt's wrinkles didn't deepen. His face already showed signs of a five o'clock shadow; it was almost six now. Did the parish women find it a sexy look? Because they constantly flocked around him, asking for help or advice, making suggestions and flagging up concerns. How much of it was genuinely essential or just attention-seeking, she didn't know. But either way, Matt didn't appear to mind.

'Great, thanks. I've a ton of work to get through before tomorrow.'

There always was a ton of work to get through.

'How's your day been?' She dished up the meal with a tomato and onion salad.

'Oh, you know, much as any other.'

'You had the parish council meeting. How did that go?'

'We're not getting very far with the fundraising so I don't know if the re-pointing will be done before next winter. Also, we're still looking for a treasurer.'

Roxanne put down her fork. 'Perhaps I—'

Matt avoided her gaze. 'We're hoping for an accountant or bookkeeper. The accounts can be quite complex.' Now he stared directly at her to give the clear message that she wasn't, in his eyes at least, suitable.

Her brain was becoming dulled from lack of stimulation outside of responding to the needs of a baby and a husband. She was about to remind him that she used to run her own business and then realised that recalling that particular venture would drive the wedge between them even deeper.

'I'm sure the accounts can be quite complex.' She spoke evenly to hide her disappointment. The current incumbent hadn't been formally trained but taught by his predecessor.

Matt must have picked up on her dissatisfaction as he said, 'Honesty is essential in a treasurer. The parish needs someone they can trust, even if they haven't been formally trained.'

There was a bitter taste in her mouth. She grimaced as

she swallowed. For the sake of their marriage, she must stay calm. For the sake of Joshua, she must pretend everything was all right.

When the main course was over, she brought the lemon cake she'd baked that afternoon to the table. As she cut it, she said, 'Shall we watch something together, when you've finished? Before bed?'

Bed used to mean something quite different. Now it meant sleep time with no comforting cuddles as they were in separate rooms. Even when they had shared a room, before Perdita's get-together, and it had led to something else, it hadn't been the kind of fun Roxanne had been used to. Matt was staid and unadventurous. But she still missed him, missed sex.

She'd attempted to introduce something new. But the disapproval had been so strong, rejection so complete, she'd not tried again. Matt's rule about having no intimacy until he'd placed a gold band on her finger had prevented her from discovering they were incompatible until after they'd married. She wondered how his departed wife had rated him. Or perhaps she'd been satisfied as she hadn't known anything—or anyone—else.

Roxanne had expected to be more involved in the parish, more than helping out at stalls and baking cakes to sell—which Matt had praised her for. But volunteers had already stepped into his late wife's shoes—as far as propriety had allowed—and there appeared to be no particular parochial role left for her. She was just an add-on to other people's activities.

He stared at her after she suggested they watch TV together. 'Oh, I don't have time. You go ahead and watch whatever you like. The newsletter deadline is tomorrow, and I need to get started on my sermon. I'll take my cake into the study.'

'Is there anything I can help with? After I've put Joshua to bed?'

Matt's expression said it all. 'It's not something a lay

person could help with.'

'I... thought you might want help with ideas or for me to listen...'

'It's my responsibility, my job.'

She clenched her fingers. 'I thought Samantha used to help you?' If she hadn't known about his first wife's condition, Roxanne would have suspected a case of terminal boredom.

'She grew into the job,' Matt said. 'We moved here together, and she forged her own path in the parish.'

'I've tried...'

'Samantha... she was...'

'Special? I know I can't replace her, but I'd love to be more involved. In the parish and with you at home.'

His glance could have cut through a diamond. 'If there's something that comes along that suits your talents, I'll let you know.'

She dug her fingernails into her arm to stop the tears that were forming. She'd pretend to misunderstand the slur. 'Thank you. I'd appreciate that.'

He didn't answer.

'We've grown apart. Too far apart.' Could they come back from this?

His gaze was icy as it held hers. 'I think the problem is more that we've got to know each other better and that... dishonesty and false pretences are two things I can't abide. I need time to get over it.'

She likened herself to a nail with Matt as the hammer, pounding her deeper and deeper into a block of wood, never to emerge again. Panic stirred in her stomach.

'Will you though? Get over it? I haven't been the same person I used to be. But that doesn't seem to be enough.'

He was silent for several seconds, then broke eye contact before murmuring, 'I've got to get on.'

Fire stirred in her belly. 'The new me—despite my best efforts—doesn't suit you at all, does it?' As it happened, it didn't suit her either. Not the way things had turned out, and she had to accept responsibility for that.

She passed him the slice of cake she'd put on a small plate.

'At the moment, neither version of you would suit.' He picked up his napkin and left.

Moments later, she heard the study door open and shut.

If Matt had stayed with her, she'd have had some cake too. But now she couldn't stomach it. Her marriage was over. It was as clear as holy water. Perhaps she'd have dessert later when the almighty sting of rejection was not so sore.

She thought of the block of wood she'd pictured earlier. She had to find a way to prise the nail out.

Having tidied away the puzzle games Joshua had got through during the meal she'd shared with Matt, she carried him upstairs to bathe him. The routine was tiresome. Would she be doing this on her own for years?

After bath time, during which she'd tried to make it fun with Joshua's plastic boat and duck, she read him a lift-the-flap book. Although her mind kept wandering off, the words surprisingly kept coming from her mouth.

His hide-and-seek book gave her an idea. Wouldn't it be good if, in her own life story, she could lift a flap and, instead of finding an elephant, a sloth or another animal, she could discover a door? An escape door.

But what would it look like, behind that door? What could she *make* it look like?

She had to devise a plan. It wouldn't be long, she was sure, until she'd need an exit. But, in her numbness, she could only imagine the kind of life she used to have. Her son was nowhere to be seen. Tears came to her eyes as she considered it, knowing how she'd be judged if she shared how she felt. But... that was just how she did feel, and she hated herself for it.

Once Joshua was settled, and the kitchen cleared up, she sat at her laptop to search for ideas: courses, franchises, ways for a solo person to make money from a business. Ways to get that nail out of the wood and be free.

There was an interesting-sounding seminar next week given by someone called Anthony Crawley: *How to Make Your Money Pay*. It wasn't quite what she was looking for, but she had capital from her last business to invest. Might there be a suitable venture to buy into rather than going it alone? Perhaps she could make useful contacts. The cost wasn't prohibitive, it was only for a day, and it was close to a crèche. Matt needn't know.

She was Roxy, Roxy Miller, and she was going to rescue herself.

14

Yesterday, Harmony had asked Saskia to come in for a special job—and here she was, awaiting instructions. It was mid-morning, the first Saturday in December, and Harmony was wearing a new dress and heels and had spent half an hour decorating her face.

'If I were a man,' Saskia said, 'I would want to give you a wolf whistle—even though that's quite unacceptable. But I expect men did that sort of thing when you were my age…'

Harmony frowned. 'You think I look old?'

'Not at all. You look great.'

'So, you don't think I'm over the hill yet then?' Harmony joked, despite sometimes fearing she was past it in the romance stakes.

'I could imagine mature men would find you very attractive.'

'By mature,' Harmony said, 'you mean…?'

'Men in their fifties or sixties. Men in their forties can attract much younger women because of their wealth. At least, that's what Mummy says.'

'Loads of forty-year-old men aren't wealthy, Saskia.'

'The ones Mummy knows are, and if they're very wealthy, there's no upper age limit to the man finding a much younger woman.'

'So, you don't think I have the pulling power to nab a man my own age?'

Saskia appeared uncomfortable. 'How old are you?'

Harmony blinked. 'Never mind. Let's get down to business.'

Saskia straightened her already straight posture.

'Fourteen-year-old Wendy has a wedding to go to, and she needs to buy a dress—and shoes and a bag. But within a budget.'

Saskia gawked at the amount printed on the envelope of cash. 'A dress, shoes and a bag? With *this?* '

'That's right.' Harmony rattled off some high street shops. 'You need to keep all the receipts and here's the money for your bus fares.'

'*Bus?* ' Saskia's perfect deportment sagged. 'But I've got a car.'

'You told me it's not insured for work purposes. Besides, it's good for the kids' independence to get around by Shanks's pony and public transport.' A familiar frown returned on Saskia's brow, and Harmony quickly added, 'Walking and use of buses.'

'What do you do? *On a bus?*' Saskia's words ended in a whisper. 'Is there a YouTube video that shows you?'

Harmony suppressed a smile. 'No idea. Wendy can go on first and you can copy her. Ask for a Day Ticket. Then you can hop on and off buses without paying extra.'

After seeing Saskia and Wendy off, Harmony went to check on Alfie, pushing the pram with Patience ahead of her.

He was sitting on the library floor staring into the hallway, ignoring the toys laid out in front of him. From the anxiety in his expression, Harmony guessed he was concentrating on the noises in the place and the children calling to one another. A plate of untouched biscuits lay beside him. Candy shook her head sadly when Harmony caught her eye.

Music might help, something beautiful and lighthearted. With Patience, she selected sheet music from the print room for Bedřich Smetana's *The Moldau.* In Czech, it was *Vltava*—the river on which Prague stood. It was one of her favourites. She'd been going to the Dower House to play in her spare time, so her fingers were nimble and sure and her sight reading had not become overly dulled.

She parked the pram at the far end of the dining room to protect Patience's delicate ears and switched on the baby transmitter at the foot of the mattress. With its monitor at the end of the keyboard, Harmony arranged the sheet music on the rack. The old, musty wood smell from the opened lid of the grand piano brought back memories of her childhood, practising for hours in the family home. She settled on the piano bench and arranged her hands as she read the first few bars.

'Would you like me to turn the pages?' Ostap, the oldest child resident, had come to stand nearby.

Her stomach knotted and her fingers curled into stiff arches, resembling the legs of a wolf spider. It would be the first time she'd played to a near-full Pinkerton Hall... She thought of Alfie and told herself to calm down.

'That would be great. Thank you.'

She took a couple of deep breaths before she began to play.

It was a demanding piece and had taken time to master, recreating the sounds of a whole orchestra on one instrument. But somehow, the memory had stayed in her fingers. As they made rapid movements, she imagined herself to be part of the river flowing merrily through the countryside.

Ostap's page-turning was faultless, so the stream of sound she created was fluent. After a while, the imagined river flowed past a country wedding, Harmony's favourite part. She became aware that more people had gathered around her. *She must stay calm.* As long as there were no strangers, she could cope.

Now she was at the part where it was a moonlit night and this too was beautiful. Did it touch Alfie like it touched her? It was then she glanced up and noticed Tim. With James. Her fingers stumbled, and she broke off.

'That was amazing,' James said.

Her cheeks burned. 'Thanks.' They were face-to-face again. The first time since Perdita's get-together.

'Please, carry on. It's lovely.'

'Yes, carry on,' the kids chorused.

But she couldn't play any more so she stood up and noticed a big box in James's hands.

'I've come to apologise. About the cockroach thing. I'm sorry I interrupted you.' His gaze swept over her.

Perhaps her preening efforts hadn't been wasted after all?

'Are you going out?' he asked. 'You look very nice.'

Some children giggled.

She'd planned to go to Bristol to follow the magazine's tip: *Be seen—and, to be seen, you have to go out and meet people.* 'It can wait. Perhaps you'll come to the office?' May as well get the awkwardness over. She fetched the pram.

On their way, Tim spotted Alfie through the open library door and the two of them locked gazes. When they were inside the office, Tim stood looking into the front library. 'Is he new? I've not seen him in school.'

'Yes. He's called Alfie.'

'Why doesn't he come to school? Has he only just arrived?'

'He's not ready to start school.'

With his gaze still fixed on Alfie, Tim asked, 'Why not?'

At first, she'd wondered whether Tim was being nosy. But now she detected concern. Why would Tim be so worried for a boy he'd never met before? 'Perhaps, if you've got nothing planned, you might like to chill out with Patrik or Anil in the entertainment area?' She glanced at James to check he wasn't going to protest.

But, to her surprise, he said humbly, 'Thank you. Tim needs to make friends.'

Was the U-turn related to the glowing report his inspector friends must have provided?

When Tim left, Harmony shut the door and she and

James sat down.

Patience had begun to grizzle so Harmony picked her up and held her close against her chest, slowly running her hand up and down the baby's back, shushing her. 'Is there anything I should be aware of as Tim will be spending time here?'

His shoulders rose and his jaw pulsed as though his muscles had stiffened. 'What do you mean?'

There was something he was hiding, but she gave a slight shrug. 'Anything that might be of consequence?'

After some apparent thought, he said, 'I don't think so.'

Then why had it taken James so long to answer, his expression become grim and he appeared to have caught the gaze of Medusa?

'No food allergies, health problems…?'

'No.' James must have been released from the Medusa spell as he stopped imitating a stone statue and handed over the box. 'I'm sorry I didn't bring a peace offering sooner. I had to wait as it was a special order. I hope this can make things right.'

He helped her release the flaps—since she had only one free hand—to reveal a huge rectangular chocolate cake decorated with Smarties.

'It's an apology to everyone,' he said.

'For sending the two nice men to look the place over?'

Crimson, James murmured, 'Yes, I'm so sorry… I should have said something straight away. I didn't know the roach had been brought in from outside.' He appeared genuinely contrite.

Thinking he'd done a good job of making amends, she smiled. 'Apology accepted. It's a very pretty cake. The kids will love it.'

'Do you think we could make a fresh start? Become friends?'

James wanted to be friends? She held his gaze, saw the sincerity and her heart flipped. 'Well,' she said with a tremor in her voice, 'why not?'

But what did friendship James's style mean? Mates? A convenient babysitting service? Or something more intimate... it was hard to tell. She needed to clarify his bachelor status before she allowed her imagination to undertake any more roaming.

'Will your wife be joining you in the cottage? Assuming she isn't already there.'

'My wife... died over eighteen months ago. I should have told you as soon as you'd asked whether there was anything you needed to know about Tim.'

So grief had been responsible for the Medusa-like reaction? 'I'm so sorry. How awful.' She wondered what had happened.

He pulled up his cuff to consult his watch. 'I've got things I need to see to.'

Was he leaving suddenly because he didn't want to rake up the past?

'It's kind of you having Tim. Under the circumstances. What time shall I get him?'

'Erm... whenever. One extra isn't a problem.'

James nodded. 'Before supper? About five?'

'Five it is.'

He rose and headed for the door.

He'd got what he wanted, wasn't interested in her, just a free day to himself. Feeling used, she doused the sparkle of hope that had started to grow. *James was not for her.*

She went with Patience to check on Alfie. Someone had shut the library door so Harmony eased it open. Tim was sitting on the floor opposite the younger boy. Tim moved a car. Alfie moved it back. Tim pushed the car along the floor to Alfie. Alfie pushed it back. Tim drove the car in a circle, Alfie drove it in a circle after Tim let go—and so it continued.

Meeting Harmony's gaze, Candy made a thumbs-up sign.

Harmony leaned forward in the chair she'd taken and

spoke softly. 'Tim, would you like a biscuit?' She pointed to the plate on the floor next to Alfie.

Tim took a cookie and bit into it, holding Alfie's gaze, who hesitantly picked up a biscuit too. As Tim was chewing, Alfie bit into the cookie. Tim waited for Alfie to swallow before he broke off a second piece with his teeth.

'Another one?' Candy asked hopefully.

Tim took a second biscuit and so did Alfie.

A wave of relief swept through Harmony. Whatever connection the boys had made, it was helping Alfie.

Candy left the room, indicating she was going to fetch drinks. After adjusting Patience's position so she could watch them all, Harmony sat with the boys.

Tim queued cars in both lanes of an imaginary road with a gap between the heads of each line. Alfie observed intently. Then Tim lined up farm animals by the gap that, she presumed, represented a zebra crossing.

The horse was at the front of the animal queue and crossed between the traffic first. Once it had safely crossed, a car from either side of the crossing moved on in its journey. Tim pointed to Alfie and then at the donkey. He got the donkey safely across the road and then allowed one car from each lane to move on before pointing at Tim.

The game continued until the cow, sheep, pig and dog had crossed. When they'd run out of cars to queue at the crossing, Tim circled them back to their original positions on his side of the crossing, and Alfie matched the actions.

Candy returned with two mugs of milk. Instead of handing them to the boys, she lay the tray down. Tim appeared to grasp what was required as he reached out for a mug and took a sip, maintaining eye contact with Alfie who, after a moment's hesitation, picked up the second mug.

With moist eyes, Harmony smiled at Candy. It would be good if they could borrow Tim all weekend. He was making headway where they'd made virtually none, and the very odd thing was that the whole time the boys were playing, Tim was as silent as Alfie.

Candy sat on the arm of her chair. 'I thought you were going out?' she mouthed.

Harmony's hand flew to her lips. She mouthed back, 'I forgot.'

Candy waved her away. As Harmony swept past the boys, she tapped their shoulders and gave a little wave. Why break their peaceful silence?

15

Harmony sat at a window table in a café overlooking Bristol's Whiteladies Road, abandoning her Sudoku grid. Patience was in the bucket car seat next to her. Every so often, she would bash one or other of the toys across the activity bar Harmony had fixed to the seat and get them spinning and rattling. She picked up a separate rattle and waved it to get Patience to grab it. When they'd done that a few times, Harmony played peek-a-boo. Patience's giggle was delightful.

A masculine voice said, 'May I join you?'

Startled, Harmony glanced up and was confused when she saw it was James. Hadn't he brushed her off earlier? She shut the puzzle compendium.

'Oh, you like puzzles?'

She nodded. 'A bit addicted to them…'

'Would you rather I left you in peace?'

Shaking her head, she indicated the seat opposite. Perhaps she'd understand why he'd left the Hall so abruptly.

He sat down, placing his coffee on the table. 'I'm sorry I was so rude earlier. Your question about my wife took me by surprise. Sympathy can make me emotional, and I didn't want to make a fool of myself in front of you—and anyone else who might have come in. Let me make it up to you and buy you a drink.'

Her heart lightened; he'd not been avoiding her. 'Oh. Thanks. Hot chocolate?'

'Does Patience need anything?' he asked.

Oh, how sweet. 'She appears quite happy—perhaps her milk could be warmed later.'

When he returned, their gazes locked. His eyes beckoned to her like the deep blue of a swimming pool in a holiday brochure, and she was still mesmerised by them when she realised he'd placed the hot chocolate in front of her. He regarded her quizzically and her cheeks became hot. Her entire body was becoming inflamed—he must know how attractive she found him.

'Thanks.' She smiled but quickly glanced away, imagining stepping into an immersion pool of iced water. Anything to sap the heat from her skin.

James settled opposite and sipped his coffee. 'We used to come here, Felicia and I.' His smile was awkward.

She checked an impulse to squeeze his hand. 'It's always difficult to fill holes in your life.'

He regarded her keenly. 'What holes do you have? It looks to me you've covered all the bases.' He grinned. 'Got enough kids for a football team.'

'There are other kinds of holes,' she said quietly, thinking of the baby she'd never given birth to, the loneliness of being a singleton.

His expression softened. 'Name one.' The sound was almost like a caress.

The sudden emotional intimacy between them began the pealing of warning bells. Was he ready to move on too or was she misinterpreting his interest? And now there seemed a real possibility of something having started between her and James, anxiety bubbled up inside her as though the cold water immersion pool had become an overheated, effervescing jacuzzi.

'I...'

'Yes?'

'I...' Fighting for breath, she began to gather her

things. 'I'm sorry,' she gasped. 'We've got to go.'

Why had she thought she could look for a fiancé? Probably only women who'd taken their final vows as a nun would be more out of practice than she was. James appeared interested in her, genuinely interested, and she should be delighted.

To dampen her fears, she'd need to know him a whole lot better, yet the getting to know him was too anxiety-provoking to take the plunge, as last time... last time, ten years ago, she almost drowned...

At her fiancé David's suggestion, Harmony had booked into a hotel to have a fun evening with her orchestra bridesmaids, Larysa and Rania. On the big day, they went ahead to the church in Long Ashton, a few miles outside of Bristol, where Harmony had been brought up. She followed a little after in a chauffeur-driven car with her dad. But when they arrived, it was clear there was something wrong.

Larysa's expression was pinched, and Mum's face was white.

'David's late and so's his best man,' Rania said.

Harmony's parents went inside the church to see if they could find out more. Perhaps there'd been an accident, and the groom and best man were caught up in traffic?

'Is everyone else here?' she asked.

'I think so,' Larysa said. 'It's packed. I suppose that's what comes of inviting a whole orchestra and their families.'

'There's David's side too.' Harmony hadn't hogged all the places for her guests.

In between scanning the cars for David's arrival, she watched the door to the church, anxious for news.

'Can you ring him?' Rania asked.

'My phone's in the hotel. We said we wouldn't get in touch before we met in the church.' He was usually punctual so surely he'd be here any moment?

Harmony's parents returned.

'We're terribly sorry but...' Mum blinked back tears.

Dad's face was pale and his expression grave.

'Has he been in an accident?'

He shook his head, and Mum started to cry.

So David was fine but just hadn't turned up? Harmony couldn't believe it. He loved her. He'd told her so many, many times. She gathered the skirt of her dress and ran inside.

The doors clanged behind her. Everyone turned around as if hoping the groom had finally put in an appearance. She walked down the aisle, aiming for his parents. They'd been in touch with him, surely?

They were on the right-hand side, at the front. His mother lowered the phone she'd just been holding to her ear and an expression of sincere, deep apology was obvious.

This couldn't be happening to her. It couldn't. David loved her.

'I'm truly sorry,' his mum said. 'He's... changed his mind.' Her anguished words rang out into the nave.

There was an immediate burst of conversation, and Harmony knew that everyone was staring at her, pitying her. *This couldn't be happening. Not after everything she'd been through...*

'Why?' She sank to the cold, wooden floor in the middle of the aisle, her knees like putty and her heart pounding so hard her ears were ringing.

David's dad said, 'She's got a right to know.'

Harmony looked up and croaked, 'I want to know. Since he hasn't been able to tell me, you *must*.'

'We want to know, too,' Mum said.

Dad nodded.

David's mum placed a hand on Harmony's arm. 'Let's go somewhere more private.'

But she was too weak to move. 'Just tell me.'

David's mum crouched down, everyone close by bending low to listen. She said softly, 'Apparently—and I'm so sorry—he does want children after all.'

It felt like a boulder had lodged in Harmony's stomach and someone had put her chest in a vice. The nave turned into a slow merry-go-round, dizziness disorienting her and her limbs were shaking. She didn't know what to do or how to feel. It was too much to take in.

One of the guests joined them. 'Has something happened to Melody?'

David's mum cleared her throat. 'I think you'll find she's with David.'

Harmony gasped. *No, no, she couldn't have...*

'*David and Melody?*' Mum sank onto the floor in a heap. 'How can one of my daughters do that to the other?' Weeping, she put comforting arms around Harmony.

It had been David's idea that Harmony spent the last night with her friends. So instead of having his mates around, he'd probably been making plans with Melody—as well as perhaps a baby.

'He tried to catch you, before you—' his mum began. 'Before you left the hotel.'

Why not before then? It was a lame excuse.

'He said he's moved out so the flat's all yours,' his mum added. 'I'm so sorry...'

So he'd left it to the last minute... His selfishness cut into her heart. Not to mention the cowardice, betrayal, dishonesty...

'I must say,' David's dad said, 'how deeply ashamed we are of our son. His behaviour is despicable.'

Had David ever truly loved her as she'd loved him? Being betrayed by her fiancé and her sister suggested that neither had ever loved her enough. The pent-up anguish gathered in her throat and she screamed.

Getting close to James felt like she was switching a plunge pool for Deep Dive Dubai—and she wasn't that strong a swimmer.

He sprang up from his seat and said, with a catch in his voice, 'Please don't go.'

She wavered.

'I'd welcome some company. I won't pry, I promise. We could tackle some puzzles together. I like them too.'

His pleading gaze was like that of a puppy in a dog rescue centre waiting for an owner. Or a child in a care home hoping they'd be chosen by a kind family for adoption. Or a lonely man missing the company of his wife.

The thump of her heart eased, and her chest relaxed. 'We'll stay.'

16

Harmony opened the puzzle book sideways in the Sudoku section so she and James could share it. She found an extra biro for him to use.

He removed his coat, revealing the expanse of his chest, the girth of his arms. As he leaned in to get a better view, a waft of cedarwood reached her nostrils. A sizzle of anticipation shot through her. She could do this; she *wanted* to do it. He'd take care of her feelings, and she'd take care of his. They'd both been hurt; he'd understand her need to go slowly. The loneliness she'd seen in his eyes was similar to what she sometimes saw when she looked in a mirror. They were two of a kind.

It was clear he was well-practised at the challenge as he was quick to work out the missing numbers. The speed at which first one grid was completed and the next steadily increased as they became more competitive—leading to a tug-of-war with the book, trying to get their number in first, and they ended up laughing.

Then James glanced at his watch. 'How about some lunch? My treat?'

'Oh, I—'

'I insist.'

'Let me change and feed Patience first.'

'I'll ask them to warm the milk while you're changing her.'

Ten minutes later, Harmony was feeding Patience in her arms, a cotton square around the baby's neck. Her little hands lightly cupped the bottle as she sucked strongly, making satisfied vocal sounds. All the while, she maintained eye contact with Harmony. Feeding was always such a special time.

'She looks so cute,' James said.

Glancing towards him for a moment, Harmony agreed. 'And she never seems to take her eyes off me.'

'I think that's working both ways,' he said with a laugh.

When Patience was halfway through the bottle, Harmony removed the teat and put the baby over her shoulder, protected with another cloth, gently patting her back. Eventually, the baby burped.

When the bottle was empty, Harmony placed Patience in the upright position to wind her again.

'You seem to be very expert at this.'

'I've had her for four months. At first, she was being sick all the time but she possets much less now.'

'I used to get regurgitated milk all over my clothes.'

'I wised up pretty quickly,' she said, 'and bought a pile of cotton cloths. The amount of washing even now is—'

'Unbelievable.'

She laughed. 'Too right.'

When the lasagne and chips came, Harmony popped Patience back in the bucket seat.

'About the inspection,' James said as they began to eat. 'I don't feel I gave a good enough apology. But I was uncomfortable about being overheard.'

She cocked her head to encourage him to explain.

'I was torn when I left the Hall. I almost came running back to help you capture the roach. But, as an Environmental Health Officer, I can't cover up any discoveries. There could have been serious consequences for me if I hadn't reported it—I had no way of telling whether it was an isolated incident. I couldn't pre-warn you of a pending inspection either.'

So she'd bad-mouthed him to Luke over the inspection for no good reason. She'd ask Miranda to pass on a message to put it right. There was no way she wanted James maligned without good cause, and now there was no cause.

'I understand,' Harmony said. 'But are you sure you didn't pre-warn me? Those steely eyes when you told me what you did for a living? The moment we'd identified the insect, it all clicked into place.'

'I didn't do it consciously... I'd been thinking about it all weekend. First thing I did Monday morning was to call one of the men who'd come around. When he updated me and followed up with a written report, I wanted to rush over with an apology. But that alone wouldn't have been good enough. I needed to make some kind of gesture as well.'

'The cake?'

'I called so many bakeries to ask about making a big cake but they were all booked up until this week. I even tried bribing a couple of them so they'd put in overtime, but it was a no-go. So, I'm sorry it took so long coming.'

It was all clear to her now and the remorse in his eyes told her he was genuinely sorry. 'I appreciate you explaining. There's no issue any more.'

He smiled in relief and ate with more gusto than previously. He'd only a third of his lasagne left and had just about finished his chips whereas she was only halfway through.

Patience started to grizzle, and Harmony wondered if she still had some trapped wind.

She picked her up. 'There, there, it's all right.' She held the baby close and rubbed her back.

'Would you like me to cut up the rest of your food so you can eat one-handed?' James asked.

Harmony was bowled over by his thoughtfulness. 'Well, thanks.'

He pushed his plate to one side and expertly cut the

lasagne and chips into bite-sized pieces. She smiled her gratitude.

They finished the meal in silence and Patience settled peacefully into sleep against Harmony's shoulder.

'James, when you found out that Pinkerton Hall was a children's home, you appeared concerned—are you worried about Tim mixing with the Hall kids?'

He met her gaze squarely. 'He's vulnerable and impressionable, and I didn't know any of you. But Patrik and Anil seem great. Tim gets on extremely well with them. Thank you for introducing them to him. It's helped him adjust to the new school.'

'They are great. You don't need to worry about them.'

'Good... There's something I should tell you, but I don't want to go into details; I'm still feeling raw about it. However, as Tim will be visiting the Hall and you asked about relevant things...'

'Yes?' she said gently.

'I used to have two sons. Now I only have one.'

The squeezing of her heart stole her breath. A double bereavement. Without thinking, she reached out to put her hand over his. 'I'm so sorry.'

She wondered if the son had been younger than Tim. Whether this was related to the mystery of Tim's burgeoning bond with Alfie.

James swallowed back tears and put his fingers over his eyelids, breaking contact with her hand, and she felt the loss in warmth from her palm.

'It's the sympathy that gets me,' he said.

She changed the subject, hoping it would help relieve the grief that had surfaced. 'Was it Perdita's husband, Saul, who suggested you find friends for Tim at the Hall?'

'Yes.'

'When you saw me coming out of the bathroom with Luke—'

James put up a hand. 'What you do, and who with, in your private life is none of my business.'

She laughed. 'That's just it. I don't.'

'Then...?'

'I'd gone to the bathroom to hide from you. I'd had the inspection that morning and—'

'You didn't want to see me.'

'Exactly. I'd been about to leave when I saw you coming up the drive. Luke—a friend who's happily married to a man called Gavin—came to ask if I was okay and we had a heart-to-heart. He knew I wanted to be considered for adopting Patience if there was no one more suitable to be found. That's what he'd been referring to when he'd said—'

'Maybe you'll soon be a mother with a baby to look after.'

She smiled.

'So you're single?' James asked, then added quickly, 'Not that it's any of—'

'I am.'

Was he keen on her or just filing away information like he would with any acquaintance? Did she care either way? Of course she did. Now she was getting to know him, the thought of getting closer was more like a sweet dream than a nightmare.

As Harmony sat in her car, now parked outside the Hall, she recalled the heartbreaking image of a man who'd lost his wife and younger son and how her whole being had wanted to reach out to him. The only reason she'd gone to that café was to follow the advice in that magazine.

It had been worth every penny.

She found the younger children having an afternoon snack of freshly sliced apples and orange segments with a drink of squash. Tim and Alfie were sitting with the rest of them.

'Hi, kids,' she said brightly, carrying Patience in her arms.

'Hi,' all but Alfie chanted back.

Hunkering down beside Alfie, Harmony gave a little

wave. 'Hi, Alfie.'

Tim began to wave to her and then Alfie did the same. She planted a grateful kiss on the top of Alfie's head. 'What did you have for lunch, Alfie?'

Tim answered. 'Beans on toast.'

'Both of you?'

Tim nodded.

Her smile encompassed them both. Then she addressed Tim. 'Have you been with Alfie the whole time?'

He nodded.

'What about Patrik and Anil?' They were at the other end of the table watching him. 'Can you all do something together?'

They all nodded.

'In the games room?' Patrik asked.

'It might be too noisy for Alfie at the moment,' she said, but Alfie shook his head.

Annie had said to keep him quiet, but it seemed it was better to let him progress now that he wanted to. 'Alfie, if it gets too much for you and you need some quiet…'

'I'll look after him. We all will, won't we?' Tim said.

Patrik and Anil agreed.

Tim was going to do well here, mixing with the others. His protective instinct was a wonderful quality. She squeezed his shoulder, feeling so proud of the magic he was bringing to Alfie's broken life.

17

When Roxy dropped Joshua at the crèche in Bristol city centre, he'd only grizzled for a moment, soon distracted by the soft play area. Didn't other babies his age have anxiety after separation from their mum? Had she done something wrong? Or was this going to make it easier? Perhaps any loving person would do.

Matt didn't know about her day or her past clothing. She'd worn maternity clothes when they'd met and had kept the best of her old things in two large suitcases under the bed in one of the spare rooms. After Joshua had been born, to fit in with Matt's lifestyle and expectations, she'd bought a new wardrobe more appropriate to parochial life.

Today, she'd donned a figure-hugging grey skirt that was only slightly tighter than before her pregnancy and a cleavage-revealing top under a half-buttoned lilac cardigan. The leopard print faux fur coat stopped her from freezing in the typical December weather. Her heels had been a little difficult to walk in at first, but she was soon sashaying again. In addition to her shoulder bag, she carried a document case for notes and seminar hand-outs.

Having the old Roxy back, with the old Roxy-walk, was empowering. To complete the former-life feeling, she slipped off the ring on the third finger of her left hand and placed it into the zipped pocket of her bag. Being married was not at all like the old Roxy.

The hotel was only a short walk from the crèche. She was very early; it wasn't due to start until ten. In the carpeted entrance, a board detailed the events for that day.

When she followed the arrows for *How to Make Your Money Pay*, she came to a large, warm room with soft seating and unbuttoned her coat. A blond man with wavy hair and wearing a crisp, charcoal suit was setting up. She almost left to find a cup of coffee, but taking in his handsome features, she thought why not be the old Roxy and strike up a conversation?

She approached, smiling. 'I'm sorry, should I wait outside? Am I too early?'

The man glanced up, revealing captivating topaz eyes. When he returned her smile, a piercing jolt shot through her, reminding her of what she'd been missing out on—the days when life had been full of possibilities.

'Not at all,' he said. 'You're welcome to stay. I'm a one-man band today.'

'So you're Anthony Crawley?'

He grinned and made eye contact for longer than necessary. 'Call me Tony.'

How she'd missed her freedom. How she'd missed... men. 'I'm Roxy.'

He tapped some keys on his laptop and the opening slide showed on the screen behind him, welcoming everyone to the day. 'I'm finished here for now. There's still time before kick-off. How about we grab a coffee?'

A clean slate, a fresh connection with a stranger. How could she refuse?

'What brings you here today?' he asked when they were seated, she with a cappuccino and he with an Americano, in an alcove by the bar.

'I've got capital from selling a franchise and would perhaps like to buy another, work flexible hours and be my own boss. Or invest my capital if there are no suitable franchises to buy into.'

'What franchise did you have?'

She almost blushed. Perhaps Matt's critical lens had rubbed off onto her. But what was the shame in a legitimate business? 'Intimate products—for personal pleasure. Or for couples or groups… to suit whatever tastes.'

Tony laughed. 'That sounds like an interesting business. Many takers?' His gaze penetrated her keenly.

'Oh, yes. But I got pregnant and couldn't keep it going.'

His eyebrows shot up in surprise. 'You've got a child? What kind of business are you looking for now?'

Wanting that hidden door behind her life's fantasy flap more than ever, she said, 'I don't know. That's why I've come here.'

'I'm not sure this is the right seminar for you—its focus is on investments. For spare capital you can manage without if something goes wrong; not your life savings.'

Hope drained away.

He must have noticed her crestfallen expression as he added gently, 'It wouldn't be ethical for me to recommend investing cash you can't afford to lose.'

She nodded her understanding. The make-believe flap in her life story was closing.

'But that doesn't mean I can't help.'

She shot an imaginary foot out to keep the flap door open.

'There's a pub around the corner,' he said. 'We could have lunch there? As the food's good, I expect the others will stay here—the lunch break isn't included in my fee so I don't need to stay. How about it?'

The traditional pub was comfortable and cosy. She claimed a table for two next to a hot radiator. While she waited for her order—as well as Tony—she sipped her white wine.

When he arrived, he raised his hand in acknowledgement before going to the increasingly crowded bar to place his order. Then he sat opposite her with a pint of beer.

'You know this place well?' she asked.

'Fairly. Although I'm based in London, I work as much as possible in Bristol so I can see my daughter.'

Her head jerked slightly in surprise. She'd pictured him as a player, not a father—although, of course, he could be both. 'How old is she?' What was the deal with the mother of said daughter?

'She was three in August and has a younger sister who's not long past one, but she's not mine.'

'Oh. It didn't work out with you then?'

Tony gave a regretful shrug. 'I wasn't interested in having a family, and she married someone else. But I found I couldn't abandon my daughter entirely after all. The arrangement we've got is working well. I'm still free, I can travel with my work and can socialise however I wish. You probably think I'm selfish?'

She laughed. 'I think you're honest. I'm not sure, if I were a man, I'd be any different.'

His gaze sharpened. 'You don't enjoy being a mother?'

She shrugged. 'Things don't necessarily work out how one hopes.'

Her grilled salmon on Mediterranean vegetables was served by a thin man in an apron.

'Thanks,' she said to the man and then to Tony, 'Tell me more about the arrangement with your daughter.' The salmon was moist, perfectly cooked.

Another server came and placed Tony's scampi, chips and peas in front of him.

He pronged two halves of a cut chip on his fork. 'The deal was I let her husband adopt Petal as long as I could be part of her life. So she's got two dads and is very happy.' The chip halves went into his mouth, swiftly followed by some peas.

'*Petal?* I know a Petal.'

'Didn't realise it was so popular. Perdita's choice, not mine.'

Roxy almost choked on a piece of courgette. '*Perdita?* I know them!'

He stared at her. 'How come?'

She wiped her lips. 'We met at the baby clinic. In Westbridge.'

'You know Posy then? Her little sister?'

Roxy nodded. 'She's a couple of months older than Joshua.'

'I'm trying to picture you at a baby clinic. You don't strike me as a mumsy person.'

She laughed. 'When I'm in Westbridge, I wear different clothes—perhaps you wouldn't recognise me.'

His gaze was speculative, and he appeared to be even more interested in her—as she was in him.

'I'm going to see Petal after the seminar's over. Best of both worlds—pop in for a fun visit and then leave the rest to Perdita.' He watched for her reaction.

She liked his unabashed straightforwardness. 'You're very candid.'

He chuckled. 'I sense you and I… might be one of a kind.'

A zing of adrenaline shot through her, just like in the old days. Except now she couldn't throw caution to the wind and book into a nearby hotel.

'Why don't we meet for dinner later?' he suggested. 'There's The Dick Whittington by the corner of Perdita's road.' Even when he was eating, his gaze didn't drop.

Disappointment washed over her. 'I can't… My husband…'

'You're married?'

'Yes—although Matt's not Joshua's father.'

'I somehow pictured you as a single mum.'

'I might be soon.' Her hand shot to her mouth. 'Please don't tell Perdita. Although many may have guessed, guessing and knowing are not the same.'

'Your secret's safe with me. I'm finding you more intriguing by the minute. Who's your husband? What does he do?'

Roxy whispered, 'He's the vicar.'

His eyebrows shot up. *'You? A vicar's wife?'*
'Shh!'
'Sorry...' he said. 'Is this a wind-up?'
'I wish it were.'
'Is that why you've come to the seminar?'
'I'm looking for... options.'

He rubbed his finger over his lip. 'I'm giving a seminar in January—an overview of what you need to start up a small business. You can book through Eventbrite. Here...' He reached into his pocket for a card. 'Take my personal number. If you're free to meet tomorrow lunchtime, I could get you started.'

18

Christmas excitement had woken Harmony early so she'd changed, fed and laid Patience on the playmat for "tummy time" sooner than usual. She was getting stronger by the week, pushing up with her forearms, holding her head high, reaching for toys—and Harmony's face as she lay softly singing next to her.

The Hall's Christmas party was that afternoon. It was always held a few days ahead of the big day, before some of the residents left to spend local authority-approved time with immediate or extended family.

Harmony had invited Tim and James along. But would they both come? After the wonderful time she and James had spent in the café, he appeared to have become more distant, as though operating a "friends only" policy. Was that because he wasn't as keen on her as she was on him— or because he was too keen and had got cold feet?

If she knew how he truly felt, she might risk thinking it was safe to let her thoughts wander.

Who was she kidding? Her thoughts roamed all over the place, including his body.

When she went downstairs with Patience in her arms, Candy was rearranging the chairs to face the stage. 'Are you daydreaming?' she asked.

'No,' Harmony lied. 'I was just running in my mind what else needs to be done.'

Candy shot her a disbelieving glance. 'I think your mind is across the road with James.'

'Don't be absurd.'

'There's definitely something going on. On both sides.'

Harmony laughed. 'James isn't interested in me.' Or was he?

'What if he were?'

Her thoughts halted when Candy's phone rang—Father Christmas had succumbed to flu.

'Can Andrei do it instead?' Harmony asked when Candy had hung up. He was a senior care worker and was usually happy to cover emergencies.

'He's got a family event. But I'll do it. Father Christmas's long hair can cover the sides of my face, the beard's big, and with sunglasses and gloves, they might not recognise me. Does anyone here still believe in Father Christmas?'

'Alfie?'

'I did amateur dramatics at uni so I can put on accents. My body shape will change too, and I'll close the curtains in here.'

'The job's yours then.'

'And you can't pull the wool over my eyes. I know you like James.'

Harmony imagined herself held against him, his lips descending to meet hers... and an unaccustomed longing filled her. If it hadn't been a children's home, she might have put up some mistletoe.

As she went upstairs to change into a dress, Nia found her. 'There's something wrong with Saskia.'

Was she ill? 'Where is she?'

Nia led her to a bathroom in the girls' wing.

There were rapid, high-pitched chittering noises, reminding Harmony of a nature programme she'd watched—but she doubted there could be an actual racoon in the bathroom. Cautiously, she opened the door, but the only creature she found was Saskia, sitting on the loo lid, phone in her hands, staring at the screen.

Harmony said gently, 'Saskia, what's wrong?'

Saskia started and the phone disappeared under the hem of her polo shirt. Her red and puffy-eyed gaze took in Nia's presence.

There was no way Saskia would talk with Nia listening... 'Saskia, why don't you come with me while I get ready for the party?' Harmony turned to Nia, 'Thank you for getting me.'

When Saskia didn't move, Harmony shifted Patience's weight to one side and put a hand under Saskia's elbow. Appearing dazed, she allowed herself to be led.

'Let's sit here,' Harmony said kindly as she took Saskia to the sofa in her apartment and placed Patience in the cot with some soft toys. 'What's happened to upset you?'

Saskia fiddled with the bunch of loo paper she was clutching.

'Let me give you a hug. I think you need it.'

But Saskia beat her to it, throwing herself into Harmony's arms. It was the longest embrace she'd ever given another woman. Was Saskia missing her mother?

'I... I only... wanted to... help,' she said between the staccato sobs when the embrace ended.

'I'm sure you did.'

'I'm in a chat group. Mummy had told everyone I was staying with my aunt in Switzerland. But my friends kept asking for photos. My aunt sent me some, but as I wasn't in them, Jemima didn't believe I was there. So I told her I'd come home and that's why I couldn't take a selfie in the mountains. That's where my aunt has a chalet, you see, on a mountain. It's very high up.

'Then, Romilly said they were thinking of letting their help go. The bathrooms weren't up to the mark, especially the lavatories. I wanted to save the help's job. It's hard to get the porcelain gleaming white with no limescale...'

Harmony was touched by Saskia's compassion. 'Yes?'

'So I suggested that Romilly buys *Flush It!* for her help

because it works very well. Then Cordelia asked how do I know that, and I said because I've used it myself. One question led to another. They know Mummy lied and that I'm working here as a low-paid help cleaning loos.'

'Does it matter? They're your friends.'

Saskia repressed a sob. 'They keep asking for cleaning advice, including how to clean an oven door. But I've not cleaned any oven doors. They asked how many loos I clean in a day and then... then...' Saskia blew her nose. 'Romilly sent a message I wasn't meant to see...'

'What did it say?'

Saskia buried her face in her hands.

'If you can't say it, can you show me?'

She passed her phone.

Romilly: Let's hope the lavatory queen doesn't make it home for Christmas

Jemima: That would be such a shame. I've already bought some Flush It! for her

Cordelia: I thought I'd invite her here to show me how it's done. I could record her scrubbing the inside of a lavatory bowl

Romilly: Oh, sorry Saskia, wrong group

'That's awful of them,' Harmony said.

'Wrong group means they've started a new group, doesn't it? And they got muddled up and sent the messages to the old one, not realising Romilly had made a mistake.'

Harmony suspected humiliating Saskia had been part of the plan.

'And,' she said, searching through her phone, 'Romilly put a picture of *Flush It!* on Instagram. She showed the page to Harmony.

The caption said, *As recommended by our dear friend, Saskia, the lavatory queen.*

'They're bullies,' Harmony said. 'They should be ashamed of themselves.'

'We made Facebook accounts a long time ago. I looked to see if they'd done the same thing there, but they've unfriended me. I can't see their profiles anymore. They're private, you see.' Saskia's head dropped to her knees again and she bawled.

Harmony drew Saskia close. 'You know, true friends stand by you no matter what. If Jemima, Romilly and...' who was the other girl? '... and Cordelia can't accept you because of your changed circumstances then maybe you could make some new friends?'

Saskia delicately blew her nose and wiped her cheeks. Harmony placed the waste paper basket nearby and passed her some fresh tissues.

'Mummy said I wasn't to socialise with anyone here.'

'What about Grandfather? What does he say?'

'He says the more I understand about real life, the more real I'll become as a person. *But I am real.* I have feelings.'

'Of course you're real and you have feelings.'

'Mummy says he's ruined my chances of having a suitable husband... They don't ever marry the help, you see, but they might have fun with them. Now everyone knows about me, no suitable man will want me as a wife, just as a plaything...'

'Oh no... What does Grandfather think?'

'He says I need a man who lives in the real world to make sure I keep my feet on the ground. He says I need to appreciate the salt of the earth and become like it myself. I looked it up. It means a genuine, worthy and unpretentious person. *Moi? Pretentious?* ' Saskia's tone became more indignant as the sentence came to a close.

'It sounds as though you're working out who Saskia truly is.'

'Yes. But why is it only me who has to work out who I am? Why don't Jemima, Romilly and Cordelia have to find out who they are?'

Harmony touched Saskia's arm. 'Life sometimes doesn't seem fair. But you've matured so much since you came here, learned new skills. That's a good thing, isn't it?'

'Mummy doesn't think that will get me a good

husband.'

'By good, does she mean someone who'll truly love you or does it mean someone who's got lots of money and wants a wife for show while he plays around with the help?' May as well use Saskia's mother's frame of reference to get her point across.

Saskia's beautifully threaded eyebrows came a tad closer together and she gently bit her bottom lip with her pearl-like teeth. 'I want to be loved. I've always wanted to be loved.'

Harmony squeezed Saskia's shoulders. 'That's what you deserve and no less.'

'I'm not going home for Christmas. Mummy and Daddy are going away and my friends only want to make fun of me.'

'I'm sure Grandfather would be lonely without you, and we'll be very glad of your assistance again after your break.'

'It's nice to be wanted,' Saskia said with a sniff.

19

'You *still* haven't said if you'll come,' Tim said. 'Harmony invited you too.'

Ever since their time at the café, James hadn't been able to stop thinking about her. Even the sound of her voice tingled his insides. But she was so close to home—what if it went wrong? And how would Tim react to his dad having a relationship with Harmony—especially with having to see her at the Hall?

When James had thought about the need to move on, he'd envisaged spending time with a woman outside of his son's life. But was Harmony even remotely interested in him? They'd got on very well at the café. However, he still didn't know much about her past or why she'd almost scarpered. She'd appeared reassured by the "friends only" mode they'd maintained. It would be safest for everyone to keep it that way.

He would do his best to keep it that way.

And look elsewhere…

'Dad? Are you coming?'

Just being in Harmony's company made James feel like he'd found some kind of haven, but she needn't know that…

'There will be a magician *and* Father Christmas.'

He couldn't let his son down. He patted Tim's back. 'Let's go then.'

They exchanged smiles, and James's heart beat with

anticipation. He was drawn to Harmony like a bee to a nectar-laden flower.

When she opened Pinkerton Hall's door in a red dress accentuating her generous curves, he made a quick grab for the large box of chocolates that was slipping from his grasp.

'I'm so pleased you both made it,' she said.

With a catch in his voice, he said, 'The chocolates are for the staff to share. To say thank you, and to wish you all a happy Christmas.'

'Thanks.' She took the box. 'A happy Christmas to you both too.'

He wished he could have bought her a gift, but that might have been too personal, made it more than it was, made her feel bad for not getting him a present. It was best to keep things neutral, pretend he was just her friendly neighbour. Which, of course, he was.

'I made these with Dad last night.' Tim showed her the bag. 'And we decorated them this morning.'

'Christmas biscuits,' James said.

'Oh, how lovely. Thank you...'

After he and Tim hung their coats in the capacious hallway cupboard, he noticed Harmony admiring his black and white jumper—or was it his chest? James turned away. He must resist the allure of her in her red dress, her pretty, heart-shaped face and her dazzling smile. They weren't for his benefit, were they? His heart squeezed with a zing.

'Let's put them in the office,' she said.

There was a playpen in the right-hand corner, and Patience was playing with some colourful foam shapes. She appeared very festive in a green top, red trousers and a red hat with a tiny white bobble on top.

'Patience looks very festive,' he said. Harmony did too...

After a sideways nod of James's silent instruction, Tim placed the two large tins next to the box of chocolates she'd placed on the desk.

She opened the tin lids. 'Wow. They're beautiful, and

the smell of cinnamon... I love it.'

The biscuits were shaped into snowflakes, stars, holly leaves, Christmas trees, baubles, snowmen and Christmas stockings.

'They're so colourful,' she said. 'It must have taken you hours.'

As she caught his eye, James's cheeks became hot. She must have guessed he'd done the bulk of the work.

'We enjoyed it,' he said. 'It's nice to do something in return. You do so much for us...'

Her face became a close match to the colour of her dress. 'I'm happy to help.'

She always was happy to help. Kindness flowed out of her.

Picking up Patience, she said, 'Tim, would you bring the tins through to the dining room?'

As she led the way, James eyed her movements; he couldn't help it.

'Whoa,' Tim said.

Did he also appreciate Harmony's outfit? But when James followed his son's gaze, he realised her knee-length, body-hugging dress was of no interest. It was the paper chains, shiny foil ceiling garlands, streamers and a lavishly decorated tree that had caught his eye. Above the twinkling LED lights, silver and purple tinsel, multicoloured baubles and snowflake ornaments was a large, silver star.

In the dining room, the long table was against the far wall, laden with covered platters and trays of food.

She pointed for Tim. 'The biscuits can go at the end of the table with the rest of the sweet stuff.' Then her gaze briefly met James's eyes. Her expression was quite impersonal as she gave a polite smile and said, 'I've still got a few things to see to and get Patience set up in the front library for the afternoon with another staff member.'

'Of course,' he said. But it was to her retreating back.

If she'd been interested in him, she'd have hung around, even if just for a while, wouldn't she? Or perhaps she considered their getting together a bad idea too. Whatever, he could relax his defences.

Candy was frantically waving at him to join her in the corridor. 'I need a favour.'

She took him into a room with a pile of empty crates that might have held the decorations since scraps of tinsel remained. On the other side were two lines of lockers with slatted bench seats in front of them. Was this the staff changing room?

'What is it?' he asked.

'Father Christmas has flu. Could you replace him? I told Harmony I would, but the outfit doesn't fit me at all and your physique would be perfect.' Candy indicated a red and white suit, hat, wig, beard, sunglasses, gloves and a cushion on one of the benches. 'With all that on, you won't be recognised.'

He'd never played Father Christmas before. 'What do I have to do?'

She pointed to a bulging sack. 'Just hand out the presents.'

James delved inside. Each gift already bore the child's name.

'Chitchat about Christmas and disguise your voice. I'm sure you'll be fine. When you've changed, you can wait in the dining room until the magician's performance is over.'

Uncomfortably conspicuous wearing the seasonal outfit, James entered the darkened dining room. His cushion-padded front gave him a paunch of which a sumo wrestler would be proud, and his skin itched behind the quintessential white beard.

The chairs faced the magician on the stage under lights and another twinkling Christmas tree. He took a vacant seat by the wall near the door, hoping the kids wouldn't turn around and spot him.

He was enjoying the magic tricks—better seen from over the top of his sunglasses—perhaps almost as much as the children.

Aware someone had sat next to him, the side of their body against his, he turned in surprise to discover Harmony. He pressed the shades hard against his face as she leaned towards him, put an arm around his neck and brought her mouth close to his ear. His throat tightened.

'Candy,' she whispered, the scent of jasmine filling his nostrils, 'you're right. I do have a thing for James.'

He stayed silent, stunned. Harmony did have a "thing" for him. A mix of temptation and longing swelled his heart. *Think of Tim, too close to home, it could go terribly wrong.* He'd use it as a mantra.

To pretend this confidence had never been made, she must continue to believe he was Candy. But as Harmony's arm was still tight about his neck, her breast pressing tantalisingly against his arm, his mind struggled to work out how he could avoid discovery.

'Isn't this the point where you reassure me of his feelings?' She withdrew her arm, her breast disconnecting with his body. 'Candy?'

He breathed in hard to settle his racing heart.

'There's no need to be nervous, you're used to acting, remember?'

Applause sounded around the room. He joined in, relieved to have an excuse not to answer.

'Candy?'

The magician bowed and introduced Father Christmas, extending her arm towards him.

A burst of Bruce Springsteen's *Santa Claus Is Coming to Town* played. By the music centre next to the stage, an older boy appeared to be responsible for the timely introduction. The kids cheered and clapped some more.

James stood up, nodded at the magician, and grabbed the sack of presents he'd placed by his feet. He avoided looking in Harmony's direction. The music stopped and everyone watched him expectantly.

As he approached the first cluster of children, he

projected his voice—adopting a low-pitched Jamaican accent he thought Candy would have used to pass as a man. Hopefully, she wouldn't appear in Harmony's line of sight until he was out of costume.

Harmony puzzled over Father Christmas. He was too tall, his accent too odd to be Candy. Unease spread as she noted this Father Christmas didn't appear to recognise many of the kids by name, so far only Patrik, Tim and Anil. Then Candy sat down next to her, and Harmony screamed. Everyone stared at her, including Father Christmas.

She ran out of the dining room and took refuge in the dark staff locker room and sat on an upturned crate, squeezing her eyes shut, desperate to erase the image of Father Christmas gawking back at her.

She also wanted to erase the one-way conversation she'd had with "Father Christmas". However she reran it, she knew she'd given far too much away, and why had James pretended to be Candy with that fake Jamaican accent? Had it been an attempt to save Harmony from humiliation—or himself?

Someone came in and switched on the light. She ignored the intrusion—they'd either not notice her or take the hint she wanted to be alone. Expecting the person to nip in and out, she was surprised the door remained silent, which meant the occupant had stayed. Opening her eyes, Harmony stared against the pain of the light, stopped breathing, gasped and then choked on her saliva.

James had divested himself of the Father Christmas outfit and was standing in just a T-shirt, socks and tight-fitting navy underpants. It had been ten years since she'd last seen a grown man with so few clothes on, seen that particular stretched cotton outline of masculinity.

At her first cough, he spotted her and his hands flew to his crotch. 'I'm sorry, I thought I was alone.'

'I didn't...' She was coughing too much to continue.

'I think you mistook me for Candy.'

'You know… I mistook you… for Candy.'

'Yes.'

'I don't think I've felt such humiliation since…' She broke off, recalling the last time humiliation had overwhelmed her. All those guests pitying her… all her work colleagues knowing of her mortification… and she'd wanted to hide from them all.

'Since?' he prompted.

'Since a very long time ago, but for a moment, it seemed like yesterday.' She charged out and headed for the dining room.

It took James a few seconds to appreciate his groin no longer needed shielding for propriety's sake. He dressed quickly.

Planning to make a retreat and come back later for Tim, James went to the dining room to let his son know. But he was grabbed and led towards a ring of chairs—as was Harmony from the other end of the room—to join an intended game. When she approached, she blushed furiously, lowering her gaze to the floor, and he flicked his eyes to the side.

His presence was obviously embarrassing her and he… he wished he hadn't heard that she had a "thing" for him. It made it so many times harder to stick to: *Think of Tim, too close to home, it could go terribly wrong.*

He'd discovered, from handing out presents, that the boy providing the music was called Ostap. Brenda Lee's *Rockin' Around The Christmas Tree* began to play. Everyone in the game danced around the perimeter of the outwardly facing chairs—well, the kids and Harmony danced, but James walked. When the music stopped, everyone had to sit down and the person left standing was "out".

He caught Tim laughing. If his son could enjoy life, surely his dad could as well, put aside his sadness for his missing wife and child. A spring came into James's step.

Why were the children passing a message from one mouth to the next ear, at the same time as playing musical chairs? It came to his turn, but the message didn't get relayed. Had Harmony similarly been left out? Then, by rights, the chair he was aiming for ought to have been taken by the girl in front. But she stumbled, leaving it free for him.

Slade was singing *Merry Xmas Everybody* when he and Harmony were the only two left in the clearly rigged game. Should he let Harmony win—which would likely be obvious to the keen-eyed audience—or do his damnedest to nab the seat? He knew from the Sudoku games they'd played that Harmony was competitive, so he opted for the latter.

When the music stopped for the last time, he slid neatly onto the seat. But Harmony, who'd passed the seat, did a quick step in reverse while clutching the chairback. Before he knew it, her bottom landed on a thigh and, as she was slipping off, he leaned towards her, grabbing her waist to save her from falling.

The kids whooped.

As she righted herself, she turned to look at him and her lips smacked bang into his.

James straightened, releasing his arm, and she removed her lips.

'I'm so sorry,' she said with fruit juice breath.

'Me too.'

'It was an accident,' she said.

'I didn't mean to... I wanted to save you from falling.'

'I know.'

She stood up and made an excuse to flee. Someone handed him his prize that softly rattled like a box of chocolates.

Tim approached. 'Well done, Dad. That was well funny.'

'It was an accident.'

'I know. But it was a funny accident.'

Why was he cool about it? James had kind of kissed Harmony and had had his arm around her waist. Perhaps the possibility of his dad having a new relationship wasn't on Tim's radar yet?

Unwilling to risk another unexpected situation with Harmony, James strengthened his resolve to go home. It would also be kind as she'd scarpered three times now because of him.

'I'm going to head off for a while. I'll come to pick you up later.'

Tim's joyful expression fell. 'You're back to being all serious. Playing the game, you looked happy—and now you don't.'

James *had* felt happy. But it wasn't as simple as all that. He put his arm around Tim's shoulder, but his son pulled away.

'I don't want to forget the past, Dad, but I don't want to live in it as well.' With hunched shoulders, he went to join his friends.

James froze. Sometimes Tim seemed wise beyond his years.

'Are you all right?' Candy placed her hand on James's arm.

'Yes. I just thought I'd go home for a while and come back later.'

'I'll see you out,' she said.

When Harmony had left the dining room, she'd only one goal—to hide from everyone as quickly as possible. She'd fled in one direction only to hear voices or footsteps approach, and she'd turned and bolted in another. Nikolai Rimsky-Korsakov's *Flight of the Bumblebee* played in her mind as she flitted and double-backed. Before she knew it, having heard footsteps on the stairs, which meant she couldn't go up, she'd opened the door to the coat cupboard and had secreted herself inside.

Although it was dark now, it wouldn't be if the door opened. She draped a coat over herself so that, should someone come seeking their outerwear, she wouldn't be discovered.

It wasn't long before the door did open.

'Can you find it?' It was Candy's voice.

'I'm sure I put it on a hanger,' James said. 'It's on some kind of stand.'

'There's no stand.'

The coat was plucked away. The astonished faces of James and Candy were too much to bear, so Harmony buried her face in another coat.

'Harmony! What are you doing in here?' Candy asked.

'I've made such a fool of myself, I can't face anyone.'

'What happened?' she asked.

James cleared his throat. 'Harmony mistook me for you—when I was Father Christmas.'

'And I might have whispered things that were meant only for your ears, Candy.'

'What things?'

'I... can't remember,' James said.

'I can't remember either,' Harmony mumbled from inside the other coat.

20

The following Monday, Harmony was with Candy in the office, tackling admin. She'd sat on the side of the desk to be close to Patience in the playpen. When Harmony answered the trilling phone and heard the voice at the other end, her heart lurched.

'Hello, Annie.'

The social worker's voice was strong. 'I'd like to see Alfie this afternoon. I should be there sometime between four and five.'

'That's fine. I'll let him know.'

'I take it he's not talking yet?'

'No, but he's doing much better.'

'Good—and I'd like to take some photos of Patience as it seems there's a possible suitable couple already waiting to adopt. I might have some news after Christmas.'

Harmony's stomach dived. Christmas was in three days. 'It's great that Patience might have parents soon. But what of her birth mother?'

'We've waited long enough.'

Where was Patience's mum? What was stopping her from coming forward to claim her baby? Did she know she was at risk of losing her child completely? Harmony swallowed an emotional lump that had formed in her throat.

After Annie had hung up, Harmony relayed the

conversation to Candy.

'You might not have Patience for much longer,' Candy warned.

Harmony picked the baby up for a kiss and a cuddle. 'I know.' The sadness that surrounded her was sweetened by the knowledge that it would be best for Patience. If Harmony's heart ended up being shredded... well, she'd known the score.

James was home early with Tim. As it was the school holidays, James had taken him to work, using the need to be based in the office to catch up on paperwork and phone calls.

Tim fiddled with his mug of hot chocolate. 'Will she be here soon?'

Felicia's closest school friend, Priya, was having him to stay until Christmas Eve. Her son, Chandran, was only a year older than Tim and they'd been friends their entire lives.

James sat opposite with a cup of coffee. 'Another half hour or so I expect. She promised to call when she was on her way.'

He considered how he'd spend his free time. Catching up on sleep, he hoped. Ever since the party at the Hall, he'd been restless in bed, wrestling with thoughts of charging across the road to ask Harmony out and buying a ticket to the moon to stop him from doing so.

His phone rang and he put it on speaker. 'Hi, Priya.'

Tim looked keenly at James.

'I'm dreadfully sorry,' she said. 'I can't have Tim after all. Mum's been taken ill, and we're going to London to take care of her.'

Tim sprang to his feet, his mouth open and his eyes wide with disappointment.

'Oh, dear,' James said. 'I'm very sorry to hear that. I do hope she'll be all right.' When the call ended, no one spoke. Then he said, 'I'm so sorry,' and went to give his son a hug, but Tim shrugged him away.

Pacing around the scant floor space of the kitchen, Tim demanded, 'Ask Harmony if I can go to the Hall instead.'

'We can't impose on her—'

'I can. She said I can go whenever I want.'

'She was just being polite.'

Harmony did far too much already, but James was very grateful all the same. However, to keep asking, to keep taking, wasn't right. This was just the kind of thing that could make things even more awkward if they had a relationship—she'd suspect him of using her. After all the work she and the other staff must have put in for the Christmas party, he couldn't ask for another favour so soon, especially after what had happened.

'No, she wasn't just being polite. She loves kids, she loves us all.'

'I love you too, Tim. I always have and always will.'

Something had gone wrong between them, since the accident, and James didn't know how to put it right. He'd hoped he might be getting somewhere when they'd made the Christmas biscuits together. But the camaraderie they'd shared then appeared to have since vanished.

Tim's hand was on the handle of the kitchen door. 'We can go over there now and ask.'

'I've not drunk my—' James broke off.

His coffee didn't matter, his embarrassment didn't matter, but Tim absolutely did. Harmony would understand about having to see James again so soon, wouldn't she?

Harmony was in the front library with Annie.

'As I told you earlier,' Annie said, 'I may have found a suitable couple to adopt Patience. I'd like to—' Annie broke off as she spotted Nia in the doorway with Alfie.

Nia's jaw was slack, but when she recovered, she blurted, 'But Harmony's engaged!'

It was news to Harmony. 'Nia! Don't—'

'*Engaged?* When did this happen?'

Harmony stared helplessly at Annie. Go with an impossible lie or tell the truth? The truth won but the words somehow got stuck in her throat and her tongue went on strike.

'You should know it's hard to keep a secret with so many children around,' Annie told her. 'When did this happen?'

'It—'

Before Harmony managed to deny the news, Nia said, 'After the Christmas party.'

'I didn't know you were in a relationship.'

Harmony was wringing her hands. 'I... er...'

'She tries to keep her personal life private,' Nia said.

'Well,' Annie replied, 'I'll make a note on the system.'

Harmony battled over what to do about Nia's lie—and the fact that denial hadn't rapidly tripped off her lips.

Nia blurted, 'Harmony loves Patience too. Just as much as if she was her real mother.'

'I'm sure she does,' Annie said. 'Whatever decision is made must be the one considered to be in the best interests of the child.'

Harmony nodded. 'Of course. I wouldn't want it any other way.' It seemed Annie wouldn't brook any thought of her adopting Patience. So did that make the lie irrelevant?

'So, Alfie,' Annie said. 'I hear you're eating better?'

Alfie fiddled with a toy horse from the farm set he'd taken to carrying around.

Harmony wasn't sure if she should admit that Tim had been instrumental in Alfie's progress. But Annie might find fault with Alfie having close contact with an outsider at this time.

'Ooh, your horse looks nice,' Annie said. 'I like horses too. Does it have a name?'

Alfie shrank closer to Harmony, his eyes huge.

The social worker leaned back in her chair, appearing to have given up on questioning the boy. 'Tell me about your fiancé.'

Harmony's neck stiffened and there was a tremor in her head that reminded her of Lady Pinkerton when she'd developed Parkinson's disease. 'Er... There's not much to tell.'

'He lives in the cottage opposite. With his son, Tim,' Nia said. 'They moved from Bristol. James is an Environmental Health Officer. He knows all about cockroaches.'

Harmony squeezed her eyes shut, but the people in the room were still there when she opened them again. This couldn't be happening...

The truth became too hard to utter. Nia would feel betrayed having acted out of kindness, however misplaced. Also, might there be the teeniest chance this might make a difference if the couple Annie had mentioned earlier did not get approved?

But it was nonsense-thinking as James would need to fall in love with Harmony for that to happen. She wished she'd stopped Nia in her tracks.

Harmony could call Annie tomorrow and endure the embarrassment of explaining or... or she and James could "split up" sometime soon, having realised they weren't compatible after all. Or—Harmony's fantasy was getting wild now—they could *actually* become engaged. Her stomach was on a rollercoaster ride, dipping in the horror of what was happening and peaking at the thought of her and James in a passionate embrace... *Stop it! Had she lost all sense?*

Annie stared at Harmony's hands. 'No ring yet?'

'We're... planning on choosing it together.' Although grateful she was supported by the armchair, it was a shame it wasn't closer to the door.

The social worker nodded understanding. 'I'm surprised you found the time to have a relationship. I thought you were always busy with the children.'

Harmony forced a smile. In for a penny... 'He's very understanding about my work.'

'Perhaps I'll get to meet him?'

She was going to be sick... 'Oh, I don't know...' Her breathing was shallow, and she'd have been glad of a paper bag if she'd been alone. Queen's *Somebody to Love* played in her mind followed swiftly by *Under Pressure*. She needed to get James on board before Annie met him!

Nia pointed to the outside. 'He's on his way now.'

Harmony's stomach almost heaved. It was lucky lunch had been hours ago.

There was James, waiting to cross the road with Tim. Annie wouldn't be meeting them some other day after Harmony had time to explain and beg. It was happening today, now. She must waylay them, wave a magic wand at James and incant a spell to get him to go along with her. Before it was too late.

She sprang to her feet, swallowing down nausea. 'I'll ask him.'

Nia was already charging towards the entertainment rooms which spelt doom of some kind as she was the Hall's equivalent of a town crier. But Harmony didn't have time to deal with it; she had to put on her metaphorical witch's hat and brave the cold without her coat.

Sometimes adrenaline could be a good thing. Fight or flight? Well, she needed to do both.

21

The last time James had seen Harmony, she'd been hiding in the coat cupboard in the Hall, too mortified to face him— and he'd been too embarrassed to face her. But now, as he approached the flower bed, the main door to the Hall opened, and she flew out towards him.

Alfie appeared in her wake, his little legs running at full pelt. Before James could take stock of what might be going on, her arms were tight about his neck.

She whispered, 'I'm so sorry about this,' before her lips were on his, her soft, coatless body pressed against him.

The jolt that shot through him made him take a step back. But she took a step forward. Not one for hints it seemed.

Then she whispered in his ear, holding him tight so he couldn't pull away. 'I'm in a mess. Please back me up. I'll explain it all later. It's to do with Patience.'

He glanced towards the front windows. A woman with an abundance of curly, wayward orange hair was staring out. Her unwavering gaze and expressionless face unnerved him.

While Harmony had been kissing him and whispering in his ear, it appeared that a panting Alfie had been whispering in Tim's ear. James hadn't realised they were close. Was Alfie a substitute for Georgie?

'Did Alfie just speak to you?' Harmony sounded surprised.

Tim nodded.

Had Alfie a problem with speaking? Tim hadn't spoken either after he'd got the news in the hospital. The mutism had lasted a few weeks.

'Dad, you must help Harmony.'

James upturned his palms and gave Harmony a questioning look. By her unevenly furrowed brow, breathlessness and appeal in her wide eyes, he knew something serious was happening.

'Dad, you need to pretend you're her fiancé. *Really* pretend.'

He took in his son's determined expression and Alfie's beseeching eyes before he dragged his gaze towards Harmony again. She was stepping from one foot to the other—from cold or anxiety?

He'd planned a retreat, not an advance. The feelings he was developing towards her would be too powerful to resist if he didn't back off.

But after the cockroach inspection, he'd told himself he'd help her, if she ever needed it. Somehow the words *Think of Tim, too close to home, it could go terribly wrong* wobbled, popped and vanished.

So when Harmony's arms went around his neck again, and she kissed him a second time, he welcomed her lips, surrendering to the feelings that had been growing from the moment he'd met her. His arms circled her waist, drew her close. His mind turned to mush and an image of actually being engaged to Harmony broke through.

'That's good, Dad. Really convincing,' Tim said.

James pulled away, clearing his throat. 'I just came to ask for a favour.' *Not to get engaged.* But, at that heady moment, it didn't seem such a bad idea.

'Whatever the favour is, I'll do it,' she said. 'Whatever the woman watching us asks, please go with it. Charm her. I'm so sorry... but *please* help me. We can reverse it later.'

'We'll do it,' Tim blurted. 'Whatever you want, we'll do it, won't we, Dad?'

'Tim,' Harmony said, 'perhaps you should take Alfie and find Patrick and Anil? You shouldn't get involved in this mess.'

'I want to be involved. Alfie does too or he wouldn't have come out, and he *spoke* to me!'

'James, would you please pretend to be my fiancé?' Her tone was desperate, pleading.

Bemused, James's mushy brain sent a message to his neck to nod. It seemed he'd just got engaged. For now. But what would being engaged to Harmony entail?

When they entered the Hall, a crowd of kids were gathered around the library.

They greeted James and Tim with enthusiasm. 'Congratulations!'

James glanced at Harmony. Her wide-eyed, horrified gaze was aimed at a girl with pigtails—had she been the one to gather the troops? Whatever Harmony had done must have got out of hand.

The orange-haired woman appeared in the doorway.

Harmony turned towards her. 'Hi, Annie, this is James and his son Tim.'

'How nice to meet you,' Annie said warmly.

'The pleasure's mine.' James gave his most charming smile as he offered his hand.

'I must say your engagement to Harmony has taken me by surprise,' Annie said, 'and you've recently moved to Westbridge?'

'Er, yes. To the cottage opposite.'

'How convenient. It seems Alfie's taken quite a shine to your son.' Annie addressed Tim. 'Did Alfie just talk to you?'

Tim looked at Alfie and then back at Annie. He nodded.

'Has he done that before?'

'No.'

'What did he say?' Annie asked.

Tim shifted his feet and glanced at Alfie.

'Well?'

'He said Patience was going to be taken away.'

To be looked after somewhere else? For adoption? James wished he understood more about what was going on.

Annie's face was expressionless. 'Anything else?'

Tim shook his head.

Could Annie tell that Tim was lying?

'Kids, there's plenty to do in the entertainment

rooms,' Harmony said. 'Off you go.'

They shuffled away.

'Now that your son's not here,' Annie said to James as they took seats in the library, 'I'd like to ask a few questions.'

'Yes?' Why did he feel like he was about to sit a French oral exam? He'd been useless at foreign languages.

'How do you think Patience, with mixed Black ethnicity, would fit into your family?'

It was about adoption. What to do? As Harmony's anxious expression was haunting him, he decided to trust her and go along with the subterfuge. She'd said her favour was reversible. As long as the woman wasn't a reporter…

He cleared his throat. 'Like Harmony, we love children. We'd help Patience connect with her racial identity. If her specific cultural background were known, we could travel to relevant places. Find people from similar backgrounds to connect with. Learn from them. I think Harmony would make a great mum.'

'And do you think you'd make a good—'

Four of the older boys burst in begging him to play football with them at the back.

'I'm sorry…' he said uncertainly. 'I'm not sure whether to stay or go.'

'Come with us, James. You promised a re-match.'

'Yeah, you promised.'

'We're going to hammer you this time.'

'You can go, James,' Annie said. 'I'll catch up with you another time.'

He stepped towards Annie. 'It was lovely to meet you.'

They shook hands.

How could he have a re-match when there had been no previous match?

22

Once Annie had left, Harmony went to find the man she'd just kissed, deliberately, twice and the man who, she was sure, had happily kissed her back. But how was he feeling now? She was afraid he was going to be very, very angry with her.

He was kicking a ball around the grassy expanse that served as part of the kids' garden. As soon as the children spied her coming down the stone steps alone, they stopped playing.

'Has Annie gone?' they asked, running up to her, panting. 'Did she fall for it?'

James came to her side, breathing heavily.

She so wished the entire afternoon hadn't happened. That she could rewind and live it differently. 'All of you—I shouldn't have gone along with what Nia told Annie. I'm sorry you got involved.' Her gaze encompassed James too. 'It wasn't my intention... I've set such a bad example.' She fought back tears.

'It was fun,' one of them said and the rest agreed. 'And we wanted to help.'

James remained silent with a watchful, questioning expression on his face.

'However much I'd like to keep Patience, it's not necessarily the best solution for her, and James and I need to discuss what to do about what just happened.'

He frowned. 'What did just happen?'

Harmony smiled an apologetic goodbye to the kids and said to James, 'Let's go to the office.'

The silent walk gave her time for thought. She'd tell all to Candy later and have a chat with Nia about getting involved when she shouldn't. But, ultimately, there was no getting away from the fact that Harmony was to blame for not stopping the misdirection instantly.

Seated in the office with James, she said, 'I'm truly sorry. It was a moment of aberration...'

He waited for her to continue.

'Nia had overheard I'd like to adopt Patience and that it increased the chances of adoption if the person wasn't single. When Annie came this afternoon and mentioned a possible suitable adoptive couple, Nia said you and I were engaged.

'I tried to put things right, but Nia carried on. In the end, I didn't know how to get out of it without making her feel terrible and me appearing dishonest for not putting a stop to it immediately. I'm so sorry.' There was a stab of pain in her chest as she waited for him to speak.

His gaze held hers. 'Do you have many moments of aberration?'

Heat suffused her face. 'Only since Patience arrived.'

'If you don't get to keep Patience, do you hope I might give you a baby?'

He thought she was after his sperm? 'I hold no hopes of you ever giving me a baby.'

His head gave a little kick backwards as though her answer had been unexpected. 'What happens when Annie finds out we're not engaged?'

Harmony raised her shoulders helplessly.

James relaxed back in his chair. 'Who is she anyway?'

She winced as she said, 'A social worker.'

His eyes snapped open wide, and his back straightened. 'You *lied* to a social worker?'

Shaking her head miserably, she said, '*We* lied to a

social worker. Most of us did...'

James's jaw dropped. 'I didn't know she was a social worker... I should have guessed. But it was all so quick and confusing.'

'I'd hoped that, perhaps in a few weeks, we could tell her it didn't work out. I don't want her to think I'm deceitful.' She wanted to add that *they'd* been deceitful but didn't think James would appreciate the reminder.

She tried to swallow the dread that was rising from her stomach, clutching her heart. 'But I'll call her first thing tomorrow and confess.' And she probably wouldn't get a wink of sleep.

With narrowed eyes, James said, 'Wait. I'm not sure that's a good idea.'

Surprise, hope and then puzzlement washed over her in quick succession.

After a few moments of silence, he said, 'I'm in no mind to call a social worker to apologise for misleading her. I'll help you so I'm not discovered in the lie either. I think your first idea was better.'

If she wasn't already seated, she'd have flopped down in surprise. 'Pretend to be engaged until we fall out and break it off? You're happy with that?'

'Unless it causes a problem with Tim. Then we'll need to have a row sooner rather than later.'

She was astonished he was taking it so well. 'Of course. Tim comes first.'

Her stomach muscles, which had been screaming with tension ever since Nia had started the lie, began to relax. Annie would be kept in the dark about the subterfuge, and Harmony might manage to eat her evening meal.

James's gaze rested on her for what felt like an age. 'What does the role involve?' His tone became light and teasing. 'More kissing when Annie's around?'

She stopped herself from saying *yes, please*. 'Er... maybe.' Perhaps acting kissing might lead to more meaningful kissing? If so, it was good that Tim didn't appear to mind she'd kissed his dad.

James regarded her intently, his blue eyes darker than usual. 'Just so we understand each other, you'd like me to kiss you whenever Annie is in the vicinity? Because, if I have to ask for your consent every time, I don't think we'd make a convincing engaged couple.'

Harmony's breath caught. 'That might be a good idea,' she said weakly, not wanting to sound too eager. He was an excellent kisser... Could she find out where Annie hung out in her spare time and then invite him to go with her? 'You have my consent.'

He laughed. 'That's what I'll do then... Until we break up.'

'It seems a sensible idea.' It was probably the *least* sensible idea. 'I'm sorry about your shoes... and your suit.' They were muddied from the football game.

'I've got other suits and shoes to wear until they get cleaned.'

She licked her lips, which had suddenly become dry. 'What should we do if, as a complete outside chance, Annie does consider us for adoptive parents? Have a sudden almighty row?'

James chuckled. 'Or I could marry you.'

The shock froze any words she might have had at the back of her throat. He was joking, right?

'I'm sorry.' He raised a hand. 'I... it came out of nowhere. I...'

'It's... Don't worry about it. It's been a confusing afternoon. I'm all topsy turvy too.' But even more so now.

23

Still seated in the office, Harmony asked James, 'What was it you wanted to ask? When I met you outside?'

'Oh.'

'I said I'd help, didn't I?'

His gaze met hers. 'Yes. Thank you. Tim was going to spend time at a friend's place but there's a family emergency. He'd like to come here for the next couple of days instead of my workplace—which is where he's been today.'

'That's no trouble at all. He's very welcome.'

'Thank you. On Christmas Eve, we'll be staying with my parents for a few days.'

She felt lost. Christmas without the prospect of James dropping by. Even if he and Tim hadn't come around on Christmas Day, she'd hoped they'd be at Perdita's Boxing Day drinks party.

'I feel embarrassed,' James said, 'having you do so many favours for him—and me.'

'Please don't. Tim's a great lad, and Alfie will be delighted.'

'That's very generous of you.'

She was about to say what else would a fiancée do but stopped herself just in time.

'Tell me about Alfie,' James said.

'I can't tell you why he's here. But Tim's been great

with him. He comes around more for Alfie now than to be with Patrik and Anil.' Then she asked, softly, 'I wonder why, but in the café, you said you didn't want to talk about...'

James swallowed. 'Tim's younger... brother would be... about... Alfie's age... now.' He stared at her, and then his face appeared to crumple. He buried his fingers in the hair of his cowlick and began to cry.

She crouched beside him and placed an arm tight around his shoulder.

'I still have dreams about what happened... that night.'

'Would you like to talk about it?' she asked gently.

He wiped his eyes and began to tell her what had happened two years ago.

James was laughing at his colleague Lars's joke when the phone rang. Still chuckling, he took the call.

'James Traffurth.'

'Hello, Mr Traffurth. I'm Dr Kapur from Bristol Royal Infirmary. I'm calling to let you know that your wife and children have been involved in a road traffic accident.'

His smile was wiped from his face. 'What happened? Who's hurt?'

'Do you have someone with you?'

'What's happened? Just tell me!'

'I am very sorry to have to give you this sad news. There was a multiple crash on the M5... Your son Tim just has a broken arm and will make a full recovery...'

'My wife? And Georgie?' James croaked, his heart almost in his mouth.

'Unfortunately, your wife and younger son were in a more critical condition. We did all we could, but I am afraid they did not survive their injuries. They died soon after arrival. I'm terribly sorry.'

The mirth of a moment ago was gone. In its place was a cavernous, terrifying void that swallowed up everything familiar, everything he believed he knew of his world and his family. He was falling, falling so fast into the dark, stark nightmare.

Lars was on his feet. 'What's wrong?'

The handset slid from James's fingers onto the desk.

His entire body felt weak. It was a gargantuan effort to whisper the words, 'Car accident... Felicia... Georgie... d... d... gone.'

'*What the...?* Tim... what about Tim?'

His dizzy head sunk onto the desk, his body skewed, unable to support itself. 'Injured.'

'Let me get you some water—'

'No. Hospital.'

'I'm not sure you're in any fit—'

'Hospital.'

'I'll take you. We'll get a cab.'

Lars helped James stagger to the waiting taxi.

They hadn't gone far when he struggled to breathe. The journey was taking too long. The car was too small. Not enough air... He grasped his chest.

'Breathe deep,' Lars said. 'You sound like you're having a panic attack. Long, slow breaths...'

James did his best but there was something hard and unyielding preventing the air from going down. How could he live without Felicia and Georgie? Cope alone with Tim? Be a good father on his own?

'Stop! I need to get out,' he rasped.

The driver pulled over, and he just managed to open the door in time to throw up by the kerb.

Lars placed a hand on his shoulder. 'Oh, mate.'

'We can go again,' James said as he shut the door.

When they stated their purpose at the emergency department reception, a doctor escorted them to a private cubicle.

'Can we have some water?' Lars asked unsteadily.

'Of course.' The doctor left.

James stared at Felicia, lying, eyes closed, on the trolley. He couldn't believe her still body would never move or hold him again. There was no chance of a third child now.

Perhaps there hadn't been anyway as Felicia hadn't wanted another baby.

Sat in the armchair by her bed, his fingers traced the contours of her bruised and battered face and stroked her hair. Burying his face in her chest, he held her to him. She was still warm. Finding her fingers, he clutched them tight and sobbed.

Lars, standing beside him, placed his hand on James's shoulder. 'I'm so sorry, mate.'

James could only nod. A large roll of blue tissue had been left in the cubicle, and he tore some off to wipe his tears away, blow his nose.

The door opened and a nursing assistant pushed in a small, metal trolley with a jug of water and two plastic cups. Soon, Lars was nudging James to accept a drink. He couldn't keep his hands steady and some of the water spilled onto his trousers. But his mouth was dry, and he sipped gratefully while clinging to his sanity.

A doctor poked her head around the door.

'Can I see Georgie?' James asked in a rasping voice.

The doctor led them to a nearby cubicle the other side of the walkway and there was poor little Georgie, the sheet up to his neck, as though in deep slumber. James squeezed his eyes shut against the pain. But he could still see Georgie, lying there. Gone.

Just an hour ago, James had been as carefree as the average person but now… now he wouldn't ever know joy again. Clutching Georgie, he keened. He felt the pressure of Lars's arms around his shoulders.

Tim… Tim needed him. 'Tim…' James croaked.

'I'll ask where he is.' Lars left the tiny room and soon came back. 'He's at the other end of the corridor. But you can't see him in this state. Best to clean up first.'

When James frowned, Lars produced his phone, tapped on the glass and then showed the screen, which had become a mirror. The reflection showed a man with red-blotched skin and eyes so red and puffy, they barely opened. It took a moment to realise it was his own image.

Lars led him to the gents.

When James's face was slightly restored, he said, 'Let's go. He's not... got anyone with him.'

Lars went ahead and James followed, focusing on the route, not wanting to see the suffering of patients, drips, machines and oxygen masks. He just wanted his only surviving son.

'We're here.' Lars pulled the curtain further aside so they could get closer.

The sight of Tim propped up by pillows, his plastered arm in a sling and his face deathly pale brought new fears.

He must have heard them arrive as his eyes shot open. 'Dad!'

James flung his arms around Tim.

'Ow, Dad!'

'Sorry.' He released his hold and cupped his son's face between the palms of his hands. 'I love you so much.'

'I love you too, Dad. Mum... and Georgie... are they okay? The doctors haven't said. I keep asking.'

They'd left it to him to break the news? He sobbed as he tried to form the words. 'I'm sorry...'

'Dad?'

'They're... not... coming... home... again.'

He expected Tim to burst into tears, but he didn't. He gathered his son gently into his arms again. This time Tim's body was rigid and the eyes in his small, pale face stared blankly ahead.

'It's a shock, I know.' Had Tim heard? Why didn't he say anything?

They'd been hit by a life-changing event, and James had no idea how they were going to get through the next few seconds, let alone the next minutes, hours, days...

Shifting slightly from the crouched position to allow some circulation to return to her calves, Harmony circled both arms around James. She held him tightly, breathing in the cedarwood scent of his aftershave, and let her head rest on his shoulder.

'After Tim found out about Felicia and Georgie,' he said in a quiet voice, 'he stopped speaking. For weeks. Alfie hasn't been talking either, has he? Everyone was surprised by what happened today. It's what brought it all back.'

That special connection between Tim and Alfie made more sense now.

'Tim must be very sensitive to loss,' she said. 'That's why he got through to Alfie before anyone else.'

'Did Alfie lose his mum?'

'I'm sorry, I can't tell you.'

'I understand.' He pulled away and fumbled for tissues. In between bouts of blowing his nose, he said, 'I'm sorry. I'm not usually like this.'

'I know. But don't be sorry. It would be odd if you didn't show emotion when talking about what happened. Thank you for trusting me with such painful memories.'

'Is there somewhere I can wash my face before Tim sees me?'

Seeing his swollen, red-rimmed eyes, her heart went out to him. 'There's a door at the back of the office that leads to a staff loo. There'll be no risk of any of the children seeing you.'

James was back in the cottage kitchen with Tim who was chattering as soon as they were through the front door.

'Thanks, Dad. I didn't think you'd do it.'

'Pretend to be engaged?'

'Yeah.'

'We'll pretend a bit longer and then break it off. Annie mustn't find out we lied, okay?'

'Your secret's safe with me,' Tim said.

James needed time to absorb his new role. He'd worried about a romance going wrong. But, if it were a *pretend* romance with his son's approval then... it meant he and Harmony could become closer while pretending it *wasn't* a romance.

Was that safer regards fallout? Or just completely senseless?

24

Roxy met Tony at the same pub they'd eaten in a couple of times before, but it was quieter today—perhaps as a result of post-Christmas abstinence. The early January weather would have made her glad to sit by the radiator again but after they'd ordered, Tony chose a table for four, explaining, 'I prefer not to sit opposite people when they eat.' When she sat down, he pulled up a chair on the adjacent side.

'I feel the same way,' she said. 'It's easier not to have to see into someone else's mouth.' She'd had enough of that, sitting opposite her drunk dad all those years, spraying out masticated food as he spoke. Mum hadn't been much better.

'You and I keep finding things in common,' he said.

She smiled.

'I wasn't always bothered,' he said. 'I had a bad experience—with Perdita, actually. Deliberately ate with her mouth open to put me off her after I discovered she was pregnant with Petal. Didn't realise she was acting a part. She'd fallen for Saul by that time, you see, and hadn't wanted me to scupper things. A word of advice; don't mess with Perdita.'

Roxy couldn't help laughing. 'Sweet Perdita? Who's kind to everyone?' Even her, despite finding out she'd wronged Perdita's friend, Faith.

'Well, she was probably like that only with me,' he said. 'I did deserve it.'

The food arrived and they began to eat. Her sea bass lay over strips of fried vegetables with Parmentier potatoes along the side. Tony's steak was medium rare with triple-cooked chips, grilled mushrooms and tomatoes. It looked good. Perhaps she'd cook steak tonight for her and Matt. He'd like that.

'What do you think of the seminar so far?' Tony asked.

'It's interesting. A lot to take in.'

They'd covered finding an idea and developing it, undertaking plenty of market research, and what to include in a business plan.

'I'll explain about an accounting app this afternoon. Have you ideas yet for social media? Any chance of getting your old franchise back? Combining the two would be ideal.'

Roxy shook her head. 'But I might be able to pair up with the person who bought it—get a percentage of sales I pass her way.'

'Then she'd be your boss, wouldn't she?'

Her lips downturned. 'If I tailor my video clips to her products to help with my face-to-face parties, then yes, I suppose so.' She didn't fancy being anyone's underling. Even having to tend to Joshua and Matt's needs was getting harder, that bit more unpalatable.

'She might already be all over social media,' Tony went on. 'If you go it alone, you could choose which products to promote, make your own deals with manufacturers?'

'I could.'

'And if you build up a sizeable following, you could get sponsorships. I could help you get started if you like?'

She paused eating. He'd do that for her? 'Well, thanks.'

'But it would be very time-consuming for you to make it a success. What will you do about your marriage? Joshua?'

'Matt moved into another room ages ago. Perhaps he's trying to put me off him like Perdita did with you—and it's worked. Other women, far more suited to being a vicar's wife, seem to be waiting in the wings, so they can try their luck with him.'

They might not mind his lovemaking or his heavy workload—and the chosen one would have the coveted status of being the vicar's wife.

'There's no way Matt would keep Joshua. Bonding just didn't seem to work out, and how could he with his job?'

'So what is going to happen with Joshua? You can't put in the hours while being a full-time mum.'

'I know,' she said.

'Would your parents look after Joshua?'

She couldn't help the grimace. Were they the reason she'd turned out to have a lack of maternal instincts? 'We're estranged.' She wondered dispassionately whether they were still alive or had drunk themselves into an early grave.

'What happened between you?'

'Some people should never have a child. I left home at sixteen.' Actually, she'd run away. Penniless.

Although she'd worked in a shop on Saturdays and had sometimes babysat in the evenings, her mum always found her earnings. Roxy had even hidden them in her school locker. But Mum had called the school, claiming money was missing from her handbag. The deputy head had opened Roxy's locker, and she'd been branded a thief. Mum had taken the cash.

'How did you support yourself?' Tony asked. 'Where did you live? Were you still at school?'

The night she'd made her escape replayed in her mind. Dad's friend Rick had been over. Her parents had been out of booze, and Rick had been flush with the readies. He must have offered to sub them again if Roxy could be "nice" to him. Her inebriated father had knocked on her bedroom door while she'd been trying to finish her maths homework.

'Roxy, be a doll and be nice to Rick, eh?'

The door had opened. Rick had leered at her, come closer, reeking of beer. She'd known what had been expected of her. He'd touched her up before now, on the sofa, in front of her parents, who'd been so out of it they'd seemed to think it was harmless.

She'd said, 'Okay,' to get Dad out of the way. He'd shut the door and she'd heard his heavy lurch down the stairs, probably back to the living room.

The moment Rick's jeans were around his ankles, she'd lunged for the door handle, charged down the stairs and out of the front door. She'd been wearing slippers, had no money and no coat. But what she had known was the way to the police station.

Tony was waiting patiently for her reply about her schooling.

'I moved into a hostel for young people who were in the same kind of situation as me,' she said. 'Finished school to age eighteen.'

She'd once visited her parents after she was settled, renting a room, working for the Ann Summers chain, to see if they showed remorse, had had a wake-up call to their addiction. They'd welcomed her with open arms. But it hadn't been long before they'd asked for cash to "tide them over". Empty bottles lay around. Nothing had changed. She'd left—without giving them anything—and had never returned.

'You were very brave to do it alone,' Tony said. 'You must have hated home.'

'I did.'

'What about Joshua's dad? Would he take him?'

Her gaze took in the ceiling as she recalled the last conversation she'd had with Andy. 'The suspected dad refused to take a DNA test. So Joshua's father is stated as unknown on his birth certificate. He's not interested, and I'm free to do what I want.'

'Are you considering paying someone to...? Because that would take all your profits and, at the start, you won't have any profits...'

'No. Not paying someone.'

'Then what?'

'I wonder if I might be able to have a similar arrangement to the one you have with Perdita. I think I'd be a better mother if I'm the second mother, like you're the second father. I've not stopped thinking about it ever since you told me.'

He stared. 'You can't just find someone like that. Perdita's Petal's mother.'

'I... think maybe I'd better not say anything else.' Her eyes were stinging, and she didn't want him to know how churned up about it she felt.

'Say it. I told you I'm a crap father and did all possible to shirk my responsibilities. I'm lucky Perdita gave me a second chance to be a dad to Petal. It's a big decision for you to make.'

'I know it's a big decision! That's why I've done nothing else but think of it—that and how I can escape.'

He put his hand over hers. 'I'm sorry, I didn't mean to upset you.' His thumb stroked her skin.

She gaped at her hand, his slight touch having more effect on her than the last time she'd had sex with The Reverend Matthew Codd, before Perdita's party.

She removed her hand.

He rubbed his chin. 'I'm not judging you—you're like the female version of me. Have you someone in mind to be Joshua's "first mother" already? If you leave Matt?'

She nodded but wasn't ready to reveal a name.

'Do you think they'll agree?'

Panic tightened her gut. 'I hope so.' What would she do if the answer was no?

'Where would you live?'

'I'll go back to Bristol, I suppose. Although, it's going to be hard to start over again.'

His gaze softened. 'Fancy coming to London? I could help get you started, advise you...'

She wasn't sure of his meaning. 'If you're suggesting some kind of partnership, I wouldn't go into business with someone I barely know, and I'm not sure I'd want to at all.

The whole point of wanting a fresh start is being free of encumbrances.'

He shook his head. 'It was a no-strings offer in every sense.' His gaze showed sincerity. 'And I know you like your freedom as much as I do. As I said, we're one of a kind. We can lead separate lives—or have them overlap every so often with no questions asked.'

She gawked at him.

'It's just a suggestion... to start with. I like you. I'm drawn to you. Let's see where this takes us?'

She liked him too. A fresh start with a kindred spirit... Nothing fazed him about her. If they genuinely were a good match, might she find some kind of happiness? But she wasn't sure exactly what she wanted or what that happy life would look like. The imagined landscape beyond the escape door hadn't gone that far.

'If you do come to London, you could start off in Deptford—it's been regenerated, lots of students and young professionals, and much cheaper than other areas.'

'Is that where you live?'

He shook his head. 'But not far from there. You could use my area too for your face-to-face sales. If you're late finishing, you could...'

'I could...?'

He shrugged. 'Stay over.'

Maybe she could.

25

After the usual Sunday roast lunch, Harmony settled herself in the younger kids' living room with Patience on her lap, making silly noises and ridiculous faces to make the baby laugh, kissing her cheeks, her hands, tickling her tummy. A movement caught her attention. Tim was in the doorway, watching.

She beckoned to him, and he joined her on the sofa, mirroring her smile.

'I keep wondering,' she said, 'what Patience will look like as a little girl, a teenager and a woman. I wonder about everyone's future when they come to stay here.'

'You might get to know. You might be allowed to keep her.'

She put an arm around him. 'That would be nice. My home's almost ready but—'

'What home?' he asked sharply. 'I thought you lived here.'

'I do, but Lady Pinkerton gave me the Dower House to live in for life.'

'The house on the way in? Dad told me what a Dower House is.'

'Did he? I lived there when I looked after her. I'll be rattling around in it on my own as it's big enough for a family.'

'I hope you can keep Patience. Then you won't be

rattling around in it so much.'

Harmony sighed. 'Annie's taken photos of her so possible adoptive parents can see what she looks like. It's part of the matching process. I don't meet Patience's long-term needs, so I doubt it would be me. I'm sorry you and your dad got involved in this.'

'It's okay. I've got more friends now because of it.'

Since New Year, Tim had been coming back at the end of the school day with Alfie, Patrik and Anil instead of attending the after-school club.

After a moment's silence, Tim said, 'Who's Lady Pinkerton?'

'A kind old lady I used to work for who made the children's home possible, before she died.'

'That was nice of her.'

'It was, and a group of people—called trustees—make all the big decisions to do with the Hall. I'm one of the trustees. That's also thanks to Lady Pinkerton.'

'She must have liked you.'

Harmony laughed. 'She must have done. I liked her too.' Loved her… She squeezed his shoulder. 'Alfie looks up to you.'

'My brother Georgie was about the same age.'

'I'm sorry you lost Georgie. It must be very tough for you. Does Alfie remind you of him?'

'Not just that.'

'Oh?'

'He reminds me of me too,' Tim said.

'In what way?'

'I know something bad happened to him. I know his mum died.'

'Is that what Alfie told you?'

'He doesn't need to. I stopped talking too when Dad told me about Mum and Georgie.'

'It must have been an unbelievably difficult time for you,' Harmony said. 'For you both.'

'Yes. But we don't talk about it.'

Her heart tightened in sympathy. 'Perhaps your dad worries it would cause you pain.'

'It hurts more because he doesn't talk about it. There are all these holes in our life we ignore.'

'I could recommend someone to your dad to help you both.'

'Does Alfie have help?'

'I can't give you information about Alfie,' she said.

'He does, doesn't he?'

'Any Hall child who has issues has access to professional support. It could help you and your dad heal and become close again; you need each other.'

Alfie's head appeared around the door frame. His face lit up when he spotted Tim, and he came to sit on the other side of Harmony. As Patience was looking sleepy, Harmony popped her in the pram she'd left by the door before pushing it to the side of the sofa. After reclaiming her seat, she put one arm around each child. Alfie snuggled against her almost immediately. Initially, Tim stayed straight but then allowed his head to drop onto her shoulder.

Closing her eyes, she imagined living in the Dower House with children around her, and a smile played at her lips before she drifted into another world.

Coming to pick up Tim, James was pointed in the direction of the younger children's living room. Could he escape without meeting Harmony? He hadn't seen her since he'd broken down in tears, and he still burned from embarrassment.

She was dozing on a large sofa, her arms around Tim and Alfie, their heads resting on her shoulders. Other children had gravitated around her, sitting at her feet whilst watching an old Studio Ghibli film.

James's heart ached at the sight of Tim snuggled up to her. He'd accepted motherly warmth while having rejected all the fatherly affection on offer. Perhaps sitting physically closer might help them become emotionally closer. James would switch the two armchairs in the cottage for a corner sofa.

When Tim spotted James, he instantly straightened as if aware his dad had clocked how different he was when with Harmony. The sudden movement awakened her.

'Tim, it's time to go.' James smiled broadly to encompass everyone on the sofa, pretending he didn't feel even more rejected at the cosy scene he'd just witnessed.

With Alfie there too, it was as though she and the two boys had made a family. How would it feel if the four of them were all one family... Or would it spoil Tim's relationship with her if he knew how his dad genuinely felt? Tim hadn't minded the pretend kissing in front of Annie, but it might be very different if it was for real. He might feel the Hall was his space, his territory and all within—including Harmony.

'Oh,' she said. 'Could I have a word with you first?'

She took James to the office, pushing the pram ahead of them. The sleeping baby appeared completely relaxed. James wasn't sure tension truly left his body, even in slumber.

'What is it?' he asked when they were seated.

Harmony rubbed the edge of her sleeve between a finger and thumb as though unsure where to start. 'Tim was talking about Georgie and how things are difficult—for you both...'

James stiffened.

'I think it might help if you and Tim see someone together. I could recommend a good counsellor.'

Resentment began to flare but immediately fizzled out. She wasn't suggesting he wasn't a good enough father. She'd been speaking out of kindness and compassion.

'I... I'll think about it,' he said and meant it. 'Thank you.'

26

On the second Tuesday of the school term, James received a call at work.

'Is that Mr Traffurth?' the caller asked.

'Yes?'

'I'm Mrs Thompson. Headteacher of Westbridge Primary.'

Fear squeezed his chest. 'Is Tim all right?'

'He's fine. But he was caught vaping at the back of the gym with Patrik and Anil at lunchtime.'

James shut his eyes. *Not again.*

'We're trying to establish who brought the e-cigarette to school and how they got it. But none of the boys will give any information. Do you know if Tim could have—?'

'Absolutely not.' Tim was away from the crowd that had supplied the vape at his last school.

'And he's not been in any trouble like this before?' she asked.

What to do? Admit it? Then Tim would get all the blame. But James couldn't lie either. 'He was led astray at his last school.'

'We need to establish the facts,' Mrs Thompson said. 'If the boys persist in keeping silent, we'll have to deal with them equally harshly.'

'I understand,' James said glumly.

He'd have it out with Tim and reconsider allowing him

to go to the Hall instead of attending the after-school club.

'Would you like me to pick him up?'

'He's in isolation,' she told him. 'Tim can go home with Patrik and Anil as usual. But they are suspended from tomorrow to give us time to consider the next steps and they can reflect on their behaviour.'

Suspended! After all he'd done to protect Tim...

After hanging up, James tried to distract himself with paperwork but his thoughts kept returning to his son. Tim wouldn't have been able to get hold of an e-cigarette in Westbridge. There was no way Ramesh or the Spar shop would have sold it to a child. An older child must be involved, one who could have bought the vape in Bristol. There were older children at the Hall.

As soon as he was home, he was going to talk to Harmony.

Harmony had only just got back from meeting Miranda at the café with Patience in the pram when Annie rang the Hall bell. What had prompted her to make an unannounced visit?

'Hello,' she said as she came in. 'I couldn't get you on your mobile so I called the Hall. Did you get my message?'

'No... What message?'

'I'm sorry, Harmony. I was at the matching panel meeting this morning. Patience has been matched, and I've come to get her.'

Jack Frost entered Harmony's body, spreading chill, icing up her extremities, freezing her heart as he'd done once before. She touched the wall for support.

'I did mention you, but we progressed the case without involving you further because a suitable couple who can already meet all of Patience's needs was found. After ten weeks, an Adoption Order will follow. But to all intents and purposes, she's going to her permanent home.'

Fighting back tears, Harmony said, 'I'm glad you've found a good home for her with the right parents. I'll miss her.'

Candy had joined them while Annie had been speaking. 'Hi, Annie. I had to take Katie to a hospital appointment. If you could wait in the library, we'll get Patience's things together.'

'She only needs a bare minimum,' Annie said. 'The adoptive parents have already bought everything she'll need. But I'd appreciate the car seat.'

'Her blanket,' Harmony croaked. 'The one her mother made for her. It must go with her—and her tiny, soft doll.'

'I'll make sure they get them.'

'Thanks.' Harmony almost choked.

Candy pointed her into the office and pushed the pram in behind her. 'You say goodbye to her now, and I'll do the rest.'

Harmony picked up the little bundle she'd so come to love and held her gently against her, wrapped in her mother's blanket. Kissing her cheek, Harmony strained against tears as she said, 'Goodbye my dear, dear Patience. I'll never forget you, and I wish you the best future you can possibly have.'

Patience's little hand reached out and touched Harmony's cheek, then Candy took the baby from her, put her back in the pram and wheeled it out.

Harmony's present world merged with the nightmarish day of her surgery ten years ago.

Harmony was still groggy from the anaesthetic when she heard the surgeon's voice.

'Ms Payne?'

She opened her eyes. 'Yes?'

'Do you know where you are?'

'Hospital.'

'And do you know why you're here?' he asked.

'I've had a hysterectomy.'

Was he checking she was sufficiently with it to take in whatever he was going to say? Was it bad news about the cancer?

'The procedure went well and there's no sign of spreading. You'll likely make a full recovery with no recurrence of the tumour.'

'Thank you. That's a relief.'

'However, I have some difficult news to tell you.'

Her chest tightened.

'Pre-surgery tests aren't 100 per cent accurate. Very rarely, we get a false negative...' He trailed off, allowing time for the words to sink in. 'I'm sorry but we discovered you were pregnant when we removed your womb. It was a very early pregnancy, a few weeks.'

Tears filled her eyes. 'I don't understand...' She'd stopped taking the pill as soon as she was diagnosed, but they'd used condoms.

'As I said, very rarely there can be false negatives... There had been no reason to undertake further tests as we'd understood a pregnancy hadn't been possible.'

It was true. She'd told the pre-op nurse she couldn't be pregnant, and David hadn't said otherwise. They'd had not made love since her last period. But it had been lighter than usual... *Had David messed up and failed to tell her?*

She looked the surgeon in the eye. 'Had you known about the pregnancy beforehand, could I have carried it to full term?' Her cheeks were wet with warm trails of tears.

'The risk to you would have been considerable,' the doctor told her. 'I would not have advised it. I'm sorry.' He nodded goodbye and went to talk to the patient in the bed opposite hers.

Every time a sob burst from her lungs, her belly burned in protest, despite the protective pressure of her hands around the wound.

When David arrived, he thought she was distraught from having had a hysterectomy. He asked a passing nurse if she needed more pain relief.

Harmony couldn't make him understand until she finally managed to say, 'I was pregnant.'

The shock on his face told her it was a blow to him too.

He'd wanted kids. But at the right time and definitely not before the wedding. Now it was impossible and the wedding had been postponed by a year.

He lowered his head as he clenched his hands together. 'I... didn't think it could happen so easily.'

It was as though Jack Frost had paid her a visit, entering her lungs, cold enveloping her and settling in her heart like an icicle. 'What do you mean?'

'The condom... it split.'

At first, shock made it impossible to talk, and then she managed to say, *'It split and you didn't tell me?'*

'I didn't think it mattered. You'd had a period since and were having the op and—'

'Didn't think it mattered? You said nothing at the pre-op appointment when the nurse asked if there was any chance I could have become pregnant.'

'I didn't think there had been a chance otherwise I would have said...'

She turned her head toward the half-drawn curtain. The man she'd trusted had betrayed that trust and now the hurt from losing her fertility had been compounded by the fact she was also grieving for a child she'd never meet. She'd never know whether they'd have been a boy or a girl, what he or she would have looked like, what kind of personality they'd have had...

In the office, Harmony sat next to the plastic waste paper bin she'd just been sick in. She'd lost Patience, and she would miss her. Her *only* hope—however tiny—of ever having a baby had gone and she'd have to learn to deal with it because it was good news for Patience. She deserved to have the best possible future. All children did.

She heard Annie say goodbye and, moments later, Candy came in. 'What's the smell?'

Incapable of speaking, Harmony just pointed at the bin.

'I'm sorry you're hurting,' Candy said. 'I truly am.' She

poured out some water from the jug on a side table and handed it to Harmony.

She used the first couple of mouthfuls to swill her mouth and spit in the bin. Then she sipped and swallowed.

Candy must have spotted Saskia as she called out, asking her to come in. 'Please could you clean this bin and disinfect it? Harmony's not well.' Then she pressed a packet of mints and a small packet of tissues into Harmony's hand.

'Does it hurt somewhere really badly?' Saskia asked. 'Does she need a doctor?'

'It hurts, but she doesn't need a doctor. I'll take care of Harmony. You take care of the bin and use a bit of discretion.'

'What colour is it?'

'It's not a cleaning fluid. It means keeping your mouth shut. No gossiping.'

'I've never cleaned up vomit before.'

'Well, now's your chance.'

As Candy led Harmony out of the office, a cello inside her head struck up the sad melody of Camille Saint-Saëns' *The Swan* from which *The Dying Swan* ballet had been inspired. At that moment, she was that dying swan, her heart deep in mourning, sure she would not survive.

27

James had contrived to arrive home earlier than usual to discuss the vaping incident with Harmony. But when he pressed the Hall intercom bell, no one answered. He waited a polite length of time before trying again. Eventually, Candy opened the door, her closed expression making her appear less welcoming than usual.

Surely Candy wasn't blaming Tim? 'Hello. Could I see Harmony, please?'

'I'm sorry, she's not available.'

'Oh.'

Kids joined Candy in the porch, almost like when he'd first visited the Hall. But now they were silent and solemn. Had someone died? Or was it because two of their own were in trouble? Was Harmony avoiding him because of the incident?

Candy waved the children back, partly closing the door. 'If you wait here, I'll get Tim for you.'

So he was expected to remain on the doorstep? 'Can we talk about the school issue?'

'I'm sorry, I'm in the middle of something... But, if you'd like to visit Harmony out of concern for her well-being, rather than about the problem at school today... well, it might be possible.'

Concern for her well-being? What had happened? 'Er... yes, yes of course.'

Candy sent the children away and led him along a corridor he'd not been down before. There were a few kids gathered down a short offshoot to the right and they appeared to be interested in something on the wall. But he couldn't make it out.

'I can't see anything,' one of them said.

'Kids, you shouldn't be here,' Candy told them. 'Let Harmony have some privacy.'

They began to melt away.

She pointed to a door with a red light shining on the wall above it—a photography darkroom? 'Take your shoes off before you go in,' she whispered.

Was that safe if there was heavy equipment in the room? Bottles of developer and fixer? 'Don't I need foot protection?' he whispered back.

'She's not going to stamp on your feet. Well, not unless you upset her, I guess.'

Nothing made sense. What had developing photographs to do with being unwell?

Feeling surreal, he slipped off his shoes and placed them next to a pair of ladies' pumps.

The scent of potpourri, not photographic chemicals, was evident as he entered the dim room. Candy shut the door behind him. Circles of coloured lights slowly shifted along the walls and ceiling. His chest contracted as the sound of musical bells was overshadowed by sobbing. Why had she been left alone in this state? Then he recalled the time delay before the main door had opened. Had Candy been with Harmony before he'd called around but had been asked to speak to him as no one else had known what to say?

There was a long heap that could be Harmony on what he took to be some floor cushions. The outlines sharpened as the circular images crossed the area, and he found it not so dark after all. She was lying on her front.

'Harmony,' he whispered.

She couldn't have heard him.

'Harmony,' he repeated a little louder. Concerned he

might startle her, he settled awkwardly beside her.

She must have felt the cushions shift because she bawled, 'Oh, Candy, I can't bear it,' and threw herself across his chest, flattening him, weeping warm tears into his neck.

James held her tight, recalling how she'd comforted him in distress.

She sat up sharply, scooting back. 'You're not Candy.'

He sat up too.

'James! Did Candy send for you?'

Why would Candy do that? 'No. What's happened?'

The coloured circles spread across Harmony's face, revealing contours swollen from crying. Sympathy clutched his throat as he drew fingers across her cheek to wipe the tears away.

She sniffed, found a tissue and then popped something small into her mouth and crunched it as though it was a nut. 'Want a mint?'

'I'm all right, thanks.' Had there been a reason she'd offered him something that would freshen his breath? 'Actually, I'd like one after all.'

She passed the tube.

After taking a sweet, he returned it. 'What's happened?'

'Annie... took... Patience.' She sounded breathless, as though fighting for air.

'She's gone?'

'Forever.' She sounded so forlorn, his heart thumped in sympathy.

He shifted so his back was against the wall, pulling her close, smoothing her hair. 'I'm so sorry.'

Her legs bent over his and she wrapped her arms around his neck, tucking her head under his chin. But the movements of her chest against him, and the exaggerated breaths, told him something else was wrong.

'Have you... got a... paper bag?'

He tensed. 'Er, no. Why?' Had she meant an airline vomit bag?

'I need it… when I… hyperventilate.'

'Does it happen often?'

'Only since… Patience arrived. I've been afraid I'd… lose her… and now I have.'

His heart wept for her. 'I've had panic attacks. I was sick after I heard about the accident.'

'I've already done that.'

That explained the mints. 'Listen… Listen to my breathing. I'll match mine to yours and then gradually shift it. If you can follow the changes, it'll make you feel better.'

'Could you… put a chair under the door handle? I don't want anyone to see me like this.'

'Sure.' He found a lightweight chair to wedge in place.

With his arms tight about her, he breathed in and out noisily to synchronise his breathing with hers. Then, to help Harmony latch on to a healthier rhythm, he began to slow and deepen it.

It must have taken at least ten minutes before her breathing was calmer.

'Thank you… I feel much better now.'

'Good,' he said softly.

'It helped, knowing you've had a panic attack too. That you wouldn't judge me for losing it.'

He gave a quick squeeze as his arms were still firmly about her. 'Oh, Harmony, of course not. Loss is terrible. You love Patience with all your heart.'

'I do.' She sniffed. 'I was going to move to the Dower House with her if… well, it wasn't to be. There's no rush now.'

'The house by the entrance? How come?'

'It's my home for life, thanks to Lady Pinkerton.'

'When you're ready to move in,' he said, 'let me help.'

'Thanks. For now, I need to focus on moving on instead of moving in. I've plenty here to keep me busy, distract me.'

Every time she spoke, his heart was being pulled closer and closer to her. Words of love were ready on his lips, but he held them back. Now wasn't the time and whatever was going on between them could go horribly wrong—for all of them. Instead, he placed a hand on her head, his thumb giving the tiniest of strokes.

She wiped her eyes with the sleeve of her top. 'Deep down I knew it was never going to happen.' Her voice wobbled. 'And I... I need to accept that.'

Could there not be some hope for her? 'Might you not have a baby of your own?' Perhaps his? He'd always wanted another child, even with the two he'd had.

'Haven't you guessed? I can't have children.'

A jolt of shock ran through him.

'I... I had cancer. The op to remove the tumour made me infertile, and I lost a pregnancy, a few weeks old.'

So it was as though she'd lost two babies. 'I'm so sorry. I bet it's common for foster parents to fall in love with the babies they're looking after. You took care of Patience twenty-four hours a day for the best part of six months so of course you bonded closely with her. I'd be concerned if you hadn't.'

She laughed. 'You're trying very hard to make me feel better. Thanks.'

'But it's all true.'

'There you go, doing it again.'

He held her tight. 'Do you think you gave Patience the love you'd have given your own child if you'd had the chance?'

'Maybe. But whenever I see someone in need, my heart always reaches out to them. Patience had been just a few days old...'

'About the cancer. Are you okay now?'

'I'm fine.'

Harmony had cared for Lady Pinkerton, she cared for the Hall children, and she'd fostered Patience. Apart from Candy, there didn't appear to be anyone looking out for her. It made him want to be there for Harmony all the more.

He cuddled her, stroked her arms. 'What should we do about the fake engagement? Is this when we break it off?'

She didn't answer.

He wanted her to say no, so he offered a get-out. 'Or do you think it might be too obvious to break it off at the same time as losing Patience?'

She clutched at the straw. 'Too obvious.'

'Then we'll still act engaged.'

'Yes.'

He felt her relax into him. Their bodies were already tight against each other, but she shifted as though trying to get even closer. He was afraid that, if he strengthened his embrace further, he'd crush her.

'Would you mind if...?' she said.

'If?'

'If we lie down?'

He'd like nothing more. Well, almost. 'Of course I don't mind.' It was the opposite of what he should be doing.

They adjusted their positions until they lay as one, by the wall, and he was inhaling the coconut scent of her hair.

'This is so nice.' She snuggled further into his body, her head on his chest.

'Mm.'

A while later, she said, 'Oh,' and sat up.

He wished he could see her expression. 'I'm sorry... You were in my arms.'

'I know.'

'I liked it.'

'I could tell...'

He wished she'd lie back down again it had felt so good. 'Did being so close affect you like it did me?'

'You mean did I have an erection?'

'Of course not. Is your heart pounding?' He searched her eyes in the dimness while waiting for her to answer.

'Not at all.'

Surely she hadn't stopped liking him since the Christmas party? Although liking and loving were quite different. 'Prove it.'

'How?'

Lifting his jumper and shirt, he found her hand and laid it against the skin of his middle chest. 'Can you feel that?'

They were facing each other.

'You did that because you want my hand on your chest?' Her tone was light now, amused even.

'Prove your heart rate is slower than mine.'

She lifted her clothing and placed his hand between her breasts. He could feel her softness and his heartbeat strengthened.

'Well?' she said.

He was becoming lightheaded and wondered if he might need a paper bag too. 'So you are affected by me.' His voice was husky, and it was an effort to keep his tone light. 'Either that or you've got a galloping horse inside your chest trying to beat mine.'

Her fingers, still in situ, caressed his skin.

Danger! Danger!

Shut up, he told the voice.

'Your breathing,' she said, 'sounds like you're on a frantic cockroach search on a playing field.'

He laughed.

His hand would have liked to have gone exploring. But when she withdrew hers, he reluctantly pulled his hand away too.

When she felt the warmth of his hand leave her skin she asked, 'Did you like touching my chest?'

He chuckled. 'I... er... always like to do several thorough tests before issuing a report.'

A frisson of delight travelled down her spine. It was difficult to swallow. 'Are we becoming more than friends? Because I worry about getting hurt.'

'I don't want to get hurt either,' he murmured.

'I know.'

He caressed the back of her hand. 'I think you're incredibly kind and caring. You give so much to the kids. You'd have made a wonderful mother.'

Her skin burned under his touch. 'Thanks, and thank you for being here—when I needed someone.'

'Thank Candy—she let me in. I had no idea what had happened. Are you feeling better now?'

'Much.' It was true. She didn't feel so alone, so bereft. She shifted position so she was leaning against the wall, and he mirrored her movements to sit next to her. 'Do you mind my asking what Felicia was like?'

'Kind. Fun. Full of life.'

'What did she look like?' This was what worried her the most.

'Tall, slim and blonde.'

'I'm not your type, am I? I don't want to be a crutch until you find someone who is.'

'You are very different to Felicia, but that's what I like about you,' he said. 'Since I met you, I don't find slim, blonde women attractive anymore. All I can think of is you—and your body. That dress you wore to the Christmas party... you looked amazing.'

Saskia had good taste... 'Thanks,' Harmony said.

'And I don't think of you as a crutch.'

'So if a pretty, slim, blonde woman started flirting with you, you wouldn't look at her goggle-eyed and have your brain travel south?'

'No, I would not.' He sounded very certain.

She pictured Melody and wondered how James would react if they were to meet.

He pressed her hand. 'At the Christmas party, you said you liked me. Well, I like you back. *A lot.* Shall we use that as a starting point for whatever is going on between us?'

Her heart lightened. 'That sounds like a great idea, and James...'

'Yes?'

'I can't tell you how much the support and comfort you've given me in here has helped.'

'Until I held you in my arms, I hadn't realised how much I needed physical comfort myself. I'll miss it when I go.'

His words got her heartbeat racing again. But they'd been in there long enough and she needed to get back to the real world—and her job.

'I must go,' she said. 'I need to send Patience's diary—a record of the time she spent with me—and her current feeding/sleeping routine off to Annie so she can pass it on to Patience's new parents. Getting stuck into work will be good for me and getting it sent will help closure.'

As she made to rise, she added, 'You should know that when you step beyond the cushions, you're in the line of sight from the viewing window, although it's very dark so it's unlikely any—'

'*Viewing window?*' He appeared to recall something. 'Candy told them to go away.'

'Children have a habit of coming back.'

'I can believe that... Harmony, before you go, there's something I came to say. Mrs Thompson—'

She sat down again. 'I know about the vaping.'

'Well, one of the reasons I moved here was to keep Tim away from a crowd that led him astray in his last school. I realise three people were involved and not just Tim, but I've decided it's for the best if he stops coming here—at least for now. He can stay at the after-school club.'

Tim had been in trouble before? Anil and Patrik never had. 'Don't you think it might be a good idea to give me a chance to talk to Patrik and Anil—and you to Tim—before you stop your son socialising here?'

'I know it might appear harsh,' James said. 'I'm just trying to keep him safe. There are kids in hospital with damaged lungs from vaping. It could ruin his health, his life. I can't have another disaster.'

Her gaze met his. 'I know you're looking out for him. But feeling rejected is a big issue for all of them here; when they hurt, I do too. I live and breathe Pinkerton Hall. The children's home was my creation with Lady Pinkerton. It wouldn't be here if it weren't for the two of us. It would be good if you, me, Tim and the kids get along. I'm not sure that putting up barriers, stopping Tim from coming here, is going to help that happen.'

'I'd no idea how instrumental you'd been to the place.'

'I just don't want us all to get hurt through hasty decisions...'

'I understand, but today's taken me back to what happened before. I feel powerless to keep my son on the right track. He needs to see there are consequences to his actions.'

'I'll have a chat with the other two and educate them about the health risks because you are right, it's serious. If we can work together to nip it in the bud... You've made a huge effort for Tim. You clearly love him...'

'Yes, of course. Very much.'

'Why do you think he vaped again, knowing you'd gone to all the effort of moving here to get him away from the old crowd? His grief seems complex because of the attention he gives to Alfie. Did Tim get on well with Georgie? Were they the best of friends?'

James took a sharp breath. 'No, they weren't, and Felicia and I... we were having problems too... I'm sorry I didn't take you up on your offer straight away. I think I do need the counsellor's contact details.'

She put her arms around him and kissed his forehead. 'I'll be here to help you through.' She'd be a guiding light through his tunnel of darkness.

28

Nursing a mug of coffee, Harmony entered the office. She'd had an unsettled night either shedding more tears or reliving James's protective embrace, wanting more, so much more. Although she was ready to move things forward, she knew she must wait for him to come to her. She needed to be sure he was ready—truly ready.

Candy stopped tapping the keyboard. 'How are you feeling?'

'Shaky, but I'll pull through. I have lovely memories, and that's worth a lot.' Harmony cleared her throat. 'Losing Patience... well, it brought back memories of my op. You see, I'd been pregnant even though the pre-op test had come back negative. I was heartbroken, and it's not something I've been able to talk about.'

'Oh, I'm so sorry.' Candy came over briefly to give her a tight hug. 'I hope you find peace. You certainly don't need any more drama this year.'

Harmony was about to agree when her gaze caught a movement on a security camera monitor. 'Hey, who's that? What's a schoolgirl skulking around the grounds for?' She changed the view on the monitor. 'Look, there she is, by the kitchen window.'

'Strange.' Candy leaned over Harmony's shoulder. 'Oh goodness. Could she possibly be...?'

'Patience's mother?'

'We've got to catch her,' Candy said. 'Let's split up.'

'Can I come too?'

Harmony spun around to find Saskia hovering in the doorway. If they didn't get a move on, the girl outside might vanish so Harmony just said, 'You're with me. Get your coat.' She was going to get togged up too.

By the kitchen window, she searched under vehicles for tale-tell feet and then straightened. She extended her gaze to the coach house and the old stables that were being converted for the school leavers to move into. It was doubtful the girl would have headed in that direction.

When the January sun came out from behind a cloud, Harmony glanced up. As her focus adjusted, she spotted the girl, her hair in two tight bunches high on her head. Her legs, in black tights, dangled from the bare branch she was sitting on. She couldn't have been more than sixteen and was wearing a familiar black uniform.

'Hi! I'm Harmony.'

The girl regarded her with horror, clutching a nearby branch as though ready to climb higher.

Candy approached from the far side of the outbuildings. 'Hello. I'm Candy. We want to help you.' She sidled next to Harmony and added, 'Come inside and we can talk about it.'

The girl shook her head.

'You're Patience's mother, aren't you?' Candy said.

The girl's eyes were at risk of popping out from their sockets.

'We can tell you about her. Show you photos.'

The girl appeared to shrink. 'Leave me alone. Go away!' she shouted in a London accent.

Saskia stepped close to the tree. She smiled and yelled, 'Hello up there. How do you do? I'm Saskia Walker-Pearson. Do you need help getting down?'

'I need the toilet.'

'There are very clean loos here,' Saskia said, and then added smugly, 'I help to keep them that way.'

Harmony raised her eyebrows. Was Saskia taking pride in her work?

'Shall I show you where to go?' she offered.

When Candy slipped away, Harmony guessed it was to use a phone.

Perhaps it was Saskia's child-like simplicity or their being close in age that encouraged the girl to feel her way down the branches until she reached the ground. The three of them trooped into the Hall. Harmony waited with Saskia outside the loo while the girl was busy inside.

There was the sound of the toilet flushing and then running water.

'The girl likes you,' Harmony whispered. 'Be like a super nosy best friend. I need all the info I can get.'

Saskia nodded.

Soon the girl appeared, eyes wide and her face pinched. 'You're not going to let me go, are you?'

'There are things that need to be sorted first,' Harmony told her.

'I want to see my baby.'

'We all loved Patience,' Saskia said. 'You should have heard Harmony when—'

Harmony stepped on Saskia's toe.

'Ow. Be careful.'

'What were you going to say about my baby?'

'She's—'

Harmony stepped on Saskia's toe again.

'Ow.'

'Did she die?' The girl's mouth opened but no sound came out.

'Goodness, no. She's been adopted.'

Not quite, but to all intents and purposes... 'Saskia!' Harmony exclaimed.

A wild panic was in the schoolgirl's eyes as though she was a gentle gazelle about to be chased by a hungry lion. *'My baby's gone?'*

'I'm so sorry.' Harmony placed a hand on her arm.

'Let's go into the library.'

'Can I get her back? *I want her back!*'

Harmony put an arm around the girl. 'I'm truly sad for you, and I'll do my best to support you. Let's talk about Patience in the library.'

'It's a lovely room,' Saskia said. 'It's got lots of books in it.' She took hold of the girl's hand. 'I'll come with you, it's all right.'

Had the girl not got on so well with Saskia, Harmony would have asked her to leave. She gestured to the sofa as it had its back to the window. Saskia sat next to the girl, who'd begun to tremble, her teeth chattering and her knees knocking together.

Harmony placed her coat on the main table and moved a box of tissues to a smaller table she dragged close to the girl. The girl kept her coat on.

Harmony drew up a chair opposite. 'Please could you tell me your name?'

The girl remained silent.

'I used to have name tags on my school clothes,' Saskia said. 'Is your name on yours?'

After a long pause, the girl said quietly, 'Mandisa. Mandisa Adeyemi.'

Well done, Saskia, Harmony thought. 'That's a lovely name.'

Candy came in briefly to hand Harmony a sheet of folded paper: *Police on their way. Annie's been informed.*

Saskia cleared her throat. 'I live with Grandfather at the moment. Who do you live with?'

Mandisa's lips tightened together.

'Is there anyone you'd like us to call for you?' Harmony asked gently.

Mandisa mumbled, 'No. I want to see my baby.'

'The social worker hoped you'd be found,' Harmony said. 'But Patience has gone to her new home now. I do have photos though.' She whipped out her phone and opened the folder she kept them in. Then she passed the phone to

Mandisa as she joined her on the sofa.

'She's so cute.' Tears streamed down Mandisa's face.

'We all loved her,' Harmony said.

Candy returned with a glass of orange juice and a plate of biscuits and laid them on the small table. 'Keep your strength up,' she urged before leaving the room again.

Saskia took a biscuit. 'Thanks.'

Harmony opened her mouth to tell Saskia the refreshments were not for her but shut it again when Mandisa also helped herself to a biscuit and then downed the juice.

Saskia twisted around, alerted by the sound of a car. Her gaze shot back to Harmony.

No-o Saskia don't say it...

'Why are the police here?'

She'd said it. Harmony made to block the exit.

Mandisa dropped her biscuit as she stepped over Saskia's feet, past the table and charged towards the door. But Harmony was there first.

'They're here to help,' Harmony said. 'You're not in any trouble.'

'Oh!' Saskia exclaimed. 'It's the man who gave you Patience who's in trouble.'

'Let me go!' Mandisa screamed. 'He's done nothing wrong! He loves me. He takes care of me.'

Had Mandisa been groomed? Groomed so well she didn't realise what the man had done?

The murmuring voices meant Candy had already let the police in.

'Please sit back down,' Harmony said. 'I'll join you in a moment.'

When Mandisa stepped away, Harmony opened the door to two female officers. One had ginger freckles and a smiley face and the other was so deadpan, she might have just visited a beauty clinic for Botox injections.

'Saskia, please could you go back to your work now?' Harmony said.

Saskia opened her mouth to protest but then changed her mind and left.

When everyone was seated, the officers introduced themselves, speaking softly and kindly. Harmony gave them Mandisa's name. At first, the officers asked simple questions and then they edged towards the central issue.

'Where were you born?' Officer Freckles asked.

In a small voice, Mandisa said, 'London.'

'And who did you live with?'

'My mum and stepdad. But they died,' she whispered with tears brimming.

Officer Botox asked, 'How come both your mum and stepdad died?'

Mandisa spoke in a rush. 'There was trouble in my mum's town. People were being killed. She took leave from her job—she was a nurse—and went to Nigeria to take my grandparents to safety. But she never came home.'

'And what about your stepdad? What happened to him?'

'He followed her, asked his brother to look after me until they were back. But my stepdad didn't come back either. I lost my phone and my step-uncle said they stopped calling him. It meant they'd died.'

Harmony wondered if Mandisa's mum and stepdad were dead and whether she'd lost her phone or it had been taken from her.

'That must be very hard for you,' Officer Freckles said. 'How old were you when they died?'

'Nearly fifteen.'

'I bet you're not much older than that now. When's your birthday?' Officer Freckles suggested a year and Mandisa corrected her.

She was sixteen. But she'd have been fifteen when she'd given birth.

'And your dad? Where's he?'

'He was in Abuja.'

The officers frowned, exchanging questioning glances.

'It's the capital of Nigeria. But Mummy lost touch with him, and she said she didn't know where he was anymore.'

'Perhaps you could give us your parents' names? And that of your stepdad?'

After she'd given them, Officer Botox said, 'And the name of your step-uncle?'

Mandisa clamped her lips together.

Officer Botox leaned forward. 'He is the one who's been taking care of you?'

The girl's eyes became round. 'He's done nothing wrong. He loves me.'

'If he's not done anything wrong there's no harm in telling us is there?'

Mandisa sat silently with fists bunched tightly on her lap.

'We could call your school to find out. But we'd prefer it to come from you.'

Mandisa considered for a while and then, very reluctantly, said, 'William Sharp. But he prefers Liam.' She gave the address.

'Is he your only relative?'

'In the UK.'

'And William—Liam—is the baby's father?'

Mandisa covered her face with her hands and moaned, her feet stamping the floor. 'I shouldn't have come. He said not to tell anyone, that no one would understand. That we'd be split up.'

So that was how he'd controlled her. Harmony tentatively took hold of Mandisa's hand, ready to withdraw it at the slightest sign it wasn't welcome.

'How did you know where to come?' Officer Botox asked.

Mandisa appeared helpless, as though she'd resigned herself to answering questions. 'I started back at school this month as I was slim again. Looked it up on the Internet during library period. Read the newspapers. They wrote the baby was found at Pinkerton Hall. I found bus routes, times… I promised not to betray him. But by coming here, I have.' Her features contorted into what appeared to be despair.

'I'm sorry we have to keep asking you questions, and we realise it's very difficult for you. But we need to understand what's happened. Why did you come today and not some other day?'

'When Liam dropped me outside school, he didn't wait for me to go inside. So I ran back out. I knew he wouldn't like it. I'd saved my dinner money for the bus fare.'

'Didn't your school want to know why you'd had such a long time off? They'd want a letter from your GP, wouldn't they?' Officer Freckles asked.

'Liam told my last school—in Peckham—we were going to Nigeria to be with Papa. Liam heard we had to get out of Peckham as it wasn't safe. Something Mummy had done had made some people in Nigeria angry. But he couldn't get hold of Papa so we never went. But Liam kept me safe. We moved to Birmingham.'

Harmony's heart was heavy with sorrow. William Sharpe had so brainwashed Mandisa she hadn't suspected he might have fed her a pack of lies to get her away from friendly faces, people who could help.

'How come you're in Bristol if you went to Birmingham?' Officer Freckles asked.

'People started to ask questions so we moved.' Mandisa burst into tears. 'He's all I've got, and he said he'd take care of me and he has. He's so kind…'

Tears filled Harmony's eyes as she put an arm around Mandisa. She didn't resist.

She screwed a tissue into a ball. 'It's all gone wrong.'

Officer Freckles said, 'It hasn't gone wrong. Although it might feel like it, you will get help now, and we will do our best to find out what happened to your mum and stepdad. You only have Liam's word for it that your mum and stepdad died, don't you?'

Over the next few seconds, Mandisa's expression

changed from what appeared to be incredulity to the dawning of possibilities. 'They might be alive?'

'You have death certificates? Paperwork to prove they died?'

Weakly, she said, 'No.'

Officer Botox said, 'We need to have a chat with Mr Sharpe. You won't be going home tonight.'

'He said I'd get taken from him, that he wouldn't be able to look after me anymore!' Mandisa shivered. 'What will happen to him?'

'It's too soon to answer that. But Mandisa, you were below the age of consent when you entered a sexual relationship with him. He took you away from your home, possibly your family, concealed a pregnancy, denied you medical supervision and abandoned the baby. There's a lot going on here. You might not see it now, but he's not a good man.'

Mandisa grabbed some extra tissues from the box.

Officer Freckles said, 'When a woman gives birth, she needs to be checked by a doctor. Would it be all right if we took you to a hospital?'

Mandisa met Harmony's gaze.

'You do need to be checked,' she said.

Mandisa nodded consent to Officer Freckles.

At Bristol Royal Infirmary, Mandisa looked at Harmony's photos of Patience again, touching her face. It was what Harmony had done herself after Patience had gone.

'I know it's terribly painful,' Harmony said. 'We'll do our best to help you deal with everything.'

After Mandisa had been declared healthy and discharged from the hospital, they met Annie at the Hall. A policewoman had already delivered Mandisa's essentials following her step-uncle's arrest, and she'd been reunited with the schoolbag she'd hidden in the grounds before approaching the Hall.

'I'd be grateful if you could provide a bed for her for

now,' Annie said. 'But I can't promise she'll be able to stay. Fostering might give her the additional support she needs at this time.'

'What about attending school?' Harmony asked. 'At the hospital, she said she wants to go.'

'Word may well get out through the media, so moving away would be preferable. I'll have to discuss it with my colleagues.' Annie addressed Mandisa. 'For now, if you want to go to school, you can. And, as you're sixteen, you can refuse to engage with our services if you want to live independently.'

Mandisa shook her head to indicate she did not want to manage without help.

After Annie left, she asked, 'Is there any way I can get my baby back?'

Annie had explained that a Placement Order had been made. Only very rarely were these overturned and there was no way a schoolgirl could offer Patience the security and stability she was enjoying now.

'I'm sorry,' Harmony said, desperately holding back tears. 'It's not going to be possible. But Annie did mention that the adoptive parents might allow you to have contact with Patience. Although that would be only once a year, it would be better than nothing.'

Harmony was having a comforting, creamy hot chocolate with Candy in the front library after all the children had settled down for the night.

After discussing Mandisa's appearance at the Hall, Harmony asked, 'When I spoke to Patrik and Anil about the vaping, neither would give anything away. Has that changed?'

'Not that I'm aware of. Honour among vapers.'

Harmony wondered whether James had had any luck in getting information from Tim.

Candy rested her mug on a small table. 'I'm puzzled about something.'

'Yes?'

'I know it's not the same as when you've got that intense biological longing to have a baby, but now that Patience has gone, why not adopt one of the children from here?'

Harmony knew she would always choose the most vulnerable and, currently, that child was Alfie. 'It would amount to favouritism. There would have to be a special reason they'd all understand.'

'They'd understand you adopting Alfie because he's so close to Tim. You and James just need to satisfy Annie's requirement for an established couple.'

'James and I aren't together and, even if we were, I don't think there'd be time to become established before Annie matches Alfie. I don't think she believes we're engaged so even the pretence wouldn't help us.'

'But you could be engaged. I know you're in love with him.'

Harmony was about to protest and then gave up. 'It's true. I am. But I'm not sure about James.'

'Come on; although he tries to hide it, I've seen how his eyes track you, how his face lights up like Christmas illuminations when he sees you. How he hangs on every word you say. He took the number of the counsellor, didn't he?'

Harmony nodded. 'Yes, but I can't rush him, and Annie's forbidden me to mention her plans for Alfie to anyone except you. I don't want to marry James—if he were to propose—just to get Alfie. This time around, I need to know, *truly* know, that the groom is madly in love with me before any discussion of Alfie comes up—if Annie allows it.

'David hadn't been madly in love with me when I turned up at the altar. He'd been madly in love with Melody.'

'Well, Melody's not around now.'

'And she'd better not be,' Harmony said.

29

The following day, Harmony strolled to the newsagents to top up her bedtime reading. She could make a start if Miranda and Roxanne were late for their meet-up in the café.

Ramesh was his usual cheerful self—or more so, grinning and appearing to shift from one foot to the other behind the counter. She greeted him before focusing on the magazine display for a big dollop of escapism. *The People's Friend* had another pocket novel out and she picked up the bundle.

As she paid, he said with glee, 'I must congratulate you. I hope you'll be very happy together.'

What? 'I'm sorry?'

'Your engagement.'

'My... engagement...' How had the non-news reached Ramesh's ears? 'I didn't know it was... er... general knowledge.' Should she tell him the truth? Did he know Annie?

'I overheard the kids talking about it.'

'I see... Well, it's a secret engagement so it would be good if you didn't tell anyone else.' She didn't want a whole town of people waylaying her to offer felicitations.

'So, it seems you were more than a little bit interested in him, uh?' Ramesh giggled. 'And he must like you very much to—'

'Please… It would be very embarrassing for us if…'

He tapped the side of his nose. 'Don't worry, *I* can keep secrets. But *you* need to be better at keeping secrets yourself if you don't want everyone to know. Once the children know…'

'You're right. I'll try to do better next time,' she said as she left. *Next time?*

Miranda was already in the café. Harmony bought a cappuccino and a slice of carrot cake before joining her at the four-seater table. They'd only exchanged greetings and updates on how they were doing when Roxanne breezed in with Joshua in her arms.

'Hi! I'll just get a drink and join you.'

It wasn't long before she was back with a server bringing her an Americano and a massive chocolate brownie covered with a generous helping of cream.

'How are you?' She popped Joshua into the highchair and gave him a cloth book from her bag. He waved it around enthusiastically. 'No Oscar?' she asked Miranda.

'He's at home with Faith's Flora and the nursery worker—laid on by Judith.' Miranda grinned. 'It means I can have time to myself if Judith doesn't need me.'

She worked as a live-in personal assistant.

'Sounds good,' Roxanne said. 'He's lucky to be growing up with another child.'

'He is. How are you?'

'Oh, not so good,' Roxanne said.

'I'm sorry to hear that.' Harmony raised the pitch at the end of the sentence to invite her to elaborate.

Roxanne appeared to hesitate and then whispered, 'Is this just between us? I know you're both friends with Perdita and her crowd.'

'It can be just between us if that's what you want,' Harmony said and Miranda agreed.

Roxanne leaned closer. 'I'm looking for a way out of the marriage.'

'I'm so sorry,' Harmony said.

Miranda nodded. 'Me too.'

'It's only Matt and the parishioners who call me Roxanne now. I'm using Roxy again.'

'I'd hoped things might improve for you,' Harmony said.

Roxy pulled a face. 'I only have to glance at another man and Matt accuses me of grooming the parishioners. Ever since Faith put the idea into his head...' She sat back and took a sip of her coffee.

Harmony felt so sorry for her. 'It must be hard for you both.'

Miranda nodded.

Tears sprang in Roxy's eyes. 'I take responsibility for the failure of the marriage. But getting out is going to be so painful for us. I never wanted it to be like this... Anyway, how are you both doing?'

'I'm fine,' Miranda said. 'But Harmony isn't.'

Harmony pulled a rueful expression. 'Patience has been adopted.' She'd called Miranda to share the devastating news but feeling unable to go through the details again so soon she'd delayed telling Roxy.

'She was gutted. Couldn't stop crying for ages.'

'Oh, no,' Roxy said. 'Life just doesn't turn out as we hope sometimes, does it?' She held Harmony's gaze. 'Would you like to give Joshua a cuddle? Or would it make you feel worse?'

He had his book open and was licking a picture of a bear.

Would holding him make it harder for her when she had to give him back? Or would she regret saying no? 'May I?'

Roxy passed the baby over to her.

'Gosh, he's a heavy lad.' To Joshua, she said, 'Hello,' in her baby-talk voice. 'I'm Harmony.'

He smiled and panted in her face, his breath smelling of biscuit and milk, his little legs pumping her thighs.

'Gosh, he's strong.' Harmony wrapped her arms around him, his padded bottom against a forearm, and caught a slight hint of soap on the neck of his wonderful baby skin. Thank goodness it was from a different product to the one she'd used on Patience or she'd be begging to keep him.

'He's a very easy baby,' Roxy told her. 'Very content.'

'That's lucky for you.' Harmony planted a noisy kiss on his cheek, and he squealed with laughter.

'Oscar's quite easy too,' Miranda said. 'We are lucky.'

Roxy addressed Harmony. 'After your experience with Patience, do you have a preference for girl babies?'

'I love all babies. But that hardly matters now, does it?'

30

After running some errands, Harmony returned to the Hall and the sound of the kids singing captivating lyrics to the tune of *Go Down Moses* drew her to the dining room. When the song ended, the young woman running the choir told them they were ready.

Harmony raised an eyebrow when she caught Patrik's eye, and he stuck his chin out as he approached. 'We're going across the road, and you can't stop us.'

Anil came up behind him. 'No, you can't stop us.'

She'd no intention of stopping them, and it was a struggle to hide her approval of the scheme. She and Candy hadn't managed to find out what had happened with the e-cigarette, and Tim had been banned from coming to the Hall.

'Take care of the younger ones,' she called to all of the children.

Several of the older kids raised their hands in acknowledgement.

The voice teacher joined her.

Harmony's grin burst through her neutral mask. 'How come they've learnt the tune to *Go Down Moses*?'

'Research on protest songs on YouTube. Ostap got them into it. They'd learned it with their own lyrics before I arrived—he'd printed out copies.'

'Do they understand the history of the song? Why it

was written? Where the inspiration for the music came from?'

'All explained in whatever it was they watched apparently. I just needed to get them to sing together and in tune. Would you like me to go with them?'

Harmony shook her head. 'It's between James and the kids.'

'We can watch though, can't we?' the voice teacher asked.

'Absolutely. The best vantage point is up the stairs. If we open the window, we'll probably hear them.'

James frowned at Tim's homework notebook. 'A project? *On spirals?*'

Tim nodded.

How could you have a whole project on spirals? 'What is it that you have to do?'

With a sigh, Tim pulled out a folder from his schoolbag. 'The instructions are in here.'

When James realised how mathematical the project was, and that he knew nothing about Archimedes, Fibonacci and Baravelle spirals, the darkness of inadequacy stole over him. He downed the rest of his coffee.

A burst of singing to the *Go Down Moses* tune shot out of nowhere. Had his son changed his mobile's ringtone? But by his blank expression, James knew his son was not responsible.

James glanced around the kitchen for a radio before he recalled he no longer owned one. Surely his dental fillings hadn't tuned in to nearby radio waves? He'd read it was possible. But his teeth weren't buzzing. He listened harder. The sound was coming from the front of the cottage.

From the living room window, he and Tim saw kids belting out the song—conducted by a boy James recognised as Ostap. The lyrics had been personalised. But Tim was not breaking free from Jewish slavery in Egypt—as mentioned in Exodus in the bible—nor escaping slavery as an African

American despite the story and music drawing from both cultures. He was simply a grounded schoolboy.

Go down, us kids, 'cross road in Westbridge land
Tell dad James
To let Tim Traffurth go.

We're in trouble in Westbridge land
Let Tim Traffurth go
By his dad we've been blamed and damned
Let Tim Traffurth go

Yes, he's our friend
Go down, us kids
Way down in Westbridge land
Tell dad James
To let Tim Traffurth go.

So us kids went to Westbridge land
Let Tim Traffurth go
Want dad James to understand
Let Tim Traffurth go

Yes, he's our friend
Go down, us kids
Way down in Westbridge land
Tell dad James
To let Tim Traffurth go!

Tim charged outside and James joined him on the doorstep. The children regarded them expectantly, their voices trailing off.

About to tell them it was up to him how he protected his son, Tim blurted, 'It's my fault. I took the vape to school. I got Patrik and Anil to try it.'

James's blood froze. 'Is this true? It was all your doing?'

'I'm sorry.' Tim appeared so sheepish, James wouldn't have been surprised if his son had let out a baa.

Patrik stepped forward. 'We chose to try it. We could've said no.'

But they were very young school kids… 'Tim, where did you get it from?'

'I had it from last time.'

It was hard not to choke on disappointment. But at least his son hadn't discovered a new "supplier" in another teenager looking to make a few pounds. There were so many illegal vapes on the market with lethal concoctions that James had feared the worst. He'd read of primary school kids being hospitalised with collapsed and bleeding lungs.

'But I told you how addictive and dangerous these things are. If they aren't legally made, they could contain lethal levels of substances too.' He didn't need another nightmare at Bristol Royal Infirmary.

'I said I'm sorry.'

Discipline hadn't worked on Tim, and he'd put Patrik and Anil at risk.

Alfie clung to Anil's arm, dragging him forwards.

James couldn't punish Alfie for his son's wrongdoing by keeping them separated. 'You want Tim to come over?'

Alfie nodded.

Well, the children had made an impressive effort for Tim but it was a shame he hadn't come clean earlier.

'Can he come?' Patrik asked.

Should James reward Tim for his misdemeanour by letting him go now? 'He has a lot of homework to get through.'

'We do too. Our friend in the year above helps us when we get stuck.'

'I don't want him just copying someone else's work. He needs to understand it too.'

'Deal,' Patrik said.

He and Anil high-fived Tim. Then Alfie joined in.

'Wait!' James said as they were about to head off. 'Tim,

you've got some letters of apology to write.'

'I'll do them later, Dad.'

What would Harmony do?

'Guys, I'm sorry the way this turned out, and I'm even sorrier it was my son who got us into this mess. Perhaps we can draw a line under it and start afresh?'

There were murmurings and nods and then the kids' attention transferred to Tim, giving playful thumps to his shoulder, hugging him. He needed friends, including good friends like Patrik and Anil. They hadn't grassed him up despite suffering for it. Alfie must have missed Tim too. They were a great bunch of kids.

As the children meandered back to the Hall, James picked up his house keys and followed. He needed to speak to Harmony.

As they all trooped back inside, he met her in the hallway. 'Can I speak to you? In private?'

She indicated the office.

When they'd sat down, he asked, 'Did you know all along it was Tim?'

'I did wonder...'

'I'm sorry. I was too quick to act and... about there being difficulties in the family before the tragedy... How did you guess?'

She touched his hand. 'James... both you and Tim strike me as people who need some healing. To be helped to forgive yourselves for surviving and for whatever happened in the past.'

The stifled sobs from James's throat loosely resembled the call of a bullfrog Harmony had heard on a nature programme the kids had been watching. She tucked some tissues into his hand and, despite a valiant attempt at holding in his emotions, they erupted in a cry of torment not unlike the sound of a snapping turtle in the same nature series.

She gently guided him to the sensory room, the

corridor empty. It was the younger kids' mealtime and she guessed the rest were either doing homework or in the entertainment room.

As he sat on a floor cushion, with knees bent and his hands covering his face, he gave great gulping, hiccupping cries that tore at her heart. With the occupied light turned on, she propped a chair under the door handle and darkened the room. She opted for twinkling stars with the background sound of the sea before putting her arms around him and holding him tight.

After a while, he said, 'Sorry.'

'No worries. We're even now, aren't we, for giving comfort?'

He gave a feeble laugh. 'I suppose we are.'

She ran her fingers tenderly through his hair. 'Would you like to talk about it?'

'I thought I was coping, getting by. But your words hit home and the past suddenly opened up and swallowed me.'

'Come,' she murmured, 'cuddle up to me properly. I bet you're short on hugs.' She could do with some herself.

He adjusted his position, his legs crossing hers as she leaned against the wall. 'How come you're so warm and snuggly?'

'I was a Care Bear in my former life.'

He chuckled. 'They're still around?'

'I believe so. Mum and Dad gave me a lavender Harmony Care Bear when I was a child. It's got a triple note on its tummy with some rainbow colours.'

Melody had been given a dark pink Love-a-Lot Care Bear with intertwined hearts. Was there an adult version called Bonk-a-Lot?

Grinning, he said, 'I'm imagining you as a little girl cuddling the teddy. That's lightened things up. Now I don't feel so alone.'

'I think we can all feel like that at times. I know I do, even though I'm surrounded by so many children.'

'We can be alone together then?'

Smiling, she squeezed his arm. 'Deal.' She began to pull away from his embrace.

'Wait.'

'What is it?'

'May I kiss you properly? I've been yearning to...'

Was it a good idea right after his emotional breakdown? Also, they weren't boyfriend or girlfriend or anything other than fake. But her heart... her heart couldn't say no. Perhaps if someone had kissed her years ago it might have helped her move on so that her last memories of intimacy weren't of David. A kiss might help them both.

Or was she just kidding herself because she didn't want to admit how much she longed for James to kiss her, *really* kiss her?

'I suppose,' she said breathily, 'a practice kiss might ensure we can give a convincing performance should Annie see us together sometime...'

His warm fingers caressed her face as his coffee lips met hers. The kiss was languorous until it deepened and his hold tightened, awakening her body leaving it aching for more. His obvious need for her, with his deep, rapid inhalations, was as welcome as ice cream on a scorching day. But as the sensations zapping around her body became more demanding, she knew she had to put a stop to it, so she wouldn't beg him to take her to his cottage and make love to her.

She tightened her lips, turned her head to one side and gently pushed his shoulders.

'I'm sorry,' he said. 'I think I'm losing my mind.'

Her stomach clenched. 'Because you're falling for me or because you regret kissing me?' When he didn't immediately respond, she added gently, 'The options I gave you have opposite meanings in case the question was too subtle for you.'

She needed to understand him, to feel safe letting her heart care deeply again.

'I am falling for you,' he told her, 'and I don't for one

moment regret kissing you. But I worry things will go wrong, that the three of us will get hurt. As for letting go of the past—I keep feeling guilty.'

'I think it's completely natural under the circumstances.'

'So perhaps we can tread carefully?' he said. 'I want to do right by Tim—and by you.'

Her heart lightened and her stomach relaxed. 'That sounds like a good plan.'

31

As James had admitted he felt alone, Harmony had invited him with Tim on the February half-term trip to Bristol Zoo Project. Everyone going on the outing was standing by the coach.

'Patrik, I'd like you to sit with Anil,' she said. 'And Tim, could you sit next to Alfie? Saskia, I'd like you to be Mandisa's companion. Together, with James and myself, we will form one of the groups.'

When Saskia had heard about the plan her face had lit up so brightly she might have been in competition with a sparkler so Harmony had extended an invitation to her as well.

Harmony's group migrated to the rear of the vehicle, apart from James who claimed a seat near the front. Once everyone was onboard, she plonked herself down next to him.

He grinned. 'Thanks for inviting me.'

She returned his smile. 'It's good to have you along.'

When he took her hand in his, warmth fed her veins with anticipation. Every thumb caress sent delightful ripples of sensation cascading around her body, making her wish they were alone in his bed, lips and fingers on an exploring expedition...

'How are you doing?' he asked softly. 'With losing Patience?'

Reluctantly erasing the scene in her mind, and dousing her longing with an imagined pail of icy water, she replied, 'Remarkably well on the surface. It's when I'm in my bedroom it's hardest. I can't help remembering the night-time feeds, playing with her, cuddling her, singing to her... Her things are in a storage cupboard now, but spaces on the floor remind me where the cot used to be—and the playmat, baby gym and box for her toys.'

'It was hard for me too,' James told her. 'Clearing out Georgie's room, the cot from our room and the baby things in the loft. It feels so final. Which of course, it is.'

'Actually,' she said, 'I've been sleeping with a small teddy I bought her—the new parents had wanted a bare minimum to go with her and it hadn't been her favourite. So she'd only taken the soft, tiny doll I'd bought her.'

'I slept with one of Felicia's scarves for a while. It's hard to let go, but I decided I must try—and I'm still trying.'

It *was* hard to let go. But there would always be a home in her heart for dear little Patience. Harmony thought of the baby's mother. 'I'll wash the teddy and give it to Mandisa. It might comfort her to have something from her daughter's cot as well as the pictures and video clips I gave her.'

Once through the entrance, Saskia and Mandisa asked to break off from the group to go around on their own, leaving the boys with Harmony and James. They headed for a route that took them past the climbing adventure course towards the giraffes and zebras.

But, before they'd gone any distance, James asked, 'Are we still pretending to be engaged? Because, if we are, you might want a public display of affection.'

She raised her eyebrows questioningly.

'That social worker's coming towards us. She'll spot us any moment now.'

She came to a halt and so did James. 'What about the moving-on guilt?'

'It's taking a break,' he murmured as he lowered his

head and gave her a brief kiss on the mouth.

When they broke away, Annie was standing next to them with a matching red-haired girl who looked about fourteen.

Harmony feigned surprise. 'Oh, hi. Er, you remember my fiancé, James?'

His warm hand encircled hers again.

'My daughter, Sara.'

'Hello, Sara.' Harmony brushed strands of hair aside that the breeze had blown into her eyes.

Sara smiled.

Annie focused on Harmony's unadorned left hand as she lowered it and she laughed awkwardly. 'I feel a bit superstitious about having a ring.'

'Oh?'

She looked at James to see if he could help her out, but he stared blankly back. So she blurted out the only thing she could think of. 'I was engaged before, and the man who'd given me the ring had to have it back. That's why we haven't set a date either.'

The breeze was making her eyes smart and when a lock of hair whipped into her face, they began to weep.

'I see,' Annie stated and added she and Sara must get on.

'You're great at acting,' James said as she wiped her eyes after Annie and Sara had left. 'It was acting, wasn't it?'

'Yes, absolutely.' It was the humiliation of the day, admitting to Annie and James that she'd been dumped...

'If you and Dad are going to keep kissing,' Tim said, 'can we split up so we don't have to see it?'

'How about you walk in front,' she suggested, 'just in case it does happen again.' She gave James a quick glance to check he agreed.

He nodded. 'That might be sensible. Just in case.'

She laughed. The day was going incredibly well and her hand felt so at home in James's. She savoured the companionship but missed his lips... Before they'd had much chance to see even an eland, she tugged him to a standstill and kissed him.

He soon broke off and surreptitiously cast around. 'I can't see Annie. Has she gone?'

Harmony hadn't seen Annie at all but said, 'She's either turned back or I was mistaken as I can't see her either now.'

After they'd resumed their walk, he peeked behind him and said, 'Don't look back,' and leaned in to kiss her. When he released her, he murmured, 'Annie just keeps popping up wherever we go. But she's out of sight again now.'

Harmony giggled to herself. James was continuing the imagine-Annie game she'd started.

He lightly tugged her hand. 'Were you really engaged?'

'Yes.'

'What happened?'

'He changed his mind on my wedding day. Left me at the altar, and I had a meltdown in front of everyone. That was the humiliation I'd referred to when I ran out of the staff locker room at the Christmas party when I'd caught you in your underwear. I should have taken the conversation in the nave somewhere private, but I couldn't wait to know what was going on from the groom's parents—he called them in the church to tell them he wasn't coming and why.'

'So he told them but not you?' James sounded affronted.

'Well, he had sent a message to my mobile, but I'd left at the hotel as we'd agreed no phones at the wedding.'

'What a bastard.'

'It took me ages to get over it,' she said. 'Having feelings again—'

'Is scary.'

'Which is why when I saw you in the café that Saturday, I wanted to escape. I realised trusting again, making myself vulnerable, was too much.'

He was silent for a moment before saying, 'If I were to

pledge myself to you, I wouldn't renege on it.'

Wow... 'Same here.' The words caught in her throat.

'Each time I see you... I feel I'm getting in deeper.' His voice was thick, like melted chocolate.

'Me too... But I don't feel like I'm drowning.'

He smiled. 'Me neither.'

'How's it going with the counsellor?'

'I'm seeing her on my own as well as with Tim. It's helping—but it's very hard. The last session we discussed my wanting a third child, but Felicia hadn't been so keen—she'd wanted to go back to being a full-time dietitian.'

'You wanted a bigger family?' How sad. Instead, it had shrunk.

'Yes, and I love babies. But she'd said I didn't show enough interest in the two boys we already had. It was true; I was bringing a lot of work home. I think I rather left them to their own devices. I still do bring work home because I have to, but it's done when Tim's at the Hall or in bed now.'

'It's easy to look back with regrets. Aren't you being hard on yourself?'

'I think of all the things we ought to have done as a family, trips out like this, weekends away. I need to know I can be a good dad.'

'You are a good dad and you care about Tim. Perhaps you should find a project you can work on to bring you closer together,' Harmony suggested.

'I'll try to think of something.'

They were walking along the raised boardwalk over Bear Wood when Harmony noticed Alfie lagging behind Tim, dragging his heels along the floor.

James must have noticed too because he released her hand before moving closer. 'Hey, Alfie. Would you like a piggyback? You're looking tired.'

Alfie stopped and nodded.

Tim turned back to join them and Anil followed. 'Is he all right?'

James crouched down. 'He's just getting some help.'

Alfie climbed onto James's back and held onto his neck as James stood up.

'Shall I be a horse or an elephant?' he asked.

Alfie giggled.

'Dad, you're like a kid.'

'There's a kid in all of us.'

Tim laughed. 'Well, you should be a kid more often.'

'Perhaps I should.'

'Alfie, which animal are you going to choose?' Tim asked. 'It doesn't have to be a horse or an elephant.'

'A zebra.'

'Are you sure?' James weaved across the elevated path. 'They're unpredictable and you never know where they might go.' He turned around and started walking away from the group.

'A horse, a horse!' Alfie shouted, giggling.

James neighed, his gait became sedate, and he trotted towards the group again.

Tim was in stitches. 'Dad, you're hilarious.'

'He is,' Anil agreed.

Although Harmony loved seeing James's playful side, her mirth was tinged with deep sadness as she wasn't allowed to tell him about Alfie being put up for adoption. Breaking confidence would be in breach of the Data Protection Act; she could lose her job.

'Tim,' she said, 'shall we look for an apple for this fine horse when we take a break?'

'I think Dad might prefer a handful of hay.'

'Or grass.' Alfie giggled, which made Harmony chuckle too.

'Oats!' Anil called out.

It was hard to get the words out she was laughing so much. 'No one's asked the horse what he might like.'

'The horse can't speak,' Tim said.

'Yes, he can,' James retorted. 'And he'd prefer a sandwich.'

'When Alfie's less tired, can I have a go?' Tim asked. 'But then you can be a naughty donkey, and I'll have to make you go in the direction I want you to go in.' He giggled. 'I'll give you a carrot when you've learnt to behave.'

'Now I know what Tim's got in mind for my evening meal,' James said, and they all laughed again.

Annie lowered her phone. She was standing on the boardwalk with her daughter, Sara.

'I thought you weren't supposed to take people's pictures and video them without consent,' Sara said.

'You're not. But they were having so much fun, I couldn't resist. But I won't use anything without their consent. If I do need their consent, they'll be only too happy to give it—even if they don't know they have—because, by then, it would have become relevant information.'

'Why relevant?'

'Because it's evidence they're already connecting as a family with that little boy. He needs to have parents. It makes me inclined to pause some admin I was carrying out.' Annie chuckled. 'Nothing beats an unexpected field trip, spotting people outside of their usual habitat and having a smartphone at the ready.

'You see,' she continued, 'when we met them earlier, they were playacting again, I'm sure of it. Although amateur dramatics doesn't appear to be their forte, and it's been fun watching—'

'They couldn't have been acting just now,' Sara said.

'Exactly.' Annie wiggled her phone at her daughter with a smile. 'I hope they realise they hold a little boy's future in their hands and get their "act" together soon. There's only so much I can do to help.'

32

The following Saturday morning, Harmony was in the café on High Street, staring into her hot chocolate, immersing herself in a James Traffurth fantasy. He was holding her close, his kiss deep and hungry, and she clung desperately to him, feeling him hard against her. Then he slowly broke off to tell her how much he loved her, dropped down on one knee, reached into his pocket—

'Harmony!'

It took a moment for the image of James to melt away. 'Mm?' Her eyes somehow managed to focus on the present to take in Roxy in a deep purple dress, her coat over her arm. Joshua wasn't with her. 'Oh, hi, Roxy.'

'I was hoping to see you. If you hadn't been here, I'd have gone to the Hall. I couldn't get you on your phone.'

'I was in a staff meeting earlier. Please, sit down.' Harmony checked her phone. Three missed calls from Roxy. 'What's up? Where's Joshua?'

'Playdate... It's rather sensitive... Do you mind if we go to the back?' Roxy pointed to the far corner to a vacant old sofa and armchair.

Harmony gathered her things. 'Not at all.'

She chose the armchair, and Roxy dumped her coat on the sofa before going to place her order. When she returned with a cup of coffee, she smiled uncertainly. 'I need to ask a favour, a very big favour. In complete confidence...'

Harmony's gut tensed. 'As long as you've not robbed a bank and want help with money laundering or some such thing...'

Roxy shook her head, apparently too anxious to appreciate the intended humour.

'Sorry, go on... You can trust me.'

She bit her lip. 'I don't want you to judge me... I know I'm an appalling wife and mother—'

Astonished, Harmony asked, 'Why would I think that?'

Roxy gave a bitter laugh. 'Well, if you don't already, you soon will. I've met someone, and I've planned my escape.'

Harmony's eyes stretched wide like ripples of rain in a still pond. At Perdita's party, Faith had suggested that Roxy would be working her way through the male parishioners. 'Does he—or she—go to your husband's church?' Should she have put a "they" in there too?

'No, he's not from Westbridge. I attended a couple of his seminars in Bristol; the second one was about starting a small business.'

'Oh.'

'He invited me for a drink and one thing led to another.'

'Bed?'

'No. I mean, one thing led to another with ideas.'

'Oh, sorry.'

'But he is very attractive.'

Harmony finished her drink. 'So he's from Bristol?'

'No, London. But he comes to the area to see his daughter.' Roxy bit her lip. 'You've met her.'

'Oh? Is she in Matt's parish?'

'She's Perdita's daughter.'

'Perdita's?'

'Yes, Petal. Saul isn't her biological father.'

'You've got a thing for Petal's dad?'

'I'm moving to London to set up another franchise, and Tony's helping me do it. We're not setting up home together but... we've got a connection. I'm sure Matt will be relieved to be shot of us.' Roxy's eyes appeared hollow.

'Joshua too? Surely not.'

'He shows no real interest in him.' She downed the rest of her coffee. 'I should never have sold the franchise... and I should never have married Matt.'

'I'm sorry...' Harmony was confused as to how she fitted into any of this. 'You said you want a favour?'

Roxy leaned forward so Harmony did too, to catch the whispered words. 'Mutual arrangement. You want a baby, and I don't want to be a full-time mum. I want my freedom back. I'd like you to have Joshua.'

The disbelief that consumed Harmony overtook any excitement about having a baby to bring up. Had she even heard right? *'Are you offering to give me Joshua?'*

'Shh... Yes.' Roxy's voice was steady, her expression calm, as though she'd practised the conversation.

Harmony shifted to the edge of her seat. 'You can't just give your child away like that.'

Roxy edged closer too. 'I can. There's no law against it.'

'I was thinking of the emotional side. You're his *mother*.'

'I know he'll be better looked after if you have him. We can make it official. I'll pay your solicitor's fees—they'll tell you what's needed, and I won't challenge it.'

'Challenge what?'

'Special guardianship. You know about it?'

'A kind of halfway between adoption and fostering. I'll have the right to make all the everyday decisions and... and you could come at a later date and try to take him back because he won't be fully mine.'

Roxy reached out to place a reassuring hand on Harmony's arm. 'Don't worry, I won't try to take him back.'

'You'll miss him. I don't believe you won't want to get full parental rights again. You take such good care of him. *You love him.*'

Roxy inhaled deeply. 'I do love Joshua—but not enough

to spend the rest of my life bringing him up *well*. Perhaps my love involves the sacrifice of parting with him to improve his prospects of becoming a happy and responsible adult. I care deeply for him, but my freedom beckons and you could give me a way out so I won't lose him completely.'

A part of Harmony leapt with joy at the possibility of having a baby to bring up. But there was a risk to her sanity if she bonded with Joshua only to have him wrenched from her later. She was happy to have helped Patience but... Harmony didn't want to risk such anguish again.

'I had bad parents.' The fire in Roxy's tone emphasised the point. 'And I wouldn't entrust Joshua to their care for five seconds. I'm a product of their upbringing. Left to myself in raising him, I know I won't do a good job because I'm having to force myself to do it. I can feel the claustrophobia getting worse by the day, and sometimes I feel like screaming.

'Please give my son the chance to be happy and learn how to form deep relationships. I didn't get that, and it shows.'

'Won't you end up committing to your new man?' Harmony asked. 'Wouldn't that give Joshua the family life he needs?'

'Tony and I may be together in some way but... he seems to be like me. How I used to be. I need to work out who I am now, what I truly want, once I've left. I hope that one day I do get a happy ending but, at the moment, I don't know what that looks like for me.'

Although Harmony felt sorry for Roxy, she needed to stay focused. 'What about Joshua's biological dad?'

Roxy gave a bitter laugh. 'Without a DNA test, I can't be one hundred per cent sure who that is. Andy didn't want to know so it's still officially father unknown.'

Harmony's heart ached for poor Joshua and Roxy. The agony of a mother giving up her child... and of a child being given up... How would it affect their lives? Surely Roxy would bitterly regret this day, this conversation? It was just as well Joshua was too young to understand. 'And if I don't agree?'

Roxy shrugged one shoulder as she tilted her head. 'Then I'll get him adopted.'

Harmony's breath caught in her throat. 'But he's your *son*.'

'You think I don't know that?' Roxy's eyes filled with tears. 'Which is why I want you to have him. I could visit when I'm in the area and we can keep in regular contact at other times with your help. He'll know I'm his mum. Tony says it works well with Petal—it's what gave me the idea. Adoption might be too hard for me, but this way... this way I think I could bear it. I'll be able to see how Joshua's doing, how happy he is, with my own eyes.'

Harmony set her jaw. 'If you leave him with me, and it becomes official, of course you'd be involved in Joshua's life. But I'd challenge an attempt to legally take him back.' She couldn't bear the thought of losing a third baby.

Roxy brightened. 'That's the spirit.'

Harmony's jaw dropped. *That's the spirit?*

Roxy's expression became grave as she put her hand on Harmony's. 'I know I'm not the best mum for him, and I believe he'll have a much better chance in life if you bring him up. You might be too sweet to see it but, believe me, I do. Now, will you take him?'

Harmony was bewildered by the speed at which this was happening.

Roxy's mouth was rigid with determination. 'It's a hard decision to have made, and I know I'll be vilified for it. I'm truly not a fit mother, and I will be less so running a franchise in London selling sex aids in the evenings and making video clips about what to do with them.'

Her face crumpled and she held back a sob behind a napkin pressed to her lips, tears streaming down her cheeks. 'Have him, please. I won't interfere with his upbringing. I trust you to do the right thing.'

Harmony's heart fluttered with hope tinged with

devastation for Joshua being abandoned by his mum. She was also afraid her dreams might be dashed again. A sense of danger and dread filled her guts.

'I'd definitely get him? It won't be another case of him being taken away like Patience was taken away?'

'Why should the authorities refuse if I state it's my wish for you to have him? I *know* he'll be better off with you. I'm sure Matt wouldn't challenge a Special Guardianship Order, even though he's had parental responsibility—what would he do with a baby when he's so busy? And I don't *want* Matt to bring him up.'

Harmony wavered. She'd love to have Joshua—*but like this?*

Nevertheless, the carrot was too big. A brief video clip of standing next to James at a wedding reception, Tim in front of them and Joshua in her arms, played in her mind. It really was a whopping carrot.

'I agree then; I'll take him.'

Roxy reached into her bag and passed her a white envelope. 'I've written a letter to authorise you to take care of him. Get it to a solicitor as soon as you can. From this moment, Joshua is living with you. When I hand him over to you this afternoon, he's moved in.'

'*This afternoon?*'

'Have you got something on?'

'Er, no, it's just that instead of being at a walking pace, I feel I'm driving a Formula 1 car.'

Roxy smiled thinly. 'Sorry. For me, it's not so quick. I've been mulling it over for ages.'

'This afternoon's fine,' Harmony found herself saying.

'Great. I'd like to have him back briefly, before I move to London, but he'll just be visiting me. You understand?'

Harmony understood very well. She was being rocket-launched into carrying out the role of a mother and blast-off was that afternoon. 'And you won't change your mind?'

'Haven't you been listening? Trust me. *Please.*'

Had she just stepped into some kind of unicorn land?

33

Back outside the Hall, more than a little dazed, Harmony showed Roxy into the silent Dower House so that she could see where Joshua would be living. It still smelt of new carpet, new furniture and fresh paint.

'This is the living room,' Harmony said, stating the obvious. 'The place is only partially furnished as I'd been waiting to find out about Patience and then it seemed too sad to move into such a big house on my own.'

There was a large corner sofa, a couple of armchairs, a large TV and a cupboard.

When they moved to the drawing room, which was bare apart from her Fazioli baby grand and a duet piano stool, Roxy said, 'You play the piano? Would you teach Joshua?'

'Of course. I'd love to.' Harmony imagined sitting on the stool with a young boy on her lap, helping his little fingers find the right keys to play.

Roxy smiled. 'It's nice to think of him having music in his life.'

The farmhouse-style kitchen had a dining table for six—a smaller size would have looked ridiculous. There was also an empty dining room that Lady Pinkerton had used as a bedroom in her final years and, next to that, a to-be study—Harmony could do some work from home.

In addition to the downstairs cloakroom with a walk-in shower—put in for Lady Pinkerton when she could no longer manage the stairs—there were utility and boot rooms with plenty of shelving for storage.

'This is huge,' Roxy said.

Harmony smiled faintly. Not if she and James...

They went upstairs.

'*Four* bedrooms?' Roxy said.

'That's why I haven't moved in yet.'

The master bedroom had a king-size bed with an en-suite in place of the original dressing room. Lady Pinkerton had let Harmony use the room when she'd moved downstairs. The other three bedrooms were empty.

'So which will be Joshua's room?' Roxy asked.

'The smallest to begin with.' Who knew who else might end up moving in? 'But for now, I'll keep him in my apartment at the Hall until you bring all his things. We have a cot from when Patience was with us.'

Roxy bit her lip. 'Please, can you keep our plan secret? Until the final handover? I don't want anything or anyone to get in the way. The sooner you can start the legal side the better.'

Harmony swallowed. 'What about Miranda?' The three of them were friends and she'd become particularly close to Miranda through regular meet-ups and phone calls.

'I'm sorry, the only sure way to protect the secret is to share it with no one. Miranda virtually lives with Faith, and Joshua might be her ex's child... I'll explain it to Miranda myself when I feel it's safe so she won't be disgruntled with you.'

'How long before I'll be able to tell? Because it's going to be very hard not explaining what I'm doing with someone else's baby.' Especially to James and Candy.

'A week? Say you're looking after him for a friend. We are friends?'

'Of course. If I get special guardianship and later marry, will that be a problem?'

'Do you have someone in mind?'

'My neighbour, James Traffurth. He's got a son, Tim. But we're not there yet—and we might not be. But that's why I'm going to put Joshua in the smallest bedroom for now. They'd have to move in with me.'

'It sounds fine,' Roxy said. 'And it would be nicer for Joshua to be in a bigger family. But I'm only giving him to you for special guardianship. No one else.'

'I understand.'

They made the arrangements to meet up later that day and then she left, allowing Harmony to perform a rain dance around the living room, which then extended around the whole of the ground floor. Well, it wasn't a proper rain dance; it was her inexpert attempt to copy rain dances from around the world she'd seen on TV. The feelings evoked when she'd watched them was how she felt now—powerful and strong, and her emotional mothering drought was about to end.

She sank onto the sofa. Reality check. Was she *actually* going ahead with this?

Well, it seemed she was as she was already searching on her phone for a suitable solicitor. She needed to get the legal side underway before Annie found out about the plan as Harmony feared something might go wrong—and so did Roxy.

Short of time, Harmony drove to the local Spar to make a start on stocking the Dower House food cupboards.

Later, as she was unpacking the car, Alfie came running towards her. Andrei was standing at the entrance to check Alfie was safe, and Harmony signalled she'd mind the boy.

'Hello, Alfie,' she said when he reached her.

'What are you doing here?' he asked, panting.

'I'm unpacking some shopping as I plan to move in soon. Want to help?'

He nodded.

She gave him a box of tea bags and another of tissues

to bring in while she started on the heavier bags.

When all her purchases were inside, she said, 'Now, where do you think I should put them?'

Together, they worked out the most appropriate homes for the items. Tea, coffee and sugar in a cupboard close to the kettle, tins near where she'd started a collection of saucepans and spreads near the breadbin.

'Well, thank you Alfie. It was very kind of you to come and help.'

'Can I look round?'

'Let me give you a tour.'

She wished she could offer him one of the bedrooms. Remembering Annie's words, Harmony knew that she and James would not become an established couple—if they ever did—before it was too late.

It was late afternoon and Harmony had already met Roxy—her head covered by a hoodie—on the secluded driveway by the side of the Dower House. She'd handed over some of Joshua's things for the next few nights. When she'd left, Harmony secured him into the car seat as there was too much to take to the Hall without the Astra and kissed him.

'Mummy's left you for now, but she will be back, don't you worry.' Any sadness he might be feeling echoed in herself; James hadn't asked to see her that evening. But hey, she'd have a baby to play with.

Joshua stared into her eyes as she crouched beside him.

'I'm Harmony.' Of course, he already knew that, but she longed for him to say her name. 'Can you say Harmony? Har-mon-ee.'

'Mummy.'

'Not Mummy. Har-mon-ee.' She repeated it a few times and then, finally, he said, without his lips meeting for the second "m", 'Money.'

'Oh, you clever boy.' She laughed and kissed him again. 'That will do. You can call me Money.' She liked the sound; it was so close to "Mummy".

She reversed the car back onto the main approach for the Hall when someone hailed her. In the rearview mirror, she saw it was James.

She killed the engine and got out. 'Hi.'

'Hi,' he said. 'I was wondering if you'd like to come over for a meal. I'm sorry for the late offer. I had so much to do that I wasn't sure I'd be back at any sensible time to invite you.'

'Oh.'

'Tim's staying later today—so it would be just the two of us.'

'Thanks, I'd love to come. But...' She opened the passenger seat to reveal Joshua.

'Money!'

'A baby!' James almost twisted his ankle as he didn't appear to know whether to step forward or stay put. *'Money?'*

'He's not got the hang of saying Harmony yet. I'm looking after him for a while. Do you mind if he joins us?'

'Oh, er, no...' He grinned. 'So you didn't just find him outside a shop?'

She blinked. Clearly, he hadn't seen Roxy. Why not pick up on the joke he'd made? 'Oh, I'm rumbled! But I could hide him at yours now if that's okay—the police aren't likely to search there.' She kept her expression serious.

His eyebrows pulled together so tightly, grooves appeared on either side of his nose. 'You are joking, right?'

She smiled teasingly; he must know it was a joke. She gathered Joshua into her arms before planting another kiss on his cheek.

He began babbling and his fingers curled around one of hers, tweaking her heart. 'You're so sweet!' To James, she said, 'Isn't he gorgeous?'

'He is. How old is he?'

'Just over fourteen months.'

He stroked Joshua's fingers and said, 'Hello. It's nice to meet you.'

There was an excuse to pat James's broad, hard chest, to grab the baby's attention. 'This is James. Can you say James?... James.' But the baby was more interested in attempting to lick James's hand, which he then lowered.

'Does he have a name?'

'Not at the moment.' She giggled. 'Then, when you hear it on the news, you can claim ignorance.'

'You're really not going to introduce my young guest?'

She bit her lip. 'I'm sorry. I promised, you see. In a week, perhaps I can tell you.'

'Is he another Patience?'

'No, he's not.'

He had a questioning expression. But she couldn't explain Joshua's presence.

'Can you give me a hand with the baby's things?'

'Sure.' James said. 'What do you want me to do?'

'Money!' Joshua shouted.

34

Harmony removed her coat and passed it to James before taking Joshua out of the buggy, which was inside the front door. James led her to the living room and placed her coat on the small corner sofa while she removed Joshua's outerwear, taking in the coffee table, small bookcase with some DVDs, and TV. Her glance took in the plain walls. Had he given all his more personal items away—the reminders of his marriage to Felicia?

'I turn the heating down when I'm out,' he said. 'I'll put the thermostat up now. It'll be warmer in the kitchen as there's a big radiator.'

She followed him into a pleasant small kitchen with a table and three chairs.

'We'll stay in here if that's okay as the dining room can be quite chilly. Usually, Tim does his homework at the table while I get the meal ready so I'm on hand to help him.'

His words conjured up a homely image of he and Tim working together, warming her heart. 'That's nice.' He was a great dad, doing his best. 'Tim's lucky to have you.' She would be too...

'You reckon?' His intent gaze brought heat to her cheeks.

'Absolutely. You're showing him all the time you love him. Consistency and stability—they're great foundations for a parent-child relationship.'

He tilted his head and smiled. 'Thanks. That means a lot because at times, I lose confidence and—'

'Oh James, you're truly doing a fantastic job.' With one arm holding Joshua, she patted James's back. Would there be a third reason to pat him that day?

He grinned shyly. 'Thanks.'

'Could I use your loo? I probably should have gone before...'

His eyes goggled. 'I'd hoped to spruce the place up...'

She pulled an apologetic expression. 'Sorry.'

'It's upstairs, the last room off the landing.'

When she passed Joshua to James to hold, their fingers brushed and the scrape of his warm skin against hers caught her breath. His eyes seemed to bore penetratingly into her. Did he guess the effect he was having on her?

Joshua's little hands went up to explore James's face and what must be stubbly skin.

'Hello, little fella.' James's tone was soft and amused as his attention switched to the baby.

She couldn't help smiling at the father-son image they made, his eyes lighting up as he grinned at Joshua, and she recalled him saying he'd longed for another baby...

The stairs from the hallway curved upwards to a landing with two open doors along one side and another at the end. She couldn't help peeping in.

Clothes were spilling out of a cupboard in Tim's room; books, 3D puzzle pieces and a part-built marble run track littered the floor. The opened construction box with additional parts sat on a large desk in front of a PlayStation. The TV was fixed to the wall, between *Star Wars* and *Guardians of the Galaxy* posters. A chaotically stacked bookshelf ran above the single bed. The cymbals, part of the drum kit in the corner, appeared to have been dulled by dust. Tim's musical activity probably remained a secret from his father.

'I don't want Dad to know,' Tim had said. 'He'd think it means I'm okay now, but I'm not.'

Harmony suspected that if Alfie hadn't wanted to join the orchestra, Tim would never have admitted he used to play the drums as he'd been clearly reluctant to talk about it.

As she passed James's room, she paused—and stared as she took in the multitude of bags and packages on the double bed. A new duck feather and down duvet, new pillows, sheets and duvet cover sets... So was James ready to start having a physical relationship with her? Is that why he'd been shopping and returned late?

A concoction of excitement and apprehension swirled around her body, butterflies flitting around in her stomach. Of course, nothing would happen tonight as she had Joshua with her; she'd pretend she hadn't seen the purchases. Then a thought struck her: what if they were presents for his parents and she'd misread the scene?

Her gratitude in reaching the bathroom was dimmed by the fact that it appeared neither resident showed much care. It must be hard for James, working full time, bringing work home and childcare kicking in the moment he was back, and she felt guilty for noticing.

Back in the kitchen, he was pointing to trees in view from the window, explaining about pollen, leaves growing in springtime and about birds building nests. Although Joshua kept following the line of James's finger, he was distracted by the feel of James's hair.

She chuckled. 'Are you getting a head massage?'

'It's more akin to being plucked ready for the oven. I should have tidied up.' His eyes showed concern as he handed Joshua back. 'I genuinely meant to clean up before you came.'

And make up the bed with the new purchases? She couldn't resist a third pat, the second on his broad chest, as she said, 'Don't worry about it. I did spring our presence on you.' Had it been because he'd been so intent on getting home and taking his packages inside that he hadn't noticed Roxy leaving?

'While the baby and I were looking at the birds outside, I remembered what we learnt at Bristol Zoo Project. About the male preparing a nest before searching for a mate and the female inspecting it to check it meets her expectations otherwise it's a no-go...

She smiled gently. 'I understand you're busy. It's hard both working and having Tim...'

'I... guess standards have slipped, and we've got used to our lax ways... Come back again for dinner tomorrow. I'll prove this owl knows how to keep house.'

She laughed to soften the joke. 'Can I bring the Hall's domestic supervisor along if there's going to be an inspection? Or invite your colleagues to have a look?'

'Touché.'

'You're lucky. She doesn't work on a Sunday, and neither do your workmates I expect, so I'll let you off.'

James grinned boyishly. 'That's a relief. I'll do my best.'

Supposedly being engaged, Annie would probably want to assess his home as well as Harmony's to ensure Joshua was spending time in suitable environments. 'I'll need to bring the baby again.'

'Unless the police have caught you?'

She laughed. 'Let's hope they don't catch on.'

After Joshua had eaten the rice, broccoli and chicken Roxy had provided, Harmony gave him, from another of Roxy's containers, a cucumber baton and a partly cooked carrot stick. With a piece of vegetable in each hand, he appeared to be busy conducting an imaginary orchestra.

The smell of pesto mixed with mushrooms filled the air and a sharp pang of hunger reminded her she'd not had enough to eat that day. But with James's sleeves rolled up, the sight of his strong-looking forearms had been a delightful distraction.

He squinted at Joshua on her lap. 'Do you realise, you've been kissing, cuddling and talking to him as though... well, as though he were yours.'

'Really?' She chuckled and then became serious. 'I wish I could explain, but I made a promise. I'm sorry that I can't break it, even to you.'

'Well, loyalty is a good quality to have.' He turned his attention back to stirring the sauce and then mixing it into the drained fusilli. 'It's ready now.'

'Can we get the buggy in here?' She replaced the lid on the tub of cut vegetables and cleaned Joshua's hands from the mush he'd created. 'Then I can strap the baby in while we eat.'

'Sure. I'll get it.'

With Joshua in the buggy, she secured a teething biscuit to his top with a ribbon. Roxy had said his back teeth were bothering him.

'What would you like to drink?' James asked. 'I've got Budweiser, red wine and orange juice.'

She glanced at Joshua. 'Juice please.'

James poured the juice and a red wine for himself, laid the table and placed the pan of pasta in the middle before offering her the serving spoon.

'Thanks. It smells good.'

When she'd helped herself, he said, 'Do start.'

'Thanks... Mm, this is yummy.' The peppery basil leaves combined with pine nuts, garlic and cheese went well with the mushrooms. She might try it herself.

'I'm going to learn to do more cooking.' His gaze met hers. 'I'm prepared to learn whatever I need to learn to make this work.'

Her heart flipped, appreciating the powerful statement coupled with his intent gaze. 'You know you said you wanted more children...' There was a catch in her voice. 'Does that apply to any child or only your own?'

'If it's any child you're involved with, I'm in,' he answered without hesitation. His gaze rested on Joshua and then lifted to settle on her.

Her heart almost leap-frogged out of her chest. If they'd been alone, the fire in James's eyes as he regarded her now would have reeled her in instantly.

As they ate, the conversation focused on the past—their childhood, school and university days. While they enjoyed the cakes he'd brought from a bakery, he asked about her music career.

'I don't understand. If you loved it so much and it was going so well, why did you stop?'

'I... my... after my engagement ended, I had difficulty concentrating. I broke down on stage mid-performance. I never played again in public. The most public performance since was when you found me in the Hall.'

'It sounds as though you were completely felled by your relationship breaking down.'

She nodded. 'I used to play with my parents but Mum had to give up. That's when they went to Italy.'

'What happened?'

'She developed carpal tunnel syndrome. She wore splints, had an injection in her wrist and then surgery, but it's a very slow recovery. Friends in Milan helped Mum and Dad find a place to live, got them teaching jobs. She can play now, just not to the standard required in an orchestra because of the hours of practice involved. It's been hard adjusting to not having them close by.

'When the family home was up for sale, I went to work for Lady Pinkerton. My job led to life at the Hall with all the children.' She explained how that had happened.

After they finished eating, he said, 'I'll clear up later. Shall we go to the living room?'

As they entered, she said, 'Have you got a clean sheet we could put down for the baby to play on?'

'Of course.'

She took away Joshua's teething biscuit, and James was soon back with a white folded bundle. He spread it out on the floor and sat at the edge.

As Joshua took the opportunity to explore the material with his mouth, she said, 'Can you watch he stays on the sheet while I get some of his toys?' They were in a bag underneath the buggy.

She returned with a posting box puzzle toy, opened it up and released the shapes that were inside. Joshua got stuck into solving it.

'Tim had one of these and then it got passed to Georgie,' James said. 'It's a shame everything's gone now... They might have come in useful.' His gaze met hers, but she just had to look away.

'They might have,' she mumbled, thinking of Joshua, and then changed the subject in case James asked about the baby again. 'You said you'd wanted to escape your Bristol life. Has it helped, moving here?'

'Yes. Tim's with a good bunch of kids now—as you know—and I... I met you...'

The air between them appeared to crackle with emotional tension, and she melted under his burning gaze.

He continued to make eye contact. 'I want to thank you for recommending the counsellor. It's tough; I'm not used to those kinds of conversations. It's probably just as hard for Tim. But we're communicating more openly, and he appears to have matured—even though he's not yet twelve.'

'I'm glad it's working out well for you both.'

He must have noticed a change in her expression as he asked, 'Is there a problem?'

She gave a feeble smile. 'I can tell you as Mandisa's been openly talking about it. Annie wants her in a foster family out of the area, so she has more support and no one knows her, as her case might hit the media. Even if her name's not mentioned, people will know it's her. It sounds very sensible. But she doesn't want to leave the Hall. I believe social workers generally get their way so I'm concerned her wishes won't be respected...'

'Isn't she sixteen? Surely, she can choose for herself?'

'To be funded, the placement has to be agreed by the local authority. If Mandisa doesn't like it, she can make her own way in life. But I don't think that's a realistic option for her.'

'That's a shame.'

Thinking of Alfie, she couldn't resist saying more. 'And Annie's going to place another of the kids with a family, but I don't think this particular child will want to leave, and I'm worried for them. I think they could be destined for a different future if only they had more time.'

'Who is it?'

She gave him a sorrowful look of apology. 'I can't tell you.'

Concerned crinkles appeared in the skin around his eyes. 'Surely it's not Alfie? When I think back to the zoo trip... It felt so good mucking around with him, like we were all one family.'

She almost burst into tears. 'I can't tell you, I'm so sorry... I could lose my job.'

His expression became thoughtful, and she blinked her tears away.

Joshua started to grizzle.

She sniffed. 'I must go, get him settled for the night.' She gathered his things and popped him back in his outerwear.

James hovered by the door as she bent to strap the baby into the buggy. 'Do fake fiancés kiss in secret?'

Joining in the fun, she straightened and said, 'You mean when there isn't a social worker to witness the event?'

His lips were close to her cheek. 'Does Annie visit the Hall on a Saturday evening?'

'Should I have brought a cardboard image of her to help you out?'

He took her in his arms. As he kissed her slowly and deeply, he stroked her head, and tendrils of desire wound their way around her body. She clung to him, her arms wrapped around his neck, her body tight against his, feeling him against her, just like she'd imagined many times before.

When he pulled away, she said huskily, still in joke mode, 'Was that a real kiss or a fake kiss?'

He looked around. 'Annie's not here, so it must be real.' He laughed a happy laugh she'd not heard since the zoo trip, and she laughed too. 'Let me help you back to your car. We could drive up to the Hall together so I can help you unload. I'll get Tim at the same time.'

As soon as he returned to the cottage with Tim, James said, 'I need your help.'

Tim replied tetchily, 'For what?'

He was probably grumpy because James had interrupted his fun.

'This place has to be spotless by tomorrow afternoon.'

'What's happening tomorrow afternoon?'

'Harmony's coming back to dinner. I'm sure she wasn't impressed with the state of the place. I wouldn't have been in her shoes. I know I can do better. *We* can do better. Will you help?'

'I s'pose it is half my mess.'

James grinned as he gave his son a grateful hug, and it was a few seconds before Tim pushed him away. Counselling was paying off.

35

Although Candy wasn't due to be working that Sunday, she was in the office when Harmony entered with Joshua.

'What's this I hear about you coming home with a baby last night?'

News travelled fast. 'I'm looking after him for a friend. I'd like to switch some shifts over the next couple of days so I can take care of him until the mum has him back.'

'Not long ago you said you had no friends—outside of here. Now you've got such a close friend you're looking after their baby?'

'Yes, I've been making new friends like you said I should.'

'Mm. The staff and children are saying you kidnapped him.'

'Of course I haven't kidnapped him! Surely you don't believe that?'

'No, of course not, and neither do they. They're messing with you.' She chucked Joshua under the chin. 'What's he called?'

'The mother's asked for privacy while she deals with the situation she's in so I'm sorry, I can't tell you at the moment.'

Candy gave her a mock stern look. 'I hope she's a true friend and isn't taking advantage of you—free baby care while she goes off for a couple of days.'

'I think she is a true friend.' Recalling the plans she'd made after Joshua had fallen asleep last night, she said, 'I'd like to reduce my hours to what I had when I looked after Patience and move into the Dower House. Andrei could step up again as deputy—perhaps permanently if we advertise and he performs best at the interview. Maybe his wife could take up his lost hours—she's expressed an interest in joining the staff team.' Then Talia and Andrei could move into her apartment and cover night-time emergencies... 'What do you think?'

'Dinner last night went that well, huh?'

Harmony chuckled. 'I can't invite James back if I'm living here, can I?'

Candy laughed. 'It's about time you had a life of your own.'

'And I'd like to sound Saskia out for a new deal.'

'What does this new deal entail?'

After explaining part of it, Candy agreed, and then Harmony phoned Saskia to invite her in for a chat.

Harmony was playing with Joshua on a large mat in the front library when Saskia joined them wearing a navy jacket and skirt with a powder blue shirt.

Her surprise was not lost on Saskia as she said, 'Grandfather said I must dress the part if we're having a formal review of my employment here. I... I thought we'd be in the office. Like before.'

'He's very correct, your grandfather, isn't he?' Harmony had much respect for "Grandfather" and his perfect manners and impeccable grammar.

Saskia nodded but her attention settled on Joshua playing with a wooden board puzzle.

'I thought we'd be more comfortable in the library,' Harmony explained. 'It's less formal.'

'Is this not an official review? I ask as you're sitting on the floor instead of a chair, and I don't know whether to join you or... sit on a chair.'

'Which would you like to do?'

She stepped out of her shoes and sat by Joshua.

'How are you enjoying working here?'

Her face became pinched. 'Have I done something wrong? Are you going to ask me to leave?'

'Not at all. I just want to know how you're enjoying cleaning.'

With a slight hesitation, she said, 'I love it.'

Had her name been Pinocchio, her nose would be growing.

Joshua threw a car-shaped piece onto the floor with a shout of satisfaction.

Saskia laughed, clapped her hands and said, 'Was that fun?'

He shouted again and laughed into her smiling face. She clearly liked babies, and he appeared to have taken to her as well.

'I was wondering if you'd be interested in a new six-month deal,' Harmony said. 'A kind of promotion.'

Saskia's beautiful blue eyes widened. 'Y... you want me to stay?' Briefly, she brightened but then her expression fell. 'What would I have to do?'

'I was thinking you could help the younger kids with their reading, teach them to keep their rooms clean and tidy.'

'That sounds fun.'

'And,' Harmony continued, 'I'd like you to take kids clothes shopping. You did well with Wendy, didn't you? You got the whole lot within budget.'

'Grandfather said I was challenged, like in a TV game show—and I won! And the buses—it was like being on fair rides with bumpety-bumps. Even though I was sitting down, I hung on. They've got bars and poles for that you see.'

Harmony smiled kindly. 'So are you interested?'

'Certainly. Thank you. As it's a promotion, do I get a pay rise?'

She mentioned an incremental increase. It wasn't much but was in line with what an entry-level support worker would be paid.

Saskia's face lit up. 'Thank you so much. Promotion *and* a pay rise.'

Harmony almost laughed at the change in Saskia's financial outlook. 'When you started, you didn't think too much of your salary.'

'Grandfather said I must learn the value of money. Now I know how many hours it takes for me to earn enough to buy new shoes, I think about whether they are worth that many hours and usually they aren't. And...'

'And?'

'Well, Grandfather said I was limiting my chances of getting a solid, dependable husband if I didn't manage to live on much less. He's right. Even you have found a man, at your age, dressed in jeans and baggy T-shirts and jumpers most of the time—and without makeup. If a man isn't going to like me in the kind of clothes I wear for work, he doesn't like *me*, does he?'

Harmony nodded. 'But I haven't exactly got James...'

'He's been kissing you.'

'Mm.'

'The boys I met before coming here knew where they'd be working; they weren't worried about their future. Although they were fun to be with, I don't think they'd make a good husband. Grandfather said I had to learn to graft. None of those boys ever did that. But I've seen that Ostap grafts. I want to end up with someone like him. Someone Grandfather would approve of.'

'There's still plenty of time for relationships, you're very young.'

'I know. But I don't want to wait until I'm your age to decide what I want, do I? It's good I know now what I'm looking for.'

'True,' she said, feeling ancient. 'Back to the reason I asked to see you—how would you feel about taking some courses, starting with a basic childcare course? You seem to have a natural leaning in that direction.'

Saskia's eyes stared into the distance and a wistful expression grew on her face. 'I think I would like to, yes... If they aren't too hard.'

'But will you stick around long enough to benefit from them? How do you feel about not living your past life now?'

'I... I'm not talking to Jemima, Romilly or Cordelia. Mummy told me they're saying I'm one of the nonessentials... That's what my so-called friends call people they don't like, and I did too because I heard them say it, but I never thought I'd be a nonessential... Mummy says it's my own fault for not keeping my mouth shut.' Her eyes became glassy with tears.

Poor Saskia... 'I don't think it's good if you have to hide who you are and what you're doing to keep friends.'

'No, it isn't.' She wiped her eyes and sniffed. 'But I'm wanted here, aren't I?'

'Very much so.' Harmony hugged her. 'I wouldn't be without you now. I'm so pleased you said you'll stay.'

Saskia was smiling now. 'What will I say my new job is called?'

'Support Assistant? Does that sound all right?'

She giggled. 'Grandfather was convinced you were going to sack me. But you promoted me! I'll get him to eat his hat when I get home.'

'Is that what he said?'

'Mm.'

'I'm glad you're pleased. But your new role means different hours—and there might be some baby care too.'

She glanced at Joshua. 'You mean this baby?'

'Yes. It would be a private arrangement with me, nothing to do with the Hall. But I'd like you to keep that part of the offer confidential for now. That means you're not to tell anyone at all apart from Grandfather until I say you can. Can you and "Grandfather" keep it secret?'

Harmony didn't think Saskia would have been able to

keep anything from "Grandfather" anyway, and since she didn't know Joshua's identity, Roxy's confidence should be kept.

Saskia nodded. 'I'm allowed to keep secrets unless it's for something bad. It's not for something bad, is it?'

'Not at all. I should have a better idea next week about hours and so on.'

'Is the baby another Patience?'

'No.'

'What's his name?'

'That's a secret at the moment. If Annie comes while he's here, I'd like you to take him to another room. Keep him out of sight until I can take him back.' Harmony didn't want Annie to meet the baby until after the final handover and Roxy had left Westbridge.

'Oh, Harmony, you didn't!' Saskia aimed such an expression of disenchantment at Harmony that she almost reeled with shame.

'Didn't what?'

'*Steal him.* It's illegal, you know.'

'Of course I didn't steal him! How could you think that?'

'I overheard something someone said when I put my bag in my locker, but I thought it must be a joke. What if the police come? Am I not allowed to answer their questions?'

Harmony laughed. 'If the police come, of course you can answer their questions. But the police won't come because I've not done anything wrong.'

There was a tap at the door and Andrei put his head around. 'Two police officers are here. If Candy had been around, I wouldn't have disturbed you.'

Her heart pounded. Was this about Joshua? Did Matt want his stepson back? But he had no legal authority over Roxy's child, had he?

Saskia gasped, her gaping mouth and horror-filled eyes making Harmony feel like she'd been transported to Antarctica to be with the Emperor penguins. 'Will I get arrested?'

'No, of course not. We don't even know what it's about.' She passed Joshua over, scooped up the play mat with the toys inside it and tidied it away behind the sofa. 'If it is about the baby, I'll explain the situation to the officers. Take him to my apartment.' She handed Saskia the key as she didn't have her work keys on her. 'Stay with him until I get there and don't worry. Honestly, I've not done anything wrong.'

Had there been a turn of events Roxy hadn't time to warn her about? Or, perhaps she'd tried. Harmony recalled she'd left her phone in the bedroom.

'It's okay,' Saskia said. 'I understand. The police came to talk to Daddy as well, and he'd done nothing wrong either.'

Harmony followed Saskia with Joshua to the door to invite the police officers to enter the library. When she recognised Officers Freckles and Botox, she was fairly certain they were not here about the baby.

'How can I help you?' she said.

'Mandisa Adeyemi. She's still here?' Officer Botox asked.

'Yes.'

'Her mother's outside in the car,' Officer Freckles said. 'Her stepdad is in London recuperating from trauma to the head as a result of a road traffic accident in Nigeria.'

Wow, what a pack of lies Mandisa had been fed.

Officer Botox said, 'We thought it best if you break the news to her.'

'Yes, of course. How come Mrs Sharpe hadn't found her before now? Surely she'd reported her missing?' The girl had been registered under her own name at school.

'Contact was maintained initially through her brother-in-law but after Mandisa's grandparents had been taken to a place of safety, Mr and Mrs Sharpe were mugged. It seems everything important—phones, bank cards, travel documents—had been taken.'

'Oh, that must have been problematic,' Harmony said.

'I believe so. Mrs Sharpe managed to contact an NHS colleague and asked her to visit the Peckham home. A neighbour said her daughter and step-uncle had gone to Nigeria to stay with her father.'

'Liam lied to everyone!'

'Yes. Unfortunately, the stepdad was then seriously injured. Once he was out of danger, his wife searched for Mandisa without success and then she suspected her brother-in-law of lying to the neighbour. When her husband was fit enough to travel, they returned to the UK. Finding no answers here either, they alerted the police. As Mandisa was on the database, the connection was made.'

The family must have been distraught. 'Could you invite Mrs Sharpe in while I find her daughter?'

Mandisa was studying at her desk. Harmony sat on the edge of the bed and said, 'I've just been given some good news. Fantastic news. But not about Patience.'

She waited for the import and possibilities to sink in so the girl could brace herself. She turned her chair around and leaned towards Harmony.

'Your step-uncle lied to you—your mother and stepdad didn't die.'

The girl shook her head. 'He wouldn't have done that.' Doubt shadowed her brow. 'Would he?'

'It seems he did.'

'It must have been a mistake then. He'd got it wrong...' As confusion cleared from her eyes, they became round. 'So they're okay?'

'Well, your stepdad is recovering from an accident so he couldn't come with your mum. She's fine.'

'*She's here?* I want to see her right now!'

'She'll be in the front library with the two police officers you've already met.'

Before Harmony finished her sentence, Mandisa sprang up from her chair like a Jack in the Box with a popped lid and ran screaming, 'Mummy!'

36

James was polishing a window in the living room when he spotted the police car outside the Hall. He recalled Harmony's comment about hiding the baby from the police. He'd taken it to be a joke. *What if it hadn't been a joke?*

Throwing down the polishing cloth, he called Harmony's mobile.

'Yes?' said a timid, barely audible voice.

What were the police doing to her?

'Don't say anything, not without a solicitor. I'll get you one if you want.' Whatever the problem was, he'd stand by her. She was too precious not to protect.

There was silence at the other end.

'Hello? Hello?' James said. 'Are you there?'

'You told me not to say anything,' the timid voice replied. 'Do you want me to say hello?'

It wasn't Harmony at all. 'It's James. I'd like to speak to Harmony, please.'

'This is Harmony's phone,' the high-pitched voice whispered, 'but she's not here.'

'Money!' a baby voice cried out.

'Who's this?'

'Saskia.'

'With the baby? I heard him just now. Where's Harmony?'

'She's downstairs with the police. She left her phone in

242

her bedroom. I know because I heard it ring. That's where I am now.'

James frowned. 'What are you doing in Harmony's apartment?'

'Hiding the baby from the police.'

Cold fingers clutched his heart. 'Thanks, Saskia.' He hung up, finding it hard to breathe as the familiar sensations of panic began to grow. *What had Harmony got herself into?*

After agonising over what to do, he finally settled on crossing the divide with the pretence he was just calling in on her. He shouted upstairs to Tim that he needed to make a quick visit to the Hall and would be back shortly. But when James was about to cross the road, he saw two police officers leave the Hall, walk towards their car and drive off.

Returning to the cottage, he called Harmony's mobile again. 'Saskia?'

'Yes?'

'It's James.'

'I know. Your name is on the screen.'

'What's happening?'

'I don't know.'

'The police have just driven away. Hasn't Harmony come up yet?'

'No. But that's good, that the police have gone, isn't it? That means she's got away with it. Whatever it is that she's done... or not done.'

He couldn't truly believe Harmony had done anything but neither could he come up with a possible explanation of recent events.

'Oh, I can hear someone coming... It's Harmony. Would you like to speak to her? She's just come in.'

'Money!' the baby called out.

James heard Saskia offering the phone to Harmony.

'Hi James,' she said warmly. 'When shall we come tonight?'

He mentioned a time. 'Tim will be here too. He's been

helping me clean the nest.'

She laughed. 'That's great. Looking forward to it, to seeing you both.' Then she hung up.

Bemused, he stared at his phone. *She'd behaved as though nothing had happened.*

Harmony hoped to have some peace that afternoon when the phone in the office rang. It was Roderick Walker, Saskia's grandfather.

After the usual social preamble, he said, 'I'm calling to thank you for your enormous success with Saskia.'

'She put in the work.'

'It seems she did.'

'I know this is early, but you deserve it. About that donation…'

After a few minutes of conversation, Harmony said, 'How would you like to become a grandfather figure to the children? Come to special meals? A concert? Parties? I could try to get permission if you'd like to.'

'That would be extremely convivial,' Roderick Walker said. 'Thank you.'

37

Early that evening, Harmony made her way back to James's.

He opened the door, grinning. 'Welcome back.'

She returned his grin, so happy to be spending another evening with him. 'Thanks. I've been looking forward to it.'

'Let me help you with the buggy.'

As James bent down to help lift it over the threshold, baby fingers clutched his hair. 'Ow!' He laughed. 'With a grip like that, he's all set for being a golfer.'

She untangled hair from Joshua's fingers while the baby chuckled and plucked him out of his seat. 'Hey, you, be a bit gentler. It hurts to have your hair pulled.'

Tim hovered in the living room doorway appearing unusually awkward. Because he wasn't used to seeing her at the cottage or he was nervous about how the evening would go? Between all of them or just her and James?

The floral scent of freshly washed laundry mingled with that of roasting meat. Her stomach reacted with a cry for food; she'd not had time to eat much at lunchtime.

'I heard you've been helping,' she said to Tim.

'Yes.'

'He's been great.' James ruffled his son's hair. When Tim jerked his head away, deep hurt crossed his dad's eyes. With a tight, pained smile he said to Harmony, 'Why don't you take a look upstairs? Then you can see what dedicated owls we've been.'

Tim frowned. 'Owls?'

'You know,' James said, 'what we learnt at the zoo place.'

'Oh...'

'I don't need to go up, I believe you,' she said. 'If I need the loo later...'

'What if you don't?' Tim said.

James smiled lazily as he leaned against the hall wall. 'I think it's obligatory.'

'Well... in that case... Could one of you take care of the baby while I nip upstairs?'

Tim raised his hand as though in school. 'I can. What's he called?'

'I think that's a state secret at the moment,' James joked.

'I'll tell you both someday soon, just not yet.' She checked Tim understood the baby's weight as she said to Joshua, 'This is Tim.'

When chubby little fingers explored Tim's face, Tim blew air onto the baby's cheek, making him squeal in delight, patting him as though asking Tim to do it again. So he did. 'He's so cute.'

Harmony stroked Joshua's arm. 'He is, isn't he?'

Upstairs, the bathroom taps gleamed, the limescale had disappeared and a perfectly folded towel hung over the rail. The bedrooms were tidy and the carpet showed vacuum tracks. Even the cymbals in Tim's drum kit shone. But James's bed had the same blue patterned duvet cover on as yesterday and the packages she'd seen were nowhere in sight. Lucky parents?

'All good?' James asked as she came down the stairs a few seconds later.

'It'll do.'

'*What?*' Tim spluttered. 'We spent hours—'

'She's messing with you,' James said, and then, doubtfully, 'You are, aren't you?'

She laughed. 'It's all good. You've been a great owl and

owlet.'

Tim grinned. 'So our nest's okay?'

'It's lovely. Very homely.'

As she took Joshua back, the baby's head turned to keep Tim in sight. He blew some air onto Joshua's cheek again and he chuckled, squeezing his eyes shut.

'Shall we eat?' James suggested. 'I've roasted a chicken and everything's ready to serve.'

'Oh great. I brought some jars just in case, but I'm sure the baby will much prefer a home-cooked meal if that's all right?'

'Of course it is.'

Harmony retrieved his eating things from a bag under the buggy and followed James and Tim into the kitchen.

James put the roasting tray on a trivet on the worktop. 'Once everyone's plate is loaded, I'll put the gravy and drinks on the table.' He began to cut the chicken.

'Tim, would you mind putting a little of everything on the baby's plate and cut them into pieces?' Harmony asked while putting Joshua's bib on.

'Dad, can you help me?' Tim said.

'Sure.'

'Shall I cut up your food so you can eat at the same time as the baby?' James asked.

It was so thoughtful of him. 'Thanks, that would be great. It's such a treat to be cooked for two days in a row.' Although she often ate with the kids, these meals were special because James had made them.

After they'd all started to eat, he said, 'I saw the police—'

Had he misunderstood the situation because yesterday she'd joked about hiding from the police? 'They came to reunite Mandisa with her mum. They left with as many of her things as they could carry on public transport—I'll courier the rest.'

'Then why was Saskia hiding—?'

Tim's owlet eyes informed James he'd been indiscreet,

and he mouthed *sorry*.

'Saskia misunderstood the baby's situation—I'll explain it when I can.'

'Can't wait.'

Tim said, 'Me too.'

Harmony laughed. She made aeroplane actions with Joshua's spoon as she fed him, enjoying watching his chubby cheeks move when he chewed. 'Thanks for calling when you thought I might need help. Even though it wasn't necessary.'

Hearing James had been anxious for her well-being felt like she'd been enveloped in an electric blanket on a cold day. She smiled. 'I'll know who to call upon if I do get into trouble.'

His steady gaze sent tingles down her spine. 'Definitely. I'd be hurt if you didn't.'

She longed to reach out to touch him, but Tim was eyeing them. 'How are you finding school now, Tim?'

'It's okay. It feels less strange now.'

He chatted and, while they had cake, she fed Joshua some Petits Filous. Once his face was clean, she asked Tim, 'Would you like to have the baby on your lap?'

His eyes lit up. 'Oh. Okay.'

She passed a gurgling Joshua over, his little fingers curling around Tim's jumper.

He smiled broadly, rubbing his nose against Joshua's, but when he tried to grab items from the table, Tim shifted his chair away, saying, 'He's so cheeky!'

'You were just the same,' James said. 'Curious about everything.'

'Was Georgie too?'

'He was, but you were more adventurous, always trying to scale the safety gates. Georgie just accepted them.'

'So I was a rebel?'

James rubbed Tim's hair. 'Maybe. I saw you as strong and confident with a desire for independence. Great qualities to have.'

He reddened at the compliment. 'Thanks.'

After everyone had finished, they went into the living room and James put a fresh sheet on the floor for Joshua. Tim joined him with a picture book Harmony had brought.

'The baby's taken to you, he likes you,' she said.

'He's very cute, isn't he?'

'Very.'

'Did you get him online?' Tim asked. 'On the dark web?'

She chuckled. 'No, of course not.'

'I love a mystery,' James said, 'but this one's too hard for me to solve.'

'For me too,' Tim agreed.

'Unless, of course,' James added with questioning eyes, 'this is a step to keeping him?'

Harmony almost gasped. She wanted to confide so badly... But she just stared helplessly at him.

He touched her hand. 'Tell us when you can. If you want help, just let me know.'

'Thanks.' He was so kind, so understanding...

'What time does this child go to bed?' he asked after they'd chatted about local news.

Checking her watch, she gave a small cry. The evening had gone so quickly. 'Thanks for reminding me.' She stood up. 'And thanks very much for the meal, both of you. It was great. When I'm all moved in to the Dower House, I'll cook for you.'

At the door, James kissed her cheek. When she kissed him back, she found his cheek was smooth as though he'd recently shaved and there was a tang of cedarwood.

'Will you be getting any more babies?' Tim asked. 'From wherever you got this one?'

'No.' Harmony chuckled. 'Now, no more questions.' She touched a finger to the end of his nose to lighten the request.

'Let me help you back up to the Hall,' James said.

'Thanks.' On the way, with him pushing the buggy, she

said, 'I thoroughly enjoyed being with you both.'

He looked her squarely in the eye. 'We should do it more often then.'

There were the tingles again, and they filled her with happiness.

When they reached the Hall's side door, James said huskily, 'I'd like to give you a proper kiss goodnight.'

Blood rushed through her veins. As she stepped towards him, his strong arms wrapped around her waist, pulling her into him.

'I can't get enough of you.' His lips grazed hers tantalisingly until he increased the pressure.

She didn't think she could get enough of him either as heat coursed through her body, desire spreading and intensifying. When was he going to invite her to spend time in his bed? Because that's what couples did, when they couldn't get enough of each other, wasn't it?

She gave a nervous shiver. It would happen soon, she felt sure of it, with or without new bedding. If she remembered what to do...

38

When James went to pick up Tim from the Hall after school the following Tuesday, Harmony answered the door, gaping at the sight of him.

He touched his face self-consciously but didn't feel anything untoward. 'Hi. I know I'm loads earlier than usual, but I've been working close by and there was no point in going back to the office. I thought Tim and I might watch a film together, get a takeaway.'

Her lips parted, but she remained silent.

It wasn't his face that was the problem, he decided. 'Has something happened to Tim?'

She gave a slight shake to her head as though pulling herself together. 'He's fine. He's in the dining room.' She stepped aside to let him in.

'Is that a band playing?' The music sounded live due to the odd squeaky mistake.

Her expression became neutral. 'Yes, and Tim's in it.'

To James's knowledge, Tim hadn't touched the drum kit at home, other than to dust it the other day, but a drum was being played right now. He followed the sound of jazz and stood at the open doorway to the dining room.

The Hall's kids were on the stage, conducted by a woman he didn't recognise, and Tim and Alfie sat by the drums. Tim was doing the clever stuff with two sticks, and Alfie just made the odd hit with a single stick whenever Tim gave him the nod. James's throat swelled from emotion.

'He wanted it to be a surprise,' Harmony said. 'We're going to have a concert. He said he'd not been able to play since…'

James averted his gaze to hide his stinging eyes and cleared his throat. 'No, he hasn't. At least, not at home.'

'He says when he plays here, he doesn't connect it so much to the past. Alfie wanted to learn to play the drums—which is what got the ball rolling.'

An internal video clip of Tim's dismissive past behaviour towards Georgie brought a rock-sized lump to James's throat. Georgie would have loved to have had Tim teach him how to play the drums. Would have loved it if his older brother had included him in lots of things. Death brought such clarity…

'I'll come back later,' James said hoarsely, his throat battling with the emotional rock-lump. 'I don't want him to think I've spoiled his surprise.'

She placed a hand on his arm. 'Are you all right?'

James nodded. 'It's… Tim wouldn't teach Georgie how to play, that's all.'

Tears shone in her eyes. 'I'm so sorry.'

'There's lots to regret, but we can only do our best to change and be more careful in the future, no?'

She nodded her understanding, blinking back tears.

Her sympathy, showing he was not alone, shattered the rock in his throat. 'I'm glad Tim's found someone he can be a role model to,' James said. 'Show care towards… He's growing up.'

'He is,' she agreed. 'Give it ten minutes and—'

'I'll come back in thirty.' As he was leaving, he said, 'Thank you for helping Tim. For helping both of us. You're the most giving person I've met.'

A deep blush rose in her cheeks. 'I…'

'Don't be modest now. You're great, more than great. You're fantastic.'

Almost as soon as James had gone, the door sounded again. Had James returned or was it Annie? She'd rung earlier to say she wanted to see Alfie.

It was Annie.

As Harmony let her in, Annie said, 'I just saw your... fiancé striding across the road.'

Feeling that she was expecting some sort of comment, Harmony said, 'When he saw that Tim was still playing in the band, he said he'd come back later for him. Alfie's with Tim now. He's been teaching Alfie how to play the drums.'

'May I watch?'

'Of course.'

They went to stand by the open doorway.

'They're quite a team,' Annie said.

Knowing they'd lose Alfie soon, Harmony swallowed hard. 'They are.'

'When they break off, it would be good to take a picture of Alfie with the drumstick.'

Annie was usually more discreet.

When the music ended, the teacher dismissed them, saying, 'Well done. Keep practising,' and the kids began to pack away and file out.

Annie was in like a shot, and Harmony followed.

'Hello, Alfie. How are you doing?' Annie asked.

Two startled heads looked up.

'Okay.'

'I've come to have a chat with you. But first, I'd like to take a photo for my records. Would that be all right?'

Alfie nodded.

Tim appeared startled.

Had he remembered about Patience's photo before she was matched with her future adoptive parents? How could Annie have acted so publicly?

When James crossed the road a second time that day, Tim must have been looking out for him as he charged out of the Hall.

'What's up?'

Tim hurried ahead. 'We can talk at home.'

Inside the cottage, he shouted, bunching his fists, 'The social worker's going to take Alfie away! You've got to stop her!'

James's initial relief that his son was all right soon turned into what felt like a hard punch in the gut. 'How do you know? Let's talk about it in the kitchen.'

Tim followed. 'Annie came to take a photo of Alfie. She did that with Patience. She's getting him adopted, isn't she?'

Now James knew for sure that Harmony had been referring to Alfie the first night she'd come to dinner. What other future had she referred to if there'd been more time? The two of them adopting the boy?

He recalled the fun they'd all had at the Bristol Zoo Project and his heart became leaden. After seeing Tim with Alfie in the band, he felt more strongly than ever that the boys and he and Harmony were meant to be together, as one family.

How long did he and Harmony—if she was willing— have left?

Not wanting to get his son's hopes up before he spoke to her, he said, 'Oh, that's too bad. I'm so sorry.'

'*Too bad?* Is that all you can say? Can't you adopt him?'

'*Adopt him?*' Tim had been thinking along the same lines as James... 'That's a big step... Why don't we chat about this over a drink? Hot chocolate?'

'Fine.'

He put the kettle on.

Would Annie allow him to adopt the boy as a single dad, to give more time for him and Harmony to get together as a couple? Or, like with Patience, did Annie want Alfie to have two parents? Had that been something Harmony had tried to covertly convey?

'So you'd like him as a brother?' James put the filled mugs on the table. 'I can understand that. He's a great boy.'

'We needn't be a bother,' Tim said. 'We could spend a lot of time at the Hall. That's where all our friends are.'

James's gut twisted. Didn't Tim want to spend time at home? And what would be the point of adopting Alfie if they didn't all do things as a family?

Tim must have read the hurt in James's expression as he said quickly, 'I'm sorry, Dad. But... I've so many friends there. It's empty here.'

'But if you have Alfie here, wouldn't that make the cottage less empty for you?' Alfie could use the dining room as his bedroom.

Tim nodded. 'It's like a morgue here.'

It was. 'We came here for a fresh start.' James had failed to make his son happy.

'But we've brought the emptiness with us. The holes.'

'Mum and Georgie?'

'Don't you feel it too?' There was hope in Tim's tone.

James did. Too much. 'Of course I do. What you're saying is that we need to fill the holes, right?'

'Right.'

'Even if I said yes, I'm not sure Annie would let us.'

'If being engaged might have helped Harmony adopt Patience, being married would be even better to adopt Alfie. You look happy when you're with her. The pretend engagement could turn real. Then we'd both have a friend.'

'Whoa, that's a big jump. But, yes, I do feel very happy when I'm with her...' And she appeared to be very happy when with him. 'Do you like her enough for her to be your stepmum?' Didn't kids baulk at their mum's position being usurped?

'She doesn't fuss over me, and I know you kiss her—even when that social worker isn't around. I don't mind that.'

'You think I fuss over you?'

Tim shrugged and drank from his mug.

'I'm responsible for your well-being so a certain amount of fussing is necessary. It's because I care about you so much—'

'I know you do, Dad. I care about you too.'

James pulled Tim closer for a kiss on his forehead. For a change, he didn't pull away.

'We could move into Harmony's house,' he said. 'She said it's too big for her. That's why she lives in the Hall. A rich lady gave it to her when she knew how much Harmony loved children. At least, I think that's what she said.'

'My understanding is she's just overall in charge with other trustees. She doesn't own it. At least, not financially. Maybe with her heart.'

'That's what she's got!' Tim exclaimed. 'A *heart*.'

James pictured a Harmony-sized Care Bear with a big heart on its tummy giving him a tight hug.

'Yours might get better if you marry her.'

'You mean I won't be so sad?'

'And grumpy.'

'I'm so sorry, Tim. I think both our hearts have taken quite a bashing. But they will get better. Even when I'm grumpy, I love you.'

'I know... same here... Will you ask her to marry you?'

'She might not be ready. Marriage is a great leap from where we're—'

'Then it'll be too late!' He thrust his chin out. 'You see her most days. You know what she's like. You chose your first wife. *Why can't I choose your second?*'

If it hadn't been such a serious conversation, and if he hadn't said it with such a core of hard intent in his eyes, James would have laughed. 'It doesn't work like that. Love is everything.' He knew Harmony liked him, but did she love him?

Tim's expression darkened. 'It's better if it isn't.'

James's heart ached. 'So no one can get hurt?'

'Yes.' Tim downed the rest of his drink and used the sleeve of his jumper to wipe the milky residue from his mouth.

James gave a slight shake of his head. 'It wouldn't be a

good basis for a marriage, not loving each other.' But he began to imagine what it would be like being married to Harmony. Wonderful, that's what.

Tim's eyebrows came closer together. 'What about marriages of con... con something?'

'Convenience?'

'That's it.'

'I wouldn't want it to be a marriage of convenience, and I'm sure Harmony wouldn't either.'

'But it would be very convenient, wouldn't it?' Tim pressed.

39

Roxy placed the white linen cloth they'd been given as a wedding present over the kitchen table and popped the polished cutlery into the pockets of folded napkins. The glasses gleamed, and she'd opened a bottle of red.

She called to Matt in the study when she placed the meat, grilled tomatoes, mushrooms and oven chips onto the warmed plates.

He sat down, taking in the white table linen. 'Steak again?'

'I thought you like steak.'

The smell of grilled or roast meat used to lure him into the kitchen before the food was ready.

He removed the cutlery from the folded napkin and spread the cloth out on his lap. 'Of course I like steak. But it's a bit extravagant, isn't it? Having it again so soon?'

'I'm sorry, you're right.'

Shortly, he'd be able to have beans on toast every night if he wanted.

She asked him about his day, and he mentioned much the same things he talked about most nights.

When she removed the plates they'd used for the main course and put out the dessert choices, small plates and cake forks, he said, 'Why do I get the feeling something is going on? This isn't how we usually eat... with all this...' He waved his hand over the offerings and touched the tablecloth. 'This feels like the Last Supper.'

It kind of was...

He glanced about the kitchen. 'Is Joshua in bed?'

'A friend's babysitting him. I asked her to keep him a bit longer so we can have a serious chat.'

'A friend? That's nice.'

It had surprised Roxy that Miranda, Perdita and Harmony had been so kind to her. She wasn't used to having friends who weren't part of a party set, where everyone had appeared to be out for themselves and no one bothered to keep in touch.

She considered her lack of long friendships. Her home life had taught her that feelings didn't matter, people were to be used, that you don't do favours... She recalled her twelfth birthday. Her mum had promised a cake, again. Like previous years, all the ingredients had been bought. But when Roxy had come home from school and found her mother in a drunken stupor on the sofa, she'd got the recipe out and had made it herself. That's what she'd done every year after that.

Perhaps she'd been erroneously looking for affection through all the trysts she'd had, knowing she couldn't cope if they'd led to more. Perhaps she'd been baking Matt cakes to show him she loved him, to help make it all right, to be a good wife.

Her throat swelled from emotion and began to ache.

Matt held her gaze, clearly waiting for an explanation about the Last Supper and serious chat.

It didn't appear they'd get past the cheesecake and fruit salad before the big reveal so she cut the cake and placed a slice in front of him. She wanted him to taste her efforts, to know that, despite wanting her freedom, she still cared about him.

But he ignored the cake.

Swallowing was an effort and her tongue felt sluggish. 'There is something I have to tell you.'

'Have you been having an affair?'

'No, Matt, I haven't.' She met his gaze squarely. 'I haven't been unfaithful to you since the day I met you.'

'Perhaps not in deed, but what about in thought?'

'Matt, I'm terribly sorry, but the marriage isn't working out. I'm so sorry I've hurt you, and that I wasn't honest with you from the start.'

'You're leaving me? Have you met someone else?'

It was hard to breathe knowing she would add to his pain. She could feel the tears overspilling her lashes. 'I've met someone who's offered to help me leave. But I'm leaving for me, not for him. We are not in a relationship.' Yet...?

He sat back sharply in his chair as though given a blow.

She wiped her cheeks. 'I'm sorry.'

Anger, disappointment and pain blazed from his eyes but quickly dampened into resignation. He appeared forlorn as though he'd known their union would end in tears. 'Why did you marry me? Was it because I'm a vicar? You went after that priest, didn't you? The similarity hasn't escaped me.'

'I think maybe I thought... perhaps felt that... if you, as a man of God, could love me, there must be some good in me?'

She believed she'd hoped for some kind of redemption, an affirmation that she wasn't so wicked after all. But being with Matt now made her feel she was bad, very bad—and she knew she was. She hadn't felt that when she'd been with Tony. He'd just accepted her as she was, despite her revelations. But he'd had some of his own unpleasant past to disclose so that was the difference.

She put out a hand to touch Matt's, but he pulled it away. 'I'm tremendously grateful to you, for giving me a home, a place to stay with my baby and for the love you gave us.' She found a tissue and blew her nose.

His face was rigid. 'Did you ever love me or did you just use me while you were in trouble?'

Her chin trembled, and her voice was thin and high-pitched. 'I believe I did love you. I tried so hard for you to be pleased with me. I wanted to be a good wife.' For a good man.

'You did your duty around the place, certainly. But honesty is... essential in a partnership.'

She sniffed. 'I know. I'm so, so sorry.'

'Is this man who's going to help you one of the parishioners?'

'No! He's from London.'

'How did you meet?'

'On a day out in Bristol.' Kind of true. 'But let me be clear, I am not leaving you for him. I'll have my own place, my own life. He's just helping me get it.'

There was an awkward silence; she was sure he didn't believe her.

'What will you do? Go back to your old work?'

Roxy shrugged. 'I'm going to try to set up another business, a franchise. But in London.'

'And your old ways?'

She blinked to keep him in focus. 'I'll never knowingly come between a woman and her man again.'

'What about Joshua? How will you manage to work?'

'I'm having help with him. It's all arranged.' Her tone suggested that he shouldn't ask more, and he took the hint.

She'd explain once she was on her way to London, and Joshua was safe with Harmony. Matt might try to cause trouble as Roxy had heard many men did when they were spurned.

'I'll miss him,' he said.

She was sure Harmony would let him into Joshua's life. 'I think there will be many women in the parish who'll be around to console you. After I've gone.'

He looked at her hollowly. 'They consoled me after my wife died, but I hadn't wanted them, I'd wanted you.'

'And I bet you're regretting that now?' she asked gently.

He rose from his chair. 'I've a ton of work to do.'

Of course he had.

Roxy cleared the table and washed up. She was going to be a dutiful housewife until she left. She'd even change the double bed so that Matt could reclaim his room and, so as not to embarrass him, she would wear her "vicar's wife" clothes until she left.

Marriage had taught her many things. The most important being that marriage did not suit her. At all.

40

Harmony was in her bedroom with Joshua, ready for the day, when Roxy called.

'I've told Matt it's over,' she said.

Poor Matt... 'How did he take it?'

'In a subdued way. But this morning, he's been banging things around the kitchen.'

Rejection always hurt.

'How's it going with the solicitor?' Roxy asked.

'He's already written to the local authority.'

'That's good. I'll tell Matt about the arrangement after I've left for London. If he wants to visit Joshua, would that be all right? He said he'd miss him and—'

'Of course that's all right.' Seeing Matt would probably help Joshua adjust.

'Thanks. I'd like to have Joshua back for a couple of days. Can we meet in an hour at the Dower House for me to get him? I'll park in the driveway again.'

'No problem.'

'After the two days, Tony will come in a hired van to help me move. We'll drop Joshua off with the rest of his stuff en-route to London.'

As Harmony had plenty of time before meeting Roxy, she pushed Joshua to the newsagents and took the buggy inside. There might be an interesting parenting magazine to help increase her knowledge of older babies and toddlers. Joshua had already been pulling himself up to stand in the cot and it wouldn't be long before he'd be walking.

'Good morning, Ramesh,' she said.

'Good morning. Who's this little fellow?'

'Oh, I'm babysitting.' She was about to approach the magazine rack when the door opened again and James entered.

He smiled warmly when he saw her. 'Hi. I didn't expect to see you.'

She smiled. 'Hi.'

'Now that you're here together,' Ramesh said, 'I'd like to congratulate you on your coming nuptials. Have you set a date yet?'

She stared at James, and he stared back. 'Ramesh overheard the kids talking. He found out a while back...'

'Oh, er... we haven't decided,' James said.

Ramesh drummed his fingers on a magazine on the counter. 'The latest Brides magazine has just come in.'

The cover image of a woman in white reminded her of her wedding dress; Harmony looked away. 'I'm not at the planning stage yet.'

Heat rose in her face and prickling sensations grew up and down her limbs as she wondered what James was thinking. Did he want her to buy it to keep up the pretence? But he hadn't said so, and she didn't want to make the lie bigger, dupe Ramesh. Plus he'd probably take it one step further and end up recommending venues, caterers and florists.

She dared to meet James's gaze, making sure her eyes didn't lower to take in the magazine's cover as he might think she was angling for marriage when presumably he wasn't. 'How come you're not at work?'

He picked up a copy of The Guardian. 'I have an inspection on the way to the office.'

'Harmony was here first,' Ramesh said quickly.

'Money!'

She explained the moniker to Ramesh and ruffled the back of Joshua's hair playfully, and he gurgled.

Ramesh waited expectantly for her to purchase something but it was too awkward to pick up a parenting magazine now. He'd have probably not given it much thought because she always had children to look after, and she'd bought them before. But James... he might read more into it than was currently safe.

'It's okay, you go,' she said to James.

'I insist you go before me. Allow me to be gallant. Take your time.'

What reason did she have now for having entered the shop?

Ramesh held out the wedding magazine and her hand automatically reached for it. But when she took in James's frozen expression, she grabbed the nearest thing that wasn't the magazine. It was from a box on the counter that Ramesh must have opened ready to re-stock a shelf. She hadn't even taken in the wording.

Silently, he replaced the Brides magazine on the counter, took the item from her hand and rang up the amount on the till. 'Would you like a bag?'

'No need.' She knew from the size of the small box in her hand that it would fit easily into her own bag.

But when she registered she'd bought a sanitary product—something she'd never need—her embarrassment with James hit a new high. Explaining at some inevitable time in the future why she'd bought a product she had no use for would be so humiliating.

'Thanks,' she mumbled.

With flames consuming her face, she stuffed the tampon box into the middle pocket of her bag. *Why hadn't she just grabbed a bar of chocolate?* She couldn't look at either man. 'I've got to go. I hope you both have a good day.' She manoeuvred the buggy outside as James held the door open.

Before she'd got very far—despite her efforts to escape—James was beside her, the newspaper folded in his hand.

'I'm sorry, I didn't mean to embarrass you. I thought I was doing the right thing—being polite by letting you go first.'

'Don't worry about it.' He'd been married, he knew all about women's periods, although not hers... And now her lack of periods had to be a closely kept secret, otherwise he'd know she'd been aiming for the bridal magazine. 'Well, I'll be off then. I hope you have a good day.'

'You too.'

It was only a few minutes after she'd reached the Dower House that Roxy's car pulled up in the private driveway, and Harmony, carrying Joshua, let her in through the back door.

He kicked his legs in excitement. 'Mummy!'

Roxy's smile transformed her face. She took him in her arms and planted a noisy kiss on his cheek.

Worried that Roxy might think Money and Mummy were too close and that Harmony was usurping her position, the words tumbled out. 'He's been calling me Money as he couldn't manage Harmony.'

'Oh, that's sweet.'

It was a relief that Roxy didn't have a problem with the moniker.

They went to sit in the living room.

'Would you like a drink? I'm set up for that now.'

Roxy shook her head. 'No thanks, I've got so much to sort out, and I want to take Joshua to the park. Here...' She fished in her bag and handed over a plastic folder. 'It's all his documents. Birth certificate, vaccinations, weight chart, GP details... And I've signed more letters to prove you're responsible for him. I've got copies of everything, but I've given you the originals.'

'Thanks.'

'I... It's been harder than I expected. But I know it's the right thing to do. I'll let you know an exact time when Tony and I'll come back with Joshua and his things.'

'Shall I let you know how he's doing? After you've gone?'

Her voice became shaky. 'I think... it would be best for me not to know for a while. I...' She sniffed and searched in her pocket for a tissue, which she dabbed over her eyes. 'I think... I need some time to adjust first... to come to terms with what I've done. It's not that I don't love him—' She broke off with a sob.

Harmony shifted closer to put her arm around Roxy. 'Are you sure you want to go ahead with this? Your heart's getting broken...'

She sniffed. 'It's the right thing for me and, in the long run, for Joshua. Together, we can give him what he needs. On my own... I can't.' Her pain was almost tangible.

'I know you love him, and I will do my utmost to give him the best life I can. You will always be his mother.'

Roxy nodded. 'Thank you... I think we should go now.'

'I'll get the car seat.'

'Thanks.' She stood up, flashed a sad smile and led the way out.

With Joshua gone, Harmony's arms felt empty. So did her heart. She needed some chocolate, a *lot* of chocolate. But not from Ramesh's shop so soon after the tampon/Brides magazine incident, so she headed for the Spar next door.

With multi-packs of Dairy Milk Fruit and Nut, Galaxy and Fry's Chocolate Cream—plus a book of Sudoku to completely hit the spot—she went to the checkout. On the way, she added some mints to the basket—she needed to keep her breath fresh around James, didn't she? After paying for the items, she bagged the haul and left.

As she reached the pavement, she bumped into Perdita and Luke. Perhaps they'd think the stash in the carrier bag was for the children? Perhaps they'd not see through the coloured material... Perdita was slim, Luke was a fitness guru and Harmony... well, she was soon to be a glutton.

'Hi, Harmony,' Perdita said. 'We were just going to the

café for some cake. Why don't you join us?

Harmony could manage cake too. 'Yes, thanks.' It would also be good not to be alone.

'I'll just be having a smoothie,' Luke said.

After they'd almost finished their drinks and cake, Perdita said, 'You're friends with Roxanne—although she said it's Roxy now—aren't you? What's up with her?'

Harmony stiffened. 'What do you mean?'

'She was deathly pale at the baby clinic. I asked her if she was all right, and she gave a wan smile and said I could talk to you about it, but not yet. She thanked me for my friendship. What's going on? It's as though I'll never see her again. Are she and Matt splitting up?'

Harmony was very sure Perdita would see Roxy again. She would likely come to Westbridge with Tony when he came to visit Petal, and perhaps they'd all go out together with Joshua.

'I can tell you about it soon,' Harmony said. Perhaps, by that time, Tony would have already told Perdita that he was helping Roxy out.

The furrow between Perdita's eyebrows deepened. 'Is it because of what happened at my get-together? Are they splitting up because of me?'

'Hang on,' Luke said. 'You can't take responsibility for Roxy hiding her past from her husband. It was kind to invite her.'

'She doesn't blame you,' Harmony told Perdita. 'She blames herself over what happened.'

'Sounds as though you like her,' he said.

'I do.' How could she not when Roxy would be entrusting Joshua to her care?

'Miranda said she's okay too,' he said. 'I'll have a word with Faith to see if she can lay her grievances to rest. After all, she's done very well out of Andy ditching her as she's nabbed Tom—who's a far better match. We don't have to be best buddies with Roxy—I never liked her and still don't. But we could let things be neutral. It's obvious she's come out the worse from this.'

'Yes, thanks,' Harmony said. It would pave the way for an easier future.

Perdita held Luke's gaze. 'You don't need to like her. But if you'd seen her looking so ill… I'm sure you'd feel sorry for her situation.'

Luke looked pointedly at Harmony. 'Whatever that is.'

41

James's head had been invaded by bees buzzing around his brain, intent on analysing the scene in the newsagents in a spiral of thought that reminded him of his son's maths homework.

Had Harmony not bought Brides because she didn't want him to think she was ready for marriage? Or perhaps she'd secretly longed to peruse the magazine but hadn't wanted to appear presumptuous?

He'd been so paralysed by discovering Ramesh knew of *and* believed in the fake engagement, he'd stupidly failed to encourage her purchase. Yet, if James *had* spurred her to acquire the publication, she'd have been reassured by the underlying message of intent, of his love. So he'd missed a serendipitous opportunity—earning him the title of Supreme Idiot of Westbridge.

Ever since leaving the newsagents, he'd been mentally kicking himself. Had they been real kicks, he'd have needed crutches by now. He shut his eyes as though it would release the twist in his guts. He'd hurt Harmony's feelings in front of Ramesh, had been a very ungallant fake fiancé.

Was that why she'd bought the tampons—to cover up the fact that her hand had stretched out to take the magazine? Or, had she wanted them all along but hadn't wanted him to guess she was on her period?

Ramesh must have been so confused…

The bees in James's head were also confused, unable to navigate the true reason behind Harmony's outstretched hand.

Well, he'd show how he felt about her at the end of the evening and, if all went to plan, he'd suggest she go back and get the publication.

But he had to wait until his morning commitments were over before he could research a restaurant and book a table. He could always cancel if she said no. But hopefully, she'd say yes.

Later, he called her phone. 'Harmony? It's James. I wondered if I could take you out for some tapas tonight?'

'Ooh, a proper date! That would be lovely. Thanks. Good timing as the baby's not with me.'

Dates were meant to be fun and light-hearted, weren't they? Whereas he was planning on them having a serious conversation. 'It's not a date. I thought it would be a—'

'Oh.' Her tone was flat. 'Is Tim coming too?'

'No! I... er... wondered if Tim could stay at the Hall until we get back. I'd like it to be just the two of us.'

'It is a date then.'

He couldn't explain over the phone. 'It's... a chance to ... get to know you better.'

There was a long silence as though she was trying to work out why he'd asked her to dinner. He squeezed his eyes shut as he reeled under the awkwardness of his invitation.

'Isn't that what you do on a date? Get to know the other person?' she said. 'Anyway, I'd love to come. I'll come to yours if that's okay so we're not spied on by curious pairs of eyes.'

Harmony thought James must have been looking out for her because the door opened when she arrived.

Date clue number one: he'd taken trouble over his clothing. His unbuttoned wool coat revealed previously unseen taupe trousers, a thick navy jumper—possibly also new—and the collar of a light-blue shirt. She'd have been happy to skip dinner and go straight to dessert in his bedroom...

Date clue number two: the porch light revealed he'd recently shaved as his skin lacked the usual dark evening shadow.

His gaze took in her short coat, loose hair, silver earrings and makeup. 'You look lovely.' He kissed her cheek.

Date clue number three was indeterminable. Was the fact that he'd kissed her at all a pro-date clue or the fact it had been on the cheek an anti-date clue?

Date clue number four: he'd recently put on aftershave. The cedarwood scent had been strong when he'd kissed her.

Date clue number five: he opened the passenger door for her. Or did he do that for every female passenger?

'I've booked us a table at the Floating Harbour.'

Date clue number six: the Floating Harbour area was a lovely setting for a romantic evening.

The original harbour had been cut off from the tidal waves of the River Avon in a 1970's regeneration project — the working dock area having been moved further south — and had been transformed for leisure, with many restaurants. The water level was carefully controlled so no boats in Bristol could get grounded again by the huge tidal range.

'The place I've chosen is on a boat,' he added. 'Is that okay?'

It was more than okay. 'Absolutely. Thank you.'

Date clue number seven: dinner on a boat...

'Where's the baby?' he asked as they were headed towards Bristol.

'Back with his mummy.'

'And will he be staying there?'

'I'm likely going to be helping out again.'

The rest of the way, they discussed their day, and she told him that she'd started to buy food for the Dower House. 'So it won't be long before I can invite you and Tim over for a meal.'

'Let me know your move date. I'd like to help.'

'As soon as it's finalised, I will.' She'd only know for sure once Joshua was back with her, and Roxy was on her way to London.

She was grateful James didn't mention Ramesh, the wedding magazine or tampons. After parking the car, his warm, protective hand took hold of hers.

Date clue number eight: strolling hand in hand along the waterside.

Date clue number nine: Under the Stars tapas place was cosy and intimate. A table for two with a vase of pretty flowers between them, a glowing candle in a bottle, light shining from the quayside opposite over the dark stretch of water... *It was a date, wasn't it?*

After sharing hummus, bread and a bowl of marinated olives, the beautifully presented main course tapas dishes arrived: harissa chicken, lamb kofte, patatas bravas and pan-fried hake. It was good they'd got the same taste in food. It was also good she'd had enough warning to leave off the chocolate she'd bought earlier.

James cleared his throat. 'I've been wondering, since the conversation at Bristol Zoo Project, how long you and your fiancé were together?'

She rubbed a thumb hard down her hand as she fought the impulse to change the subject—she didn't want to talk about David on her first proper date with James. But she answered anyway.

'Four years. We lived together for the last two.'

He stroked his brow as though nervous. 'Do you mind my asking...'

'Mm?'

'Why did David change his mind?'

Harmony twisted the napkin in her lap. 'He found someone he preferred who could give him children.' She stared at her plate.

'I'm sorry, that was such a painful question for me to ask.'

Yet he had... Best to get it over with. 'He'd been packing while I'd been at the hotel getting ready to marry.'

He covered her hand with his. 'What a snake.'

She recalled how she'd spent her wedding night snipping her dress into confetti, her hands blistering despite swapping the scissors between them. 'I couldn't afford the flat on my own so moved back with my parents until I worked for Lady Pinkerton.'

'I hope he stayed with the woman, had kids, after causing all that anguish,' James said in a hard tone.

The romance of the evening began to dissolve. 'No, she dumped him. He had some kind of breakdown, lost his job, then accepted a post with another tech firm in Tampa, Florida.' A picture of Melody, so beautiful, so beguiling, swam in front of her.

The waiter came to take their dessert order.

James asked for vanilla and strawberry scoops of ice cream, and she opted for a raspberry sorbet.

'Is that why you invited me out?' she asked when the waiter left. 'To ask about my past?' Had she been more "under the spotlight" than "under the stars"?

James shifted in his seat. 'I wanted to have a serious discussion. About Alfie—Tim's told me that Annie's going to get him adopted.'

So Tim had connected the photos Annie had taken of Alfie with the one she'd taken of Patience before she'd been placed for adoption.

'I'm not allowed to discuss it.' Harmony's eyes stung with regret—for the fact that the social worker had forbidden her to talk about it and because it felt like there was nothing romantic about the evening after all.

The waiter returned with their desserts and they began to eat again.

James's expression appeared earnest as he leaned towards her. 'Do you think I could adopt him? Tim's desperate to have him as a brother and I... I loved playing around with Alfie on the zoo trip. He needs a family, a father...'

Annie had said that Alfie must go to a couple so there'd be a safety net if something happened to one of them—he had no other family as backup—and, as he'd been brought up solely by his mum, at least one of them must be female. There was no way James could adopt him by himself.

Date clue number ten: James had been right. It definitely *wasn't* a date.

His gaze appeared to be assessing every nuance of her expression. 'Or maybe we could adopt him together.'

Her throat began to ache, and she tried to stop moisture welling up in her eyes. 'Is this why you invited me out? To get Alfie for Tim? And interview me for suitability as a... a what?'

'As a wife. We could be one big happy family. Marry me.'

'*Marry you?*' What about love? She swallowed back tears; she didn't want to cry. Not here.

'I thought you might want to hurry things along too, to keep Alfie.' He must have noticed her distraught expression as he added, 'I'm so sorry if I've misread the situation...'

She'd hoped James would invite her back to his place after dinner, see his bed dressed with the new bedding, hear him whisper words of love. But this... this was so unexpected, she couldn't take it in. She fished in her bag for a tissue and found a packet on top of the tampon box she'd forgotten to put in the girls' emergency supply cupboard.

Getting a proposal like this couldn't hurt her more than if a knife had been stuck in her back. Had he said he loved her, she would have said yes. But even then, there was no way Annie would let them adopt Alfie as they weren't an established couple—they'd not been living together. Only if the social worker couldn't find a match in the next few months, there might have been an outside possibility of adopting the boy.

Hiding behind her hair, Harmony picked up her bag. 'I'd like to go home. Let me pay half.'

'No. You're my guest tonight. I insist.'

She didn't care about the money, but it was easier to give in. 'Thanks.'

After he'd paid, they walked back towards the car, hands by their sides with no risk of touching.

Tears filled her eyes as she took deep breaths. Then, unable to stop the hurt spilling from her tongue, she said, 'Was your last marriage proposal business-based?'

Under the light of the street lamps, she saw his face redden, colour spreading to his throat. She'd shamed him, hurt his feelings. Letting out a sob, she stuffed knuckles into her mouth to prevent more wounding words from being unleashed.

People were staring, but she glanced away, hoping they wouldn't intervene. They couldn't help an aching heart.

He put his arms around her, muttering another apology, but she brushed them off.

'I'm truly sorry,' he said. 'For not giving you the romance you deserve.'

'I'm sorry too—for snapping at you.'

'I deserved it. I'm honestly so, so sorry. I think the time pressure dislodged a few brain cells.'

It was better to run with his introduction of levity than make things worse. 'It must have done—like mine had been dislodged when Patience arrived, and I threw you a curveball by asking you to be my fake fiancé.'

'You certainly did.'

'But you're not talking about a fake marriage are you?' she asked gently.

'Not at all. I thought we could have a real one...'

'Moving in together, marrying... that's a different level entirely...' She sniffed. 'You and me—I don't think we're quite there yet, do you?'

'We could be? We could throw our hat in the ring with Annie—'

Back to Annie... Harmony had to tell him now. 'She's not going to consider us. We don't fit her requirements for

Alfie.'

Harmony had left the Hall full of excitement but now her mood had deflated like a tired party balloon. She longed to curl up in bed, be alone.

James parked outside the Hall's main entrance and they entered the building together so he could pick up Tim.

Saskia, who'd offered to teach some girls how to put their hair up, came hurrying towards them, speaking in a rush. 'Your sister's come to visit!'

Harmony's heart hardened, and her muscles felt like threads of steel. 'My... sister?'

'Yes. Your sister. Musical.'

Her skin began to smoulder. 'You mean Melody?'

'That's it!'

'Who let her in?' Her voice was deep and scratchy. People couldn't just turn up at the Hall without an appointment, including her sister. Surely Candy would have refused entry?

Had Melody been genuinely contrite for ruining Harmony's life, she might have managed to reach a level of tolerance. But her sister's smug arrogance and refusal to admit wrongdoing had made that impossible.

42

James watched Harmony undergo a disturbing personality change. Her lips set in a thin line, her nostrils flared and her eyes stared as though she'd caught mad cow disease.

'Who let my sister in?' There was a scalpel edge to her voice as she repeated the question.

Saskia took a step back. 'I... did.'

'Where's Candy?'

'Seeing the emergency doctor. Patrik hurt his ankle.'

'Where's Melody?'

'In the front library.'

Bemused and curious, James followed Harmony's determined footsteps. After all, Melody could be his future sister-in-law. Yes, well, after this evening, perhaps that was a tad optimistic...

She was sitting on a chair. Cream cowgirl boots, a short skirt, a wide belt cinching her waist, a skimpy top, a pink bolero jacket with beads, multi-coloured dangling earrings and the face of an angel framed by flowing blonde hair.

Had Harmony worried about Melody when she'd asked him about his attraction to slim blondes? Well, he loved Harmony and wasn't interested in anyone else, including her sister, whose physical appearance interested him as much as a toy doll.

Harmony whispered something into Melody's ear.

She shook her head. 'I want to stay.'

'Get out,' Harmony hissed.

James approached.

'Hel-lo.' Melody's gaze appeared to wander appreciatively over his body.

His face felt like it had caught fire.

She smirked.

Harmony scowled. 'If you don't go, I'll call the police. This isn't a hotel. I've told you before and nothing's changed.'

'I don't think that's entirely true.' Melody's unruffled gaze drifted over James again. 'You didn't have *him* the last time I looked in on you.' Then she addressed James. 'This is the welcome I get. She's had it pretty cushy here but can't be supportive to a sister in need. Always left me out, even when we were kids.'

'I didn't leave you out of anything,' Harmony snapped. 'Not when we were kids. It was you who didn't want to learn to play an instrument.'

'I might as well not have had parents,' Melody said. 'Always shut in a room with Harmony. The talented one.'

'I think you've proved your talents lie elsewhere,' Harmony said. 'Now go and leave me in peace.'

He wanted to help, to prove he could protect her. 'Melody, Harmony has asked you to leave. So please go.'

'I'll call the police if you don't,' she said.

It wasn't good for the scene to be played out in front of the kids he'd heard shuffling up behind him. A quick glance over his shoulder proved Tim's presence too.

Melody swept a hand in front of her. 'Now that you have all this, you selfishly keep it to yourself. Well, I bet they don't know the half of it. You always did play things close to your chest—the mountain range that it is.'

James blinked, having always admired Harmony's breasts, and she gasped.

She thrust her hand into her bag. But as Melody lunged to snatch it—presumably so that Harmony couldn't retrieve her phone—it fell onto the floor. The contents spilled out.

Melody grabbed the tampon box. 'What have you got these for?'

'Mind your own business.'

James frowned. What was the issue with the Tampax?

'Well, they're obviously not yours...'

'Shut up, Melody.'

Had Harmony had an early menopause?

Saskia was by his side. 'I don't understand.'

He didn't either, but he felt sure he was about to.

'Unless someone's donated a womb.' Melody laughed.

Harmony glared.

James's heart chilled. *Harmony had no womb?* Poor, poor Harmony, and that meant... she *had* been about to take the magazine, didn't it? So, this morning, she *had* wanted to marry him? But it didn't seem like she did anymore.

Instead of uncovering the reason for Harmony's outstretched hand at the newsagents appeasing the bees, they redoubled their buzzing and, mentally, James produced a smoker to calm them down. He'd make everything right, he reassured them. The "how" would have to come later. Perhaps some imaginary honey could give his cognitive functioning such a boost that the solution would present itself.

'I don't think Harmony's sister's very nice,' Saskia whispered.

'No,' he whispered back, wondering how best to shield Harmony from this vixen.

'Leave. Now!' Harmony yelled.

Melody turned to him. 'She sweet-talked an old lady into setting this up—so that she could have all of this while feeding her obsession with the kids she can't have.'

In his mind, her face became pointed, her ears became triangles and she'd grown a long, bushy tail.

'You've caused enough trouble. You need to leave now.' He wasn't going to let her do more damage. He began to wheel her suitcase to the door.

'Get out!' Harmony screamed. 'And never come back.' Tears were streaming down her face.

Melody bit her lip as though realising she'd gone too far. 'Can you give me a lift to the station?' she asked James.

At least she was willing to leave without police involvement. Driving her would be the quickest way to get Melody away and spare Harmony more anguish. He'd be back before 9.30...

'Shall I give her a lift?' he asked Harmony, who'd followed them out of the front library. 'To get her away?'

He expected an indication of approval but her eyes were round with an expression he didn't understand. However, as she didn't suggest an alternative solution, he said to Melody, 'Come on,' and began to wheel her suitcase out of the Hall.

As they approached his car, Melody said, 'You're so kind. Unlike Harmony. She's always been jealous of me.'

James harrumphed. 'Back there, it sounded quite the other way around. Is that what turned you into such an attention seeker?'

'I can't help it if I'm more attractive than she is. She's always been envious of my looks, hasn't been able to get a man in years...' A hand rested on his arm. 'If you ever...' Melody's hand began slow, sensuous stroking. '... need some company...'

James tossed the hand aside. 'You don't care a jot about your sister, do you?' He opened the boot to stash her case. 'I love Harmony so I couldn't possibly be interested in you.'

He realised that was the first time he'd spoken the words out loud. Stupidly, he was saying them to the wrong sister. Surely Harmony would have known how he'd felt? Why else would he have asked her to marry him?

She hadn't said she loved him but the magazine/Tampax incident and how she reacted to his clumsy efforts in the restaurant suggested she did. Very much. He ought to have made a very romantic proposal — and at the right time, not racing ahead because of Alfie. If he'd known Annie wouldn't consider them as adoptive parents, he'd have played it so differently. But he understood Harmony hadn't been allowed to divulge anything—and he'd not be able to tell Tim as he'd be sure to repeat it...

When they were seated, Melody squeezed his thigh. 'I can be very discreet.'

He shivered as ice formed in his heart. What a sister! He bet Melody had been the one who'd lured Harmony's fiancé away—which would explain Harmony's sudden personality change in her sister's presence.

What an idiot he'd been in agreeing to give Melody a lift. No wonder Harmony had looked at him oddly. It had probably brought back memories of her ex's betrayal. Well, James wouldn't betray Harmony. He loved her and no one else, and he would prove it.

He might have been crowned Supreme Idiot of Westbridge but even fools could learn. 'I've changed my mind. I'm ordering you a taxi and, if you touch me again, I'll report you for sexual assault.'

She removed her hand.

He called up the taxi app on his phone and tapped the pay-by-cash option—he wasn't going to risk paying for a fare to Land's End, John O'Groats or wherever she chose to go.

'I can understand,' she purred, 'why you'd want to keep things sweet with Harmony. She's onto a good thing here. Great you don't mind about the cancer. Such a shame she'd been pregnant at the time of the op. I hope you weren't expecting to have children.'

'You don't respect confidentiality, do you?' His jaw ached from clenching his teeth, and it was a gargantuan effort to keep in his seat. So he got out to wait—and ensure Melody did get in that taxi.

She opened the front passenger seat, and James went to stand guard. 'You're a real troublemaker, aren't you? I hope, after tonight, neither Harmony nor I ever set eyes on you again.'

Harmony was too wound up for curling up in bed and wanted to vent some steam. From her hiding position on the floor behind the locked office door, her ears ached from listening out for Candy's return.

Eventually, there was the pressing of the keypad and then the door opened. Candy switched the lights on.

Harmony squinted against the sudden brilliance. 'Hi.'

Candy squealed.

'Sorry for scaring you. How's Patrik?'

She waved a hand. 'Just a sprain. What's up?'

'Is anyone around?'

After Candy checked the hallway, she shut the door. 'All clear.' As she sat on the nearest chair, she wore an expression of concern. 'Why are you on the floor in the dark?'

'Melody came.'

'That woman! What did she want? After the last time...' Candy tutted, the strands of her short, twisted curls waving as she shook her head.

'Same thing. Brought luggage.'

'Boyfriend chuck her out?'

'Either that,' Harmony muttered, 'or she lost her job again.' Melody had never settled in one place for long. 'She told everyone I had no womb and that's why I can't have children.'

Candy joined her on the floor, stretching out her legs. 'Ooh, Harmony. She's nasty, through and through.'

'Yes. James offered to drive her to the station.'

'He was standing by his car when I drove in.'

'Really? Did you see Melody?'

'Nope, but the passenger door was open. I didn't stop to talk as I parked by the side entrance.' Candy peered out of the window. 'He's still there. Checking his watch. I bet he's called a taxi.'

Harmony tensed. 'Oh. I thought she was well clear of

the place... I wonder why he changed his mind. The way she was dressed... she looked so pretty, and his wife had been blonde and slim, so she's likely just his type. I know what Melody's like. Mistress of seduction.'

'James wouldn't fall for cheap tricks.'

For a moment, Harmony was back in that church with no groom. 'I completely trusted David. Yet the unthinkable happened. When he moved out, he took the crocheted blanket Nana had given me when I'd graduated from university. It must have taken her ages to make, and it was so beautiful. Floral patterns inside different border designs, all in pastel colours. How could he have done that?'

'Did you ask for it back?'

'I didn't want anything to do with him, and I didn't have the heart to tell my parents. Nana had died by that time.'

'He and your sister sound a right pair,' Candy said.

Harmony sniffed. 'James asked me to marry him—because he thought it would give us a good chance of adopting Alfie. Tim worked it out and told him, you see, after Annie, for some reason, took photos of Alfie in front of the whole orchestra. James hasn't said he loves me, and I can't settle for a lukewarm groom who might back off.'

Candy was shaking her head. 'No, no, no... His offer of marriage wouldn't just be for Alfie.'

Harmony hoped Candy was right. 'I need James to say he loves me—and I'd love a wedding where the groom actually turns up. But I... I can't bear the thought of spending another wedding night snipping up another dress.'

'You cut up your dress?'

That night in the empty apartment was so vivid; the loneliness and emptiness about to swallow her up. 'Into what might have been a thousand tiny pieces. Like I felt my heart had been shattered.' Harmony met Candy's gaze. 'If James and Melody have even so much as exchanged phone numbers, nothing will ever happen between James and me.

I'm *never* coming second to her again.'

Perhaps she should have told him about Melody at dinner, but Harmony had thought it had been a date and her sister's name had no place when on a date, especially a first date.

'I need to get to bed,' she said.

'You're not waiting for James to come back in?'

In a thin voice, she said, 'There's been too much drama tonight already. I could probably benefit from a week in a sensory deprivation tank.'

As she opened the office door, there was the not-so-rare sight of Nia's back and pumping feet racing towards the stairs, a drawing book in her hands. Harmony remembered she'd promised to look at her latest likeness of the farm cat that strolled the grounds. The girl hadn't heard everything, had she?

Of course she had; she was Nia.

43

When James arrived back at the Hall, Candy let him in.

'Is Harmony around?' Might she be in the sensory room?

Candy shook her head regretfully. 'Gone to bed.'

He just *had* to see Harmony. To let her know he'd guessed about Melody being the one to cheat with her ex-fiancé, to apologise for the messed-up proposal. 'I was hoping to talk about what happened...'

Candy shook her head.

'Her sister—I sent her off in a taxi. She's toxic, isn't she?'

'She certainly is.' Candy tapped her watch. 'It's time Tim was in bed.'

'I... messed up. Proposing to Harmony.'

Candy nodded sympathetically. 'Perhaps you can un-mess it up?'

In the cottage hallway, Tim railed at James. 'You messed up, Dad! You messed up!'

James's body felt so heavy with regret, every movement and word spoken was an effort. 'Please don't talk to me like that.' Surely Tim didn't know about the disastrous proposal?

In a daze, James managed to grope his way to a kitchen chair. He'd tried calling Harmony while waiting for his son to be found, but her phone had been busy. It wasn't her phone that should have been engaged…

Tim sat opposite. 'Nia waited outside the office to show Harmony a drawing of the cat she'd done—it was really good. But when she heard—'

James supported his head in his hands. 'Heard what?'

'She said Harmony had cut her wedding dress up into tiny pieces, and if you've even swapped phone numbers with her sister, she'll never have you! She's not coming second best to Melody again.'

So James's instinct about Melody had been correct. 'Melody's a nasty piece of work. I'm not interested in her.'

'Nia said you didn't say you loved Harmony. You do love her, don't you?'

'I thought you were anti-feelings?'

Tim stamped his foot. 'Feelings are *everything*, and we're all getting hurt because of you!'

James rubbed his gritty eyes. 'I want to make it clear. I'm not offering marriage to Harmony just so we can adopt Alfie. It's because I *do* love her enormously. Even if she says yes, it doesn't mean social services would approve us. Remember what happened with Patience? I don't want you to end up heartbroken.'

Tim was likely to end up heartbroken anyway, and poor Alfie. They'd all be sad, wishing for what could not be.

James regretted not telling Harmony how much he loved her. But if he *had* started with the romance, and she'd accepted his offer of marriage, it still could have gone terribly wrong. She might have felt manipulated the moment he'd brought up the subject of adopting Alfie.

The only way James could have safely expressed his and Tim's hope of adopting Alfie would have been if Harmony had accepted a very romantic and loving proposal and then brought up the subject *herself*. Except it didn't seem her job would have allowed her to or that she and James fitted whatever criteria Annie had in mind, making the whole thing pointless.

Was this a *Catch-22* situation? He'd read the book in his teens.

His heart was burning and sinking into the depths of hell. 'Well, Tim, do you have any bright ideas?'

Tim's mouth opened wide. 'You want *me* to help *you*?'

'Yes. What do you suggest?'

With a puckered brow and squinting eyes, he had an air of concentration James was familiar with.

'I don't know. Isn't that your job?'

James recalled how much Harmony liked puzzles. 'I've an idea. But I'll need your help. It's going to be hard to pull it off.' It would involve so many people...

'What's the idea?'

James explained.

'Wow, Dad. That's brilliant.'

The imaginary honey he'd eaten must have supercharged his brain. Tim's approval meant the world to him. James stood up, holding out his arms. After a brief hesitation, Tim stepped into them.

'I can't do it without you.' James planted a kiss on his son's forehead before they parted. 'I need you and love you so, so much.'

'I know, Dad. I love you too. I won't let you down.'

'Then let's get some paper and plan this thing, work out who's doing what. But Harmony mustn't get wind of it. If it's not a surprise, it'll be a flop.'

'I know. I'll tell them. We all want the same thing. We all want Harmony happy and they like you.'

James's chest filled with warmth. 'They do?'

Tim nodded. 'We'll be like family with them... Unless you mess it up or it doesn't work.'

'It will work.' *It had to.* 'Harmony will be in no doubt that I truly do love her.'

'The fact that you're going to take time off work to do this should convince her. You never play truant.'

'I'm going to use my annual leave. It'll be above board.'

'Of course it will,' Tim said flatly. 'Can I have the day

off to help too?'

It was like déjà vu and James was going to have to refuse again, like he had done on the day of the move. Except this time, it wasn't possible to give a different answer. 'I'm sorry, Tim. You won't have finished your side of things before I have to leave. I'm hoping to make the first drop off in Bristol before my early morning meeting starts.'

Tim sighed. 'All right, but I want to be with you at the end. I want to see what happens.'

'I'm sure you will. It'll take Harmony ages to complete.' But Tim would be so disappointed if it didn't work, and James... well, he'd be utterly broken. He checked his watch. 'I'll call Candy, get her on board. It's late, but I hope under the circumstances...'

He and Candy had exchanged numbers in case of an emergency with Tim. This was an emergency.

44

Harmony lay stretched out on the bed, chatting to Miranda over the phone, empty chocolate wrappers screwed up on her bedside table. She'd called after James's dinner invitation for one of their catch-ups, and Harmony had promised to let her know how the evening had gone. Or hadn't...

'Don't worry,' Miranda said. 'James just proposed to you. So why would he be interested in Melody?'

Because Melody was a siren? 'Well, he changed his mind about driving her so you're probably right. Perhaps she made a pass at him and he saw her for what she is. But when he proposed, he didn't mention love. I don't think that's an unreasonable expectation.' What woman—other than those prioritising pennies and pounds perhaps—would be happy with a proposal that *didn't* mention love?

'Of course it isn't an unreasonable expectation,' Miranda said. 'But wait and see what his next move is.'

'It will need to be convincing...'

'Let's hope he's like a good magician and can pull a rabbit out of the hat.'

Harmony hoped he could find both a rabbit and a hat.

'Just think,' Miranda said, 'you could have regular sex if you're with James.'

Harmony's mind wandered over to the first floor, main bedroom of the cottage. 'I'd hoped sex was going to be an after-dinner treat. Instead, on the way home, I made do with an after-dinner mint.'

Miranda sighed. 'I'd like to have sex, at least once. It would be such a bonus if love were involved.'

Harmony's heart went out to her. 'I hope you find a man who loves you so you can have it more than just the once.'

Harmony was finishing off getting ready, having had a restless night, disturbing herself with the things she'd said to James—and should have said—on their non-date.

There was a quick, double knock at the door.

Candy was outside her apartment. 'Can I come in?'

'Er, yes. Why don't you come into the bedroom? I'm not finished getting ready.'

She scanned the room and went to stand by the dressing table.

A sudden pain in Harmony's chest made her ask, 'Is this about James?'

'He was desperate to talk to you,' Candy said, making her feel worse. 'And you definitely have no worries over Melody.'

'Thanks, it's good to know.' Harmony padded into the en-suite to comb her hair and then poked her head around the door to say, 'I'm pleased he still wants me. But, for marriage, I need to believe he truly loves me.'

Candy started at Harmony's sudden reappearance and began to cough. She reached into her trouser pocket for a tissue, dabbed her mouth and put the tissue back. 'Did you get much sleep last night?'

'Hardly.' Harmony bobbed back into the bathroom to smooth her hair into the scrunchie.

'I think you should take the day off. There's no pressing admin apart from some post on your keyboard that needs to be actioned. Then chill out.'

'Yes, I think you're right.' She could organise more belongings to take to the Dower House.

'Well, I'd better get on,' Candy said and left.

When Harmony went to the dressing table to put on her jewellery, she couldn't find her grandmother's ring. She moved the toiletries, looked under the furniture, in the drawers. Nothing. She searched the medicine cabinet and scanned the surfaces and floor. Even her bedside table yielded only the usual nighttime stuff. She checked under the saga she was reading and the latest puzzle magazine, then gave up and headed for the office.

A white rectangular envelope lay on her keyboard. Her name was written on it with the loops and flourishes James used in the visitor book. So this was the post Candy had referred to?

She slipped a fingernail under the flap, removed the white slip of paper and began to read.

From the moment I first saw you, I was drawn to you like a bee to a nectar-laden flower. A beautiful mother, I'd thought, surrounded by her children, showing love for them all...

The note as a whole didn't make sense. It was as though it was the beginning of a story and then... nothing. She turned it over and then examined the envelope. In the top right-hand corner, there was a small number one. Or had James's pen slipped? Or had he made a mark to check that the pen worked?

She concluded the mark had been deliberate. It was a clue! That would lead to more clues? If so, she hoped they'd be more reliable than the date clues she'd been given yesterday evening.

James must have recalled how much she liked puzzles. She remembered her conversation with Miranda the night before. James had found the hat! A fizzing excitement filled her core, making her spirits soar, her heart pound as she wondered what rabbit she was going to pull out of it at the end because this—if she was not mistaken—was a treasure hunt!

So where was clue number two? She re-read the note. She'd first met James and Tim at the Hall's entrance.

But there was nothing outside—until she turned to come back in and discovered a white envelope taped to the frame of the door bearing the number two.

Having snatched it free, she scurried back into the office to read the contents.

It was clear you truly loved the kids, despite not being their mum. I wish Tim and I had never discovered the cockroach in the library. But, I'm not at all sorry I've become closer to you.

She bit the crook of her finger to stop the threatening tears. The treasure hunt was charting the progress of their relationship, and she was touched by the effort James had expended. Candy must be in on it. The staff too as there was no one around. Tim and the rest of them? She smiled. She bet they all knew about the novel game, and she loved it.

The next place to search had to be the library as that was where James had discovered the cockroach. Sure enough, there was an envelope on the table with a three in the right-hand corner. Harmony carefully opened it so that she could keep the series of envelopes and notes safe.

When I saw you and Luke, coming out of the bathroom together at Perdita's, I was madly jealous.

Surely, James hadn't been to Perdita's to leave the next clue? Harmony re-read the note. No doubt. She called Perdita's mobile.

After saying hello, Harmony said, 'This is a very odd request, but may I take a look outside your upstairs bathroom for something James might have left for me?'

'By all means. But it was Tim, not James, who came.'

So Tim was helping his dad. How fantastic was that?

'Shall I put the kettle back on? It's only just boiled.'

'That's kind of you, but I have a lot to do, and I don't know how many envelopes I'll have to find.'

'I don't know either,' Perdita said. 'It sounds great fun!'

Harmony giggled. 'I know. No one's ever done anything like this for me before.'

It was only a short walk to Perdita's. A little while later,

Harmony was on the driveway approaching the house. Two cars were parked by the bushes.

Perdita opened the front door with a grin before Harmony reached the top step. 'How lovely to see you!'

'Same here.'

They hugged.

'How are you?' Harmony asked.

'Having a great morning. So many visitors so early. It feels like my birthday.'

'Oh, are others here?'

'Just Luke now,' Perdita said. 'He's appointed himself as a guard.'

Harmony frowned. *A guard?*

'I'll come up with you to help you find it.'

Harmony didn't need a guard or any assistance.

'Good morning,' Luke said as she crested the stairs. He was wearing sports leggings, a T-shirt and a hoodie.

'Hi, Luke. I wasn't expecting to see you.'

'Two clients claimed to have emergencies so I came to have a natter before heading off to the gym. When Perdita said you were coming to pick this up,' he indicated the white oblong on the floor, 'I volunteered to guard it against interference.'

Guard it against what? Harmony cocked her head questioningly.

Luke grinned. 'Petal wanted to draw on it, Violet thought it was dropped recycling...'

Violet was Perdita's husband's resident aunt.

'... and Perdita wanted to steam it open,' Luke finished.

'You snitch!' she cried. 'That was a joke!'

'That's why you boiled the kettle?'

'That was part of the joke. To make it more believable.'

'I believed it all right.'

She addressed Harmony, 'I would never steam open someone else's correspondence. It *was* a joke.'

Harmony laughed. 'I believe you.'

'Well, now that Harmony's here, she can satisfy your

curiosity,' Luke said.

'And you're not equally curious?' Perdita asked.

Luke raised his eyebrows. 'Of course, it would be nice to know...'

Harmony retrieved the letter. 'I'm sure that if James wanted you to know what was inside, he wouldn't have sealed it.' She gave an apologetic smile. 'I need to go.'

45

In the car, Harmony opened envelope number four.

It wasn't until we were chatting and solving puzzles together in the café on Whiteladies Road that I truly began to get to know you and the amazing, caring person you are. You'd already started to capture my heart.

A hungry longing grew in her chest. She couldn't wait to finish the game; she wanted to be with him. She *wanted him*.

It took her over half an hour to reach Bristol town centre. Within seconds of entering the café, the server passed envelope five into her hand.

Things were racing along when you asked me to pose as your fiancé by the circular flower bed. I know that when you love, it's with all your heart. I love that about you.

Her heart didn't just skip when she read that James loved something about her, it was as though she'd been trampolined high into the air… It was going to be all right, wasn't it?

On her return from the city centre, she soon spotted a white rectangle protected in a transparent sandwich bag, weighed down by a smooth, grey stone in the circular flower bed. She took out note number six.

I came to see you about the vaping incident but found you in distress in the sensory room. As I held you crying in my arms, I needed you as much as I thought you needed me. I wished so much to make life better for you, to heal your wounds. You'd already started to heal mine.

Her throat swelled as she recalled the strength of James's arms about her. She'd have happily clung to him all night, despite barely knowing him. But in the sensory room, he hadn't felt at all like a stranger. He'd felt warm and comforting, the kindness he'd shown her settling deep in her heart.

James had dropped off the envelope at the café on Whiteladies Road very early that morning, before his meeting—but that had overrun. Although he'd since been to Under the Stars tapas restaurant, would he manage the rest in time?

He called Candy. 'Hello. Do you know how far along Harmony's got? I'm concerned I won't be back before her.'

'She's just found the note in the flower bed.'

His heart dived as fast as an osprey after its next meal. 'It's too late then to make clue number seven harder to find? I've yet to get to Clifton for a ring and the traffic's a nightmare.'

'Don't worry, it's already going to be a challenge, and she's not got anything else planned for the day—she won't be in any hurry.'

There were three more clues for Harmony to find before needing to go to Under the Stars. By that time, he should be back in Westbridge and the ring would be on her bed...

Harmony hurried past Candy in the office; she didn't have time to chat. With the sensory room at maximum brightness, Harmony cast about her for the seventh envelope. She searched the easiest places first, then headed for the box where the sensory toys were stored. Had it fallen between the gaps?

By the time almost all the toys had been removed, she realised it had been a wasted effort. The other letters had revealed themselves with relative ease so it was frustrating that her labours had so far yielded no reward. Becoming convinced she had an audience, she flung the door open and caught Candy spying through the one-way mirror.

Harmony clutched Candy's arm. 'Where is it?'

'I...'

'Please? Help me?'

'Why the rush? It's meant to be fun.'

'It is fun, *enormous* fun, but I must be done before four as I've got an appointment.' Roxy had called to confirm the arrangements for handing over Joshua. 'At this rate, I'm not going to get all the clues.'

'What appointment?'

'It's personal, but I can't miss it. I have to be there, envelopes or not. Now, will you help me?'

Candy must have read the urgency in Harmony's face as she slowly nodded. 'Fine. You're cold. In fact, you're freezing.'

So Harmony walked towards the back of the room.

'Getting warmer.'

She made for the far-right corner so that she could work her way along the back wall.

'Colder.'

She headed for the left corner.

'Warmer... very warm. In fact, you're hot now.'

But she'd already searched the toy box. Half-heartedly, she picked up a toy she'd shifted before.

'Not so warm now.'

That was a relief. It had been a dampening prospect to have to take the toys out again. Perhaps it was under a mat next to the toy box?

'Even colder.'

Candy had got to be kidding? *Under the toy box?*

'You're hot now,' she said as Harmony dragged the toy box to a new position.

Raising the mat it had stood on, she peeked underneath.

'You're boiling now.'

She certainly was. Sweat had formed in her hair, prickling and tickling. But she'd got envelope number seven. She gave Candy a quick hug and went into the office to peruse her new finding.

The kids came to the cottage in support of Tim. The calm way you handled the vaping situation showed me that you are incredibly special. Harmony, I <u>need</u> you in my life.

Wow. He *needed* her. Well, she needed him too...

Short of time, she drove to James's cottage. The place appeared empty. She imagined him spending the day navigating streets like a lead in an action racing film, dodging obstacles, going down one-way streets, launching across water—to leave the notes for her. He'd gone to so much effort...

Envelope number eight was taped to his doorstep.

I sorely regret not encouraging you to buy Brides magazine. I'd love you to go back and get it now. Perhaps we could look at it together?

He was clearly repeating his proposal—and he'd used the word love again.

When she entered the newsagents, Ramesh was grinning. Although that wasn't unusual, the tone of the grin was different.

'Hello, Harmony, how are you today?'

'Good thanks. You?'

His grin was still plastered across his face. 'Very good.'

'I've come in search of an envelope.'

'Envelope? We sell many kinds.' Ramesh pointed. 'Shelf next to the magazines.'

'One that James might have left for me?'

He shook his head, but his lips were still stretched to the maximum.

'Perhaps someone else left an envelope for me on his behalf? With a number nine on it?'

'Oooh,' he said, overdoing the surprise element, 'do you mean this?' He plucked it out of a drawer under the counter.

'Yes, thanks.'

Ramesh grinned again. 'Tim came this morning, before school.'

Tim's involvement meant so much to her.

'James suggested I should buy the magazine you recommended... And I'd like a bottle of water and this...' She held up a Galaxy bar she'd picked from the display under the counter. Much better than a box of tampons.

'Will you set a date soon then?'

She smiled, shrugged and handed over the money.

'Will you let me know when you have? I do love a wedding.'

'*If* there's a wedding, I'll make sure you get an invitation.'

Somehow, Ramesh's wide grin became even wider, exposing his gums.

Back in the car, she read note number nine.

It had been a magical day out with the kids on the trip to see the animals. It felt like we were a family. But I know it wasn't a magical evening at Under the Stars. It would be lovely if we could go back to make better memories. Heart-warming ones.

Reading the note itself warmed her heart. But it also became heavy because she wasn't sure she'd have time to drive to the Floating Harbour and back before four. Should she call a taxi for the driver to fetch the envelope?

46

James had discovered there were two jewellers with onsite workshops in Clifton, which meant there'd be a goldsmith to alter the ring size if necessary. He squirmed at the memory of what he'd asked Candy to do; he hoped Harmony would understand. *But it had been her grandmother's ring...*

In the first jeweller's shop, the only man serving was occupied with a customer dithering over necklaces. James browsed the rings on display and went back onto the street to look at some more. None of them stood out as "the one". So he headed for the other establishment.

Harmony had decided she must—as far as she could—play the game as James had intended. He'd gone to so much trouble, he'd be hurt, and she'd feel awful, if she used a taxi service to retrieve the next envelope. She knew she must complete the hunt without cheating and was already well on her way to Bristol's Floating Harbour. If she ended up being a few minutes late for Joshua's handover—which also seemed a terrible thing to happen—she'd let Roxy know. But after the restaurant, she'd have to drive straight back to the Dower House, no matter what.

When James entered the second jeweller's, a woman with short, brown hair in a puffy pink anorak was being served by an elderly man in a suit. The name badge identified him as Donald. She'd brought in a gold watch that apparently had something wrong with the clasp.

James was gratified to see a young, sandy-haired man with the name Wayne on his badge appear from the back of the shop.

'How may I help?' he asked.

'I'm looking for an engagement ring that I can take home today.' James fished out the ring Candy had purloined from Harmony's room. 'This will give you the lady's ring size—I understand you can make alterations on the spot?'

He hoped that the third finger on Harmony's right hand matched her left.

'Donald does have a number of jobs waiting,' Wayne said.

The other customer turned to James. 'Including mine. My employer's keen to get her watch back.'

'I'd be happy to gift a box of chocolates for the inconvenience if she allows my alteration before—'

The customer's expression was stony. 'I'm the one who'd be standing here, waiting.'

'Of course.' He changed tack. 'I'd be quite happy to gift *you* the chocolates. Or a box to each of you.' Was there also a family that might be inconvenienced? 'I need the ring as a matter of urgency.'

Her stony expression remained.

Now that he'd had time to take in her appearance, he suspected he'd seen her somewhere before. But she'd shown no particular interest in him, so he must be mistaken. All the same...

He addressed Donald. 'I'll pay a premium to get any necessary adjustment carried out straight away.'

'My employer has been a long-standing customer of this establishment,' the woman said, 'and I will not step aside for you.'

'I wouldn't want to keep a valued customer like Mrs Gold waiting unnecessarily.' Donald took the watch into the back of the shop.

Mrs Gold... There must be many Mrs Golds. But not one where her assistant was someone he thought he recognised.

'Do I know you?' she asked. 'You keep staring at me.'

'You look familiar.' Where could he have seen her? 'You weren't at one of Perdita's get-togethers, were you? With Judith Gold?'

'Well, yes...'

He held out his hand. 'James.'

Boggle-eyed, she said, '*James?* As in Westbridge James?'

Westbridge James? Well, it was up from being the Supreme Idiot of Westbridge—a title he hoped soon to ditch forever. 'I don't believe I've had the pleasure...'

'No one has,' Miranda said.

'*Sorry?*'

'Oh, er, I'm Miranda.' Her grip was strong.

She appeared to expect a reaction when she'd said her name. 'You seem to know more about me than I do of you.'

'Harmony hasn't mentioned me?'

'*You're a friend of Harmony's?* Oh... er, this is rather awkward. The ring is for her.'

Miranda's eyes bulged even more. If he hadn't known it was from surprise, he'd have suspected her of having a serious medical condition. 'But I thought...'

'Yes?'

She appeared confused. 'It doesn't matter.'

'I need to be back in Westbridge before her so I can give it as part of a surprise. Timing is crucial.

'May I suggest,' Wayne said, 'that sir chooses a ring and then we can determine whether it needs to be adjusted?'

'Good idea.'

While he was unlocking a drawer, James said to Miranda, 'My son and I set up a treasure hunt, and the treasure needs to be in place before Harmony gets to the end of it. Our future together depends on it.'

Her bulging eyes were safely back in place and were now lit like sparklers. 'I'll do everything I can to help.'

'Thanks, I appreciate that.'

Wayne presented a display of stunning platinum diamond rings. 'Although our readymade pieces represent a small selection of what we can provide, we do have them in a variety of sizes.'

The moment James spotted it, he felt sure he'd found "the one". 'May I take a closer look at this one?'

Miranda leaned forward with apparent interest.

'I think this is it,' he said as he held it up to the light. The ring was exquisite, and he could totally imagine it on Harmony's finger.

'Why do you think this is "the one"?' Miranda asked.

James turned sharply to face her. 'Is this some kind of test?'

She shrugged. 'I'm a nosy friend with an insatiable curiosity.'

Should he give it a go to see if Miranda agreed with his thinking? 'Well,' he said, licking his lips in the hope it would somehow oil his brain at the same time. 'A smaller ring might not stand out so well on her finger, whereas this one's centre diamond is big enough to give a good sparkle. But it's not so big as to be ostentatious—Harmony's far from that.

'And these shoulders with the triple diamonds mounted in petal-shaped settings make the ring look more like a flower. But a delicate one. The petals only sit over the ring, they don't go around in a full circle. So it's an elegant, streamlined look. It would suit Harmony's simple lifestyle, yet it's far more interesting than a single diamond on its own.'

'Everything you said is true,' Miranda said, in what sounded like awe.

Although he couldn't imagine Harmony not liking such a ring, tastes varied and he shouldn't assume. He glanced at Wayne. 'If the lady doesn't like—'

'You can exchange it within seven days if it's returned in perfect condition.'

'I'm sure she'll love it,' Miranda said, with more than a hint of envy in her voice.

James smiled at her. 'Thanks.' To Wayne, he said, 'I'll take it. Now about the size...'

Harmony charged to Under the Stars restaurant, retrieved envelope number ten from someone who'd been wiping tables and belted back to the car. She read the note:

I wholeheartedly love you and can't imagine life without you. I hope you'll believe how much I love you when you get to the room I've never seen.

Her heart flipped. He'd said the words. Her stomach flipped too. But there was still something that could go wrong...

The car was now in gear and moving homewards, the remaining third of the Galaxy bar in her stretched mouth. She glimpsed the clock on the dashboard. Was it called that as people did lots of dashing?

If Joshua's handover at the Dower House went ahead as planned, she must speak to James before she went to her bedroom at the Hall and claimed what she suspected would be a ring. After all, it was a treasure hunt...

Wayne had compared the selected ring to Harmony's grandmother's ring and had gone out to the back to find a closer size.

James tapped his foot while waiting for the man to come back.

Wayne returned. 'A slight adjustment will be required. The next size down is the closest we've got. Would you like us to enlarge it?'

'Yes, as quickly as you can, please.'

'The watch repair can be paused,' Miranda said.

James smiled gratefully. 'Thanks.'

'We can either stretch it or add a little extra platinum,' Wayne said.

'Which is faster?'

'We'll stretch it, shall we?'

James nodded, but after Wayne disappeared, he worried he'd made the wrong decision.

Miranda must have noticed as she said, 'Don't worry, it'll be fine. It'll look great.'

Wayne returned without the ring.

'Will it be too thin, if it's stretched?' James asked.

'Not with our rings.'

He checked his phone. He'd put it to silence before entering the first shop, and now he saw there was a text message from Candy: *H got an appointment in Westbridge at 4. You need to hurry.*

It was almost four now. Had Harmony already collected the clue he'd left at Under the Stars? Well, even if she had, she would be delayed getting to her room because of her appointment. If she'd made it to her room, Candy would have surely told him. So he still had a chance, hadn't he?

After the alteration was complete, James paid a princely sum and pocketed the rings.

'I hope she says yes,' Miranda said as he opened the door to the street.

He flashed a grin. 'Me too. I'll get you a huge box of chocolates. You deserve it.'

'Thanks.'

'And Mrs Gold?' he asked.

'No need. I'd have to explain I'd let you jump the queue. She's not known for being accommodating.' Miranda's cheeks reddened. 'As you saw, I've learned a lot from her...'

'Well, it didn't stop you from becoming friends with Harmony.'

She smiled. 'No, it didn't. Harmony's great.'

'That's why I want to put a ring on her finger.' He checked his watch. *Oh, dear! Oh dear! I shall be late!...* as Lewis Carroll's White Rabbit in *Alice in Wonderland* had apparently said.

When James had been at school, he'd been good at

sprinting, so he put on a spurt to get back to the car while hoping Harmony's appointment was a lengthy one.

He should have taken the whole day off. Perhaps he ought to listen to his son more often—he'd been making a lot of sense lately.

47

As Harmony drove by James's cottage to turn into the Hall's approach, she noticed the absence of his car. She hoped he'd be back by the time Joshua's handover was complete so they could talk about the baby before she went to find the treasure.

She pulled up behind a van and Roxy's car in front of the Dower House; there was no need for secrecy now. Roxy was standing with Joshua in her arms next to a blond-haired man. Her pale, makeup-free face revealed a sprinkling of freckles across her nose and her eyes were red-rimmed. Even her clothes appeared sad; wrinkled chinos and a misshapen short coat.

Although she'd made it on time, Harmony worried all the same. 'I'm sorry, have you been waiting long? I had to get back from Bristol.'

'It's fine,' Roxy said. 'It's only been a few minutes.'

Joshua kicked his legs and waved his arms. He was such a cutie.

'Hello, Joshua!' Harmony smiled, taking a brief hold of his little chubby fingers inside his green mittens. She'd have liked to have taken him for a cuddle but this was not the time.

'This is Tony,' Roxy said, 'and Tony, this is Harmony.'
'Money!'

Harmony shook Tony's hand and they exchanged

greetings.

'It's a great thing you're doing, for Roxy,' he said. 'If she'd had to leave him with anyone else...' He shook his head.

It was good he was so supportive. 'I'm delighted to have Joshua.'

He reached into the van and picked up a collapsed playpen.

'Do you mind if we get this done quickly?' Roxy's words were unsteady as they went inside, her expression pinched. 'Otherwise, it's just stringing out the agony.'

Harmony's heart went out to her, and she placed a hand on Roxy's arm. 'Of course not. You haven't changed your mind?'

She shook her head. 'It's hard, so terribly hard, but I'm still certain it's the right thing to do. So that list of all Joshua's things I sent you... Could you show Tony where you'd like everything to go?'

'Yes, of course.'

It took seconds for him to unfold the playpen in the living room.

'I'll show you where to put the cot,' Harmony said, 'and I'll bring in the less bulky things while you're putting it back together.'

Roxy was with Joshua on the sofa, nuzzling his face while he grasped locks of her hair between his mittened thumb and fingers. Harmony shut the living room door behind her and Tony to give her friend some privacy.

'The stuff that's not labelled is Roxy's,' Tony said.

'Okay.'

When the last of the tasks was completed, they gathered outside.

'I know you'll look after him well and treasure him.' Although Roxy spoke calmly, sadness showed in her eyes. 'I've changed my mind about contact. Can I call you later or tomorrow to see how he's settling in?'

'Of course.' Harmony's words came out thickly, like

cold, gloopy custard.

'I'll be back to see him soon.'

She squeezed Roxy's arm. 'Whenever you want.'

Roxy closed her eyes as she gave Joshua a big kiss, and he turned towards his mum to touch her cheek with his mittened hand. Then she passed him into Harmony's arms.

Having a baby, a little boy, to bring up just didn't feel real. 'Thank you,' she whispered, 'with all my heart, I thank you.' She choked on the words, a sob escaping her mouth. Her joy was at Roxy's emotional expense.

Roxy outstretched her arms and they hugged. She kissed Joshua's cheek again. Tears were streaming down her face, which turned Harmony's emotional tap on full.

Tony put an arm around Roxy. 'Are you sure this is what you want?'

'I am.' She wiped her eyes and assumed a stiff, stoical expression, her lips firmly closed, but the tremble in her chin was still discernible.

Harmony had to trust that this was what Roxy—the greatest friend Harmony hadn't known she'd had—truly wanted, and they would be a team. 'Will you be all right, driving your car?'

Roxy gave a bitter laugh. 'Don't you know, I'm as hard as nails?'

'I know that's not true.'

'Well, I was and... well, for the journey at least, I will be again. I'm so grateful for my freedom—and now I won't have to worry about what's become of him. I'll know he's safe with you.'

After the final farewells, she and Tony turned the vehicles around and drove away. Harmony bet that, once Roxy had got to her new home, she'd become inconsolable. But she'd have Tony to comfort her, help her get settled. She wouldn't go through the separation alone.

As Joshua watched her leave, he began to cry.

Harmony kissed the top of his head. 'It's okay. Mummy will be back soon. Mummy will always be in your life.'

The softness of his smooth wet skin pulled at her heart. Inhaling deeply, she shut her eyes and breathed in his baby scent. Stroking his back eased his sharp breaths, and she took him to the sofa to cuddle him until he was completely calm.

Joshua was hers to take care of and she must find James. As she stepped out of the house, she saw him running across the road with Tim in his wake and her heart gave a somersault. James had probably only just arrived home. Had Tim been waiting outside the cottage for him?

'James!'

He gave a startled double-take as they approached. 'Oh, I'd hoped to be back before you—' His expression appeared perturbed. A hand went to his pocket as he turned to Tim, as though he intended to pass something to him.

'The treasure hunt—it's been fantastic—'

'You've not got to the end already, have you?' His eyebrows pulled together above wide eyes and his hand returned to his side. 'I've been so scared I'll mess up again.'

She reached out to touch him. 'No, you haven't messed up at all, quite the opposite. I haven't got to the end yet, but I must tell you something first.' Her breath caught in her throat.

Faint lines on James's forehead deepened. 'What is it?'

'It's about Joshua, the baby.'

'He's called Joshua? So it's no longer a state secret?'

She gave a tentative smile. 'As of a few minutes ago, I'm free to talk about him. I'll be raising him as his special guardian.' Her stomach clenched as she waited for his response, searched his face—and Tim's.

They exchanged puzzled glances.

'It means I'll be bringing him up,' she explained. 'But not as his mother. If the court approves. Does my having Joshua make a difference to the end of the treasure hunt?'

James laughed. 'You know I love babies!'

She laughed too, and Tim grinned. Joshua, picking up the happy vibes, chuckled for the first time since his mother had left.

James leaned in to kiss her lips. 'Having this gorgeous baby doesn't make even the slightest difference... I thought you had a real make-or-break issue... But, as it is, I'm thrilled.'

'Me too,' Tim said. 'But Dad...'

James patted his pocket. 'Tim, do you think you could—'

Tim tugged at James's sleeve, nodding towards the Hall. *'Dad!'*

The mirth that had bubbled inside Harmony evaporated. 'Oh, no.'

Social Worker Annie, marching ever closer, must have been visiting the Hall and spotted them.

Edvard Grieg's Peer Gynt Suite No. 1 *In the Hall of the Mountain King* began to play in Harmony's mind. It picked up speed as Annie got nearer, increasing the sense of threat and doom. Surely she couldn't object to Harmony keeping Joshua? She'd got the legal side started, was following his mother's wishes, moving into the Dower House, cutting her hours.

'Annie,' Harmony said, 'I wasn't expecting you.'

'I took the opportunity to check in on you and meet this little fellow.' Annie reached out to touch the baby's hand. 'Who exactly is this little chap?'

'I've applied to be his special guardian.'

'I know. The letter from your solicitor was passed on to me. Harmony, I need—'

'Money!' Joshua shouted.

Annie pulled her head back in surprise.

Tim laughed. 'It's his name for her. He can't say it right.'

Everyone else smiled, including Annie. 'How sweet. I'd thought he'd somehow developed a bigger understanding of how the world worked.'

Harmony grinned. 'No, but he's very bright, great with puzzles.'

Annie nodded kindly.

Much preferring this version of the social worker, Harmony asked, 'What is it you need?'

'To know more about the situation. Who is Joshua to you?'

'I'm good friends with his mother.'

Laughing, James put his arm around Harmony. 'Tim and I couldn't be happier that we've been given this opportunity to have Joshua in the family as well.'

'Yeah.' Tim came to stand the other side of her. 'Can I hold him?'

Was this a show of solidarity for Annie's benefit? 'Remember how heavy you found him before when you held him,' Harmony warned. 'So be ready to take his weight.' Now Annie would know that this was not Tim's first involvement with the baby.

She studied James's face. 'Who exactly is the mother?'

He grinned, giving a good impression of being relaxed at the sudden interrogation. 'I'll let Harmony tell you. It's her story, after all.'

Harmony burbled through the information in the solicitor's letter. 'His mum is Roxanne Codd, the vicar's wife. She and Matt have separated and Roxy's unable to manage Joshua on her own and does not wish to. She wants me to bring him up, and I agreed.' Phew. Now James knew the background.

Annie's lips tightened. 'Mm... Where's his mother now?'

'On her way to London where she'll be living.'

She appeared to absorb the information.

Now or never... 'There's something I'd like to ask,' Harmony blurted. Since Annie had been indiscreet when she'd photographed Alfie so publicly, the cat was out of the bag anyway—the worst she could say was no. 'James and I would love to adopt Alfie. We all get on so well...'

Annie glanced pointedly at Harmony's unadorned left hand. 'Alfie needs parents who are an established couple.

You're not even living together.'

'They will be,' Tim said. 'They'll be married soon, won't you, Dad? Show Annie the ring.'

When James fished in his pocket before producing a cube-shaped box, Annie's eyebrows launched the furthest up her brow Harmony had ever seen them. Dropping her gaze to the box, she managed to lean in before Annie as the lid flipped open, but Tim's head also dipped, head-butting the social worker.

She rubbed her forehead. 'Ouch.'

'Sorry,' Tim said.

'It should fit perfectly now,' James assured.

From the brief glimpse, Harmony had seen that the ring was lovely. As he slipped it onto her finger, she met his intensely blue eyes. John Donne's words came back to her. She was no longer an island. Together, she and James would find their way in life with the support of family and friends, and her whole being filled with confidence. Everything was going to be fine. More than fine. Fantastic.

Glancing down, she admired the stunning glints in the central diamond, rocking it to pick up the light.

'The size wasn't quite right,' James said. 'Harmony lent me her grandmother's wedding ring so that the jeweller could adjust it.' He fished in his wallet before presenting the second ring.

Dazed, she placed it on the third finger of her right hand before realising the significance of Candy's unusual early morning visit, coughing by the dressing table with the handkerchief over her mouth. That was probably where she'd hidden the ring when Harmony had unexpectedly peered out of the en-suite.

'Let me take Joshua,' James said to Tim. 'He might be getting too heavy for you.'

Annie watched Joshua's reaction. When the baby happily started pulling at James's hair again, showing no signs of anxiety, she appeared satisfied. She sniffed as she glanced over to the cottage. 'Alfie would need to have his own room. Joshua too.'

'Harmony's got the Dower House,' Tim said.

'Money!'

'It's my home for life. James and Tim are helping me move in.'

'Then we're moving in,' Tim said.

Harmony blinked at the sudden surge forward in her relationship with James and almost burst out laughing. It was like the fake engagement all over again, but this was so much more serious. One wrong move now might make it go horribly wrong for Alfie...

'Are you going to sell the cottage?' Annie asked.

'He's not sure,' Harmony said, at the same time as James said, 'No.'

'You do need to get your stories straight.'

'We're making it up as we go along,' she said by way of excuse.

Annie fixed her with a hard stare. 'I can see that.'

James coughed. 'What Harmony means is that we keep discussing our plans but we haven't come to any firm decision yet.'

Annie's expression was inscrutable. 'Well, perhaps Tim could give me a tour of your new home?' Switching her gaze to rest on the boy, she added, 'I'd love to see your room and where Joshua is going to sleep.'

That was going to be a tall order since Tim had never been inside before. Clearly Annie was still suspicious.

'You're more than welcome to look around,' Harmony told her, 'but Tim's not quite made up his mind as to which room he'd prefer. Joshua's cot is in the smallest bedroom.'

'Then Tim can show me his options and tell me what he thinks about them.'

There was the sound of light, rapid feet on gravel and her gaze shifted. Alfie was sprinting towards them.

'We're showing Annie Harmony's house,' Tim called out. 'Where we're all going to live together.'

Harmony exclaimed, 'Tim! Nothing's been decided,' at

the same time as Annie said, 'I don't think it's appropriate at this stage to include...' She trailed off when Alfie joined them and pushed into the Dower House ahead of them.

'Harmony's got a piano, there's a big TV on the living room wall and there are *four* bedrooms.'

'Alfie,' Harmony said, 'I don't know what Tim's said to you—'

Annie smiled. 'Let him be. This is the most vocal I've heard him.' Addressing the boy, she said in a soft tone, 'Would you like to show me around?'

'Can I live here?' he asked.

'It's not up to me,' Annie said. 'But... it's not impossible.'

48

The tour must have satisfied Annie that the Dower House was going to meet their current and future needs as she said, 'I'll pop in about this time next Thursday to see how you're all settling in.'

'That's fine,' Harmony said. It had to be; she couldn't put Annie off.

What did James think? She didn't dare glance his way as Annie might pick up on the fact something was off.

'Can Alfie move in too?' Tim asked.

Alfie jumped up and down, aiming pleading eyes at Annie.

Her face softened as she spoke to him. 'Harmony and James would have to be approved as adoptive parents first. Then your case would need to go to the matching panel. Only if that stage is reached can you move in. It can be a long process and there is no guarantee...'

Annie turned to Harmony. 'I'll bring some paperwork next week, including consent forms for sharing relevant data with relevant professionals.'

'Of course,' Harmony said. 'I'm happy to share anything.'

'I suspected you might say that,' Annie said with a sudden grin.

But Harmony couldn't see the joke. Had there been a joke?

As Annie was leaving, Candy showed up. 'I've come to see what's going on. Is there a problem?'

'No problem,' Annie told her. 'I'll visit next week after Harmony, James, Tim and Joshua have had a chance to settle in—and I'll bring the necessary paperwork to kick things off regarding Alfie.' Then she left.

Candy's gaze burned into Harmony. 'What is going on, and how come I don't know anything about it?'

'We've asked Annie if we can adopt Alfie,' Harmony said, 'and she didn't say no.' She stepped back to allow Candy in. 'Come and sit down.'

They all sat on the corner sofa. Joshua began babbling on James's lap, attentively looking from one face to the next.

Candy's gaze rested on Joshua. 'What's he doing back here?'

'I'm going to be Joshua's special guardian. I can tell you now that his mum is Roxy, the vicar's wife.' Harmony turned to James. 'I'm so sorry I couldn't tell you about it either—I had to keep my promise. Do you mind?'

'You don't mind, do you, Dad?' Tim sounded desperate for everything to work out with no last-minute hitches.

'Well, of course I'd have liked to have been told.' James turned to Harmony. 'But I'd guessed Joshua might end up living with you.'

'I would have preferred to have been told too,' Candy said. 'But I understand the situation was very sensitive. What will happen about The Reverend?'

'He's very welcome to visit Joshua.'

'Harmony's marrying Dad,' Tim said. 'And we're all going to be a family.'

Harmony glanced at James and then back at Tim. 'You know, I need to have a chat with your dad before we—'

Candy pointed. 'But you're wearing a ring. A very nice ring. With that other one you've found.'

Harmony laughed. 'You were so sneaky this morning, taking it.'

Candy pulled a rueful expression. 'Sorry.'

'It's fine, but I did panic for a while.'

'Blame me,' James said. 'I was—'

'It's all right, everything's fine now.' More than fine. It was wonderful. 'The ring was put on my finger earlier to appease Annie. We still need to talk about it.'

'Do you think,' he said, 'we could have some time alone? I don't believe what happened outside with Annie breathing down our necks counts as a marriage proposal and acceptance either.'

'Are you going to marry my dad or not?' Tim asked heatedly.

Of course she was, but she wanted to tell that to James first, in private.

He motioned for the others to go. 'Leave it to me.'

'Come boys,' Candy said. 'And let's take Joshua back with us.'

'No!' Harmony had only just got him, and he'd been unsettled earlier. It could confuse him. What if he cried, and she wasn't there to console him?

'I understand how you feel, but you need this time to talk to James. Properly. I'll bring Joshua back the moment you call—or you can come and get him.'

'What if he starts crying?'

'If I can't soothe him quickly, I'll give you a call to let you know he's coming back.'

'We'll play with him and help him eat,' Tim said. 'He likes me.'

It would help Joshua bond with Tim...

'You know it makes sense,' Candy said. 'It's only for a short time, and he knows the Hall, the library. Tim and Alfie can eat in there with him. He'll enjoy it.'

Torn, Harmony didn't know what to do.

'Let's see if he cries when I pick him up,' Candy suggested.

Joshua didn't fret.

'Now I'll put him in the buggy and we'll see if that

upsets him.'

Joshua was fine.

'Let me push him,' Tim said. 'He knows me.'

'Me too,' Alfie said. 'I want to push him too.'

It appeared the decision was made. Well, it wouldn't be long before Joshua would learn where he was living and who his main caregivers would be.

'Does he have a travel bag?' Candy asked.

Tim said, 'It's the striped one in the hall. I'll get it.'

Harmony accompanied them out of the living room with James following, holding her newly adorned hand.

Tim picked up the travel bag. 'When can we start packing, Dad? Can we move in tonight?'

Harmony couldn't help grinning at Tim. It seemed like the usual obstacles put in the way of blending families weren't going to apply.

'Let's talk about practicalities later,' James suggested. 'I'll come and get you.'

Tim shrugged and then left with Alfie and Candy—and Joshua strapped in the buggy.

'About Melody,' James said when the door shut. 'She made a pass at me, and I got out of the car and called a taxi.'

'I was worried because I know what she's like—and was like, with David. But you've put all my fears to rest. Thanks for seeing her off the premises.'

'I guessed she was the one he cheated with. She's toxic.'

'She is.' Harmony returned to the sofa with James, their knees touching. 'I'd like to know what's real because a lot was said in front of Annie…'

'Well, if you're in agreement…' Tenderly, he took hold of her hand. 'It appears that I, Tim, and probably Alfie sometime in the future, are moving in—and you and I will be getting married. But first, let me say something about yesterday's clumsy proposal.'

She was about to protest, but he raised his hand. 'I'm extremely sorry it was such a bad proposal. I'm not sure there was any right way to do it with Alfie in the picture—if I'd approached it differently, you might have felt manipulated. So I shouldn't have mentioned him but—'

'If you hadn't, I wouldn't have brought him up with Annie just now and we'd have probably lost him for sure.'

James nodded. 'The regret we all might have felt—'

'I understand.' She squeezed his hand. 'After what Annie had said, I was convinced adopting Alfie would be impossible. But then, knowing already how you and Tim felt, I decided it was worth the risk.'

'Well, something seems to have changed her mind.'

'Do you think it was related to bumping into her on the zoo trip? Because it was after that she took Alfie's photo in front of Tim. Do you think she wanted him to spill the beans since she'd stopped me from confiding in you?'

'There's no telling how her mind works,' James said in a bemused tone. 'Now...' He dropped to one knee.

'Would you like the ring back? You know, like on the clipboards when they're filming and they write "Take 2".'

He laughed. 'Go on then.' She passed him the ring, and he said, holding it out to her, 'Harmony Payne, I absolutely adore you. Please marry me. I promise I will cherish you for the rest of my life.'

Her heart swelled. 'Yes, I'll marry you! I've loved you for ages.'

'And I love you so, so much.' He slipped the ring back on her finger, where it belonged. 'If you'd like to choose a different ring—'

'No! I love it. Thank you.'

Sitting beside her again, he stretched his arm across her shoulder. 'Just as well I didn't make it back in time or I wouldn't have had the rings in my pocket. Candy would have put them in your room.'

So much had happened since Under the Stars restaurant. 'The stars are in alignment today, don't you think?' She was so happy, she felt as light as a helium balloon. Any more good things and she might float skywards.

'The stars are definitely in alignment. I met Miranda in the jeweller's shop getting a clasp repaired for Tom's mother.'

'What a coincidence.'

He nodded. 'After we realised the connection, Miranda let me push in.'

'Oh good. I'm glad you've met her.' She'd call her later to tell her everything, including that James had indeed pulled a rabbit out of the hat and the said rabbit was now sitting prettily on the third finger of her left hand. 'The treasure hunt, so romantic—'

He grinned. 'I remembered you like puzzles. Tim was a fantastic help and Candy, Ramesh, Perdita, the rest...'

'It's wonderful you and Tim found a project to work on together—and you've become part of the community here. I like that.'

'Perhaps *we* could do something together now?'

Her insides somersaulted. It was happening...

'Oh.' His face contracted with regret. 'I didn't have time to buy... and I wouldn't have wanted to presume...'

Her brow puckered. 'Are you suggesting a trip to the shops right now? To pay a visit to Ramesh perhaps?'

He snorted. 'No! Not Ramesh! But I just want to make sure you're happy with the situation. I've not been with anyone since...'

'Well, neither have I.'

'Then there's nothing stopping us...' he murmured.

'No, there's nothing stopping us...' Frantic butterflies fluttered in her belly.

James leaned back on the sofa. 'I wanted to invite you into my bed after the zoo trip. But I realised I needed to get new bedding and a new bed.'

'Because it was the marital bed?'

'Exactly.'

She touched his arm. 'I saw lots of new bedding on your bed the first time I came to dinner, but it wasn't there the next day.'

His cheeks became pink. 'I was worried you'd seen them and think I was being—'

'Presumptuous?'

'Exactly. So I hid them on the floor, the other side of the bed.'

She chuckled.

'The day I invited you for that no-notice dinner, I'd been chasing around shops to find a comfortable bed that could be delivered the same day.'

So that's what he'd been up to. 'Has it come?'

'No. The earliest I could have it was in ten days.'

She laughed. 'Some seduction plan.'

He chuckled. 'I know.'

'Well, as you're moving in, and I do have a brand new bed upstairs, perhaps you could cancel that other bed and we skip the ten-day wait?'

He nuzzled her neck. 'Sounds sensible.'

Gathering her to him, lightly brushing her lips with his, he teased her mouth with little kisses. Pressed against his cheek, rough with five o'clock shadow, her nostrils filled with the scent of cedarwood. As he languorously explored her mouth with his, waves of desire melted her as though she was a slab of butter left out in the hot sun.

While her fingers caressed the warm nape of his neck, she imagined what it would feel like to lie naked, her body becoming one with his.

He broke the kiss, leaving her breathless. 'I want you so badly,' he murmured.

'Me too.' But her throat constricted. 'It's been so long... I've got frantic butterflies in my stomach.'

'We can take it at your pace... I don't mind waiting, even though it's very hard.' He stroked her back, firing delicious ripples of sensation up and down her spine.

Waiting? 'That's... kind of you.' Reluctantly, she pulled far enough away to study his face. 'Have you changed your mind?'

'No.' Releasing her, his expression concerned, he said, 'But since you mention nerves... I've no idea what you like...'

'I think this might be the way to find out.' With her palm on his denim-clad thigh, she exerted enough pressure to confirm her intent.

James came in to kiss her again and, as it deepened, heat rushed downwards, consuming her with longing. She relaxed into him and the butterflies in her belly began to settle. 'Let's go upstairs.'

Gripping her hand, he helped her to her feet, and he didn't let go until they were in her bedroom—their bedroom. He tucked a stray lock of hair behind her ear. 'I'm going to help you out of your clothes.'

She nodded and swallowed her nervousness.

He unbuttoned her shirt and slipped it from her shoulders. She removed his shirt and the white T-shirt underneath. Desire swirled through her veins—but then she gasped.

'What is it?' he asked.

'Remember the viewing window in the sensory room?'

'Ye-s.'

'Katie's into astronomy and there's that big tree—'

'You're kidding, right?'

'She's got a powerful telescope. I could see the surface of the moon through it so viewing the inside of the house would surely be a doddle? Someone might have borrowed it if she's not into climbing trees herself.'

'I'll shut the curtains.'

'Duck first. You're not fully clothed. I wouldn't want them to—'

'You think they can't guess? Maybe not Alfie but—' He closed the curtains.

'It doesn't mean they have to have it confirmed. We'll make the bed up again as though it's never been used.'

He glanced at her askance. 'Isn't closing the bedroom curtains in the daytime, under the current circumstances, a signal to the entire community? As good as a radio broadcast. The kids can see the windows from—?'

'Oh. Yes, they can.'

'Do you want me to open the curtains again? I could have been trying them out, checking they were running smoothly.'

'Yes. And help me drag the mattress onto the floor. They won't be able to see—'

'This is fun,' he said.

'You won't be able to say it wasn't memorable.'

'There's a lot to do with you that's extremely memorable.'

They tugged the mattress and its bedding onto the floor on the side of the bed away from the window.

'Let's hope no one else wants a tour of the house before we make it look like nothing happened in here,' she said. 'And I hope Annie's not forgotten something and comes back.'

'I'll just tell her it's something engaged couples engage in.'

Harmony giggled.

'Is it always going to be like this?' he asked. 'Living in a goldfish bowl?'

'How about we put up net curtains? Then we only have to worry when the lights are on.'

'That will be one of my first jobs.'

'Let's get under the covers.' She slipped under the cool duvet, removing her jeans and socks.

'Are we undressing under the covers because of the children? I'm sure it would be impossible—?'

'No. I'm feeling shy.'

In his underwear, James joined her, his head next to hers on the pillow, the duvet up to their shoulders. 'Do we have a lock on the bedroom door?'

'You're worried they'll break in downstairs?'

'I'm worried there will be three children in the house and they'll burst in unexpectedly.'

'I get it,' she said. 'That'll be your first job. Nets second.'

'Deal.' He sat up. 'You didn't leave a window open downstairs, did you?'

Had she? 'We can check after. Crawl to the door, shut it and put the chair under the handle.'

James crawled around the room, following her instructions, and then slid back between the sheet and the duvet. 'That was a bit harsh on the knees. My skin's burning.'

'Sorry.' Would it spoil things…?

He stroked her temple and kissed her neck. 'So, it's definitely happening?'

'Mm…' Her lips twisted as though she was considering her answer.

'You don't seem so sure. I'm picturing a union representative on the factory floor who calls out, "Down tools!" Do you want me to stop?'

She gave a tinkling laugh. 'No. I just meant to be playful, that's all. It's definitely happening. Now.' Despite his sore knees.

Lying in his arms, consumed with happiness, she savoured the steady thump of James's heart and the soapy scent of his skin.

When she craned her neck to make eye contact, he raised an eyebrow. 'Well…?'

'Mm…' She pretended she was thinking about how to answer, but it had been wonderful, and she was floating in the clouds she'd been at risk of heading for earlier. She recalled the explosive ending of Igor Stravinsky's *Firebird Finale* that had not long ago played in her mind as her pleasure had become complete. 'It was lovely. I think I could be persuaded to do it again.'

'Right now?' He sounded disconcerted.

'A few minutes to recover?' she asked hopefully.

'That should be fine.'

'And how are your knees?'

He chuckled. 'This is more fun than worrying about carpet burns, thanks.'

'Was I completely out of practice or—?'

'It was well worth the wait.' He shifted onto his elbow and kissed her tenderly before breaking off to look seriously into her eyes. 'You'll still marry me?'

Her smile was slow in coming as she wanted to tease him some more. 'Yes, James, I'll still marry you.'

He lay back down and pulled her into his embrace again for another kiss. 'Yay,' he said softly. 'You're going to be my wife.'

'Yay,' she whispered back. 'You're going to be my husband.'

'And this husband-to-be is going to take a week off work to help us all get settled in.'

Epilogue

Three months later

The pretty, dainty notes of Luigi Boccherini's *Minuet* matched the lightness in Harmony's heart as she stepped towards James down the terracotta-carpeted aisle clutching Candy's arm, Alfie following as pageboy. Harmony passed by Mum, Dad, James's parents, Miranda, Lars—who was one of James's closest friends—and Saskia with Joshua, in the Mayoral Room of Bristol's Old Council House.

James's pale seersucker suit complemented her knee-length ivory shift dress and the ivory flower hairpins she'd found on Etsy to decorate the fancy plait up-do Saskia had created. He smiled the whole time it took her to reach him. Tim, his best man, was grinning too.

James squeezed her hand. 'You look absolutely lovely.'

She squeezed back. 'Thanks. You too.'

Last summer, she'd not imagined she'd soon have a husband as well as a family but, fifteen minutes later, that's what she had.

After signing the register, *Morning Mood* from Edvard Grieg's *Peer Gynt Suite No.1* struck up, representing the dawn of the new beginning of their lives. Tom, Perdita's photographer friend, snapped away with his camera and then everyone dispersed to make their way to Westbridge.

'You know,' James said as he sat at the front of the minibus next to Harmony, 'although I suggested we travel to the venue together so you needn't worry about my being late... or failing to put in an appearance... Well, we've exchanged vows now, and I'd like my freedom back.'

She hadn't taken any freedom away. 'What do you mean?'

'Tim's been keeping tabs on me. In fact, it feels like the whole Hall's been keeping tabs on me.'

'We have.' It was Alfie's voice from the row behind.

As Harmony swung around in synchrony with James, Tim elbowed Alfie in the ribs. 'It was supposed to be a secret.'

James chuckled. 'British Intelligence won't be recruiting from you lot.' He turned to Harmony. 'Did you know what they were doing? Were you the domestic equivalent of GCHQ?'

'No, of course not!'

'Boys,' he said. 'Can the spying stop now?'

Tim shrugged. 'I s'pose.'

Alfie shrugged too. 'I s'pose.'

James leaned over to kiss Harmony, his lips soft and caressing, filling her with the promise of another delectable night in bed.

'Dad! Can't you save that for when you're alone?'

Alfie giggled.

'You're going to have to get used to it,' James said. 'Men kiss their wives. Often.'

'I don't remember...' Tim broke off as though in confusion.

'This time around, it's going to be different. We will all show our love for one another as often as we feel we'd like to. That will include me kissing and hugging you, Alfie and Joshua.'

'You already do... now,' Tim grumbled, but with a smile on his face.

Saskia was minding Joshua on the other side of the minibus. 'Am I part of this family now? I'm at the house most days.' Her eyes were bright and wide as though she was expecting to be knocked back.

'You are,' Harmony said. 'But I don't think I'd approve of James hugging and kissing you.'

Saskia shuddered. 'I wouldn't either. But an occasional hug from you and saying something nice from time to time might be good.'

'Well,' Harmony said, 'although it's not usual for an employer—'

Saskia looked away. 'I understand.' Silver glistened on her lashes as bright sunlight streamed through the window.

'But I'm quite a casual employer, so I don't see why I wouldn't hug you sometimes. Haven't I already?'

Saskia beamed. 'I can't wait until our holiday.'

The original plan had been that only Harmony and James would go with Tim, Alfie and Joshua to Cornwall—to visit, among other places, the Eden Project.

'It would be a great educational opportunity for Tim and Alfie,' James had said. 'To learn about the diversity of flora and fauna in different climates.' Then he'd added, 'Why not go the whole hog and invite Patrick and Anil too, now that we've swapped the hybrid for a 9-seater?'

The vehicles had been switched after the cottage had been let. Having the extra boys was a good idea, but she wanted to have *some* time alone with James... 'In that case, let's invite Saskia along to help.'

'Sounds like a plan,' James had replied.

Now he put his arm around Harmony. 'I'm so in love with you—and so, so happy... Hey,' he said with a laugh, 'when Tom's got us the sample photos, should we choose one to send to Annie? To prove the deed is done?'

The notion appealed for all of two seconds. 'One must never antagonise a social worker, and she's on our side now. The Special Guardianship Order for Joshua came through yesterday, she's approved Patrik and Anil joining us on holiday, and Alfie's been placed with us pending formal adoption. She only needs a copy of the marriage certificate.'

When Candy stopped the minibus outside the Hall, Saskia said, 'Did someone forget to deliver the crisps on time? And why are they there?'

Harmony stood up to follow Saskia's gaze. A very large Walkers multipack crisps box had been left on the top step of the Hall. *Not another baby, surely?* Harmony was out first to peer inside, the others crowding around.

'So there aren't any crisps.' Saskia sounded disappointed.

Harmony touched Nana's folded crocheted blanket in disbelief. Surely David hadn't come here? But then the truth hit her. It hadn't been David who'd taken it from their flat but Melody. Although Harmony scanned the area, her sister was nowhere to be seen.

'It's the blanket Nana made for me when I graduated. It's been returned.' Harmony fished in the box for a note but found none. Well, Melody had done one right thing, and Harmony was grateful to have the blanket back. 'Melody must have brought it as my parents wouldn't had left it here.'

Candy glanced around. 'She's not still here, is she?'

'I doubt it.'

James carried the box into the office and then they trooped through to the rear garden, Harmony taking Joshua from Saskia. The guests who'd travelled by car from the Mayoral Room were already there. The marquee was decorated with bunting, fabric linings and flower displays.

Everyone had chipped in with the catering. Children and staff from the Hall, people from the area, Harmony and James's friends and family had come to celebrate. Saskia's grandfather, Roderick Walker, sporting a small moustache, was standing next to Violet, Perdita's aunt-in-law. Ramesh with his wife. Harmony had never had so many friends or felt so loved in the past few years as she did right now.

As she and James stepped onto the grass with champagne in hand, Joshua on her hip, everyone raised their glasses and shouted, 'To James and Harmony!'

'Money!'

Tom took a photo of them with Tim and Alfie before

Saskia walked Joshua to Roxy, who'd been clapping with the rest of them. Her face lit up as her son toddled towards her and she scooped him up for a kiss and a hug. Then she and Tony, who was beside her with Petal, exchanged happy smiles.

Alfie ran off to join Robbie, who was inspecting something in one hand, a magnifying glass in the other.

Ramesh came close. 'You see,' he told Harmony. 'I told you that James is the one.'

'You did indeed. Thank you, Ramesh.'

James coughed. 'He said that to you too?'

'You can't fight what's meant to be,' Ramesh said.

'Apparently not,' James agreed.

He grabbed Harmony's hand, raised their arms above their heads and kissed her. Everyone cheered. When her laughter settled, she cast around her. The grounds, the people, her family. Then there was an unfamiliar feeling in her heart. The clutching, burning angst of the past melted away, leaving peace and serenity. Erik Satie's *Gymnopédie No.1* began to play in her mind, and she took a moment to appreciate the slow, gentle music.

She knew that if she'd not been left at the altar all those years ago, she'd never have had a family like the one she had now or such a dedicated husband. She stretched to kiss James on the lips again. He pulled her close and her heart gave a little skip.

She'd found true love.

About the author

Mari Jane Law lives in the UK and loves cats and chocolate. She also loves books, TV series and films that make her laugh. Through her writing, she discovered she could make other people laugh too. She is a member of the Romantic Novelists' Association's New Writers' Scheme and The Society of Authors.

She hopes those who buy or borrow her work have as much fun reading it as she had in writing it.

There will be more to follow in the *Love & Mishaps* series, so you can meet some favourite characters again, to see how they're doing, as well as enjoy new quirky romance stories—happy ending guaranteed!

Reviews

If you enjoyed reading *Love & Misdirection*, please consider leaving a comment on Amazon and Goodreads to help other readers decide whether this book is for them, and to help the author!

Find out more at:
www.marijanelaw.com
X: www.twitter.com/MariJaneLaw1
Threads: https://www.threads.net/@marijanelaw
Facebook: www.facebook.com/marijane.law.1
Goodreads: https://tinyurl.com/566avtb6
Amazon author page: https://amzn.to/3lFWe2o
YouTube: www.tinyurl.com/2ryst3w9

Book One — Love & Pollination

Convent girl seeks love. But there are one or two hiccups...

Perdita Riley is facing the greatest dilemma of her life. Why had she taken Violet Freestone's advice on how to make herself look more alluring? It led her into the arms of a womaniser.

To cheer herself up, Perdita goes shopping, where an extraordinary encounter deposits her, literally, into the lap of Saul Hadley. She would like to stay there, but...

Will she find a way to deal with what has happened? Can she manage the complications of her growing attraction to Saul?

This hilarious situational romantic comedy will keep you gripped until the very end. *Shortlisted for Choc Lit's 2019 Search for a Star competition*

Paperback: ISBN-13: 978-1913410056

Paperback: ISBN-10: 1913410056

eBook: ASIN: B08772BTFZ

Buy it from Amazon: https://shorturl.at/esSzN

Book Two—Love in the Cupboard

A Catholic priest seeks a wife. A betrayed woman needs an honest man. What could possibly go wrong?

When Father Thomas Sheridan encounters Faith in a dark cupboard, he believes he's found his future wife. But Tom isn't brave enough to reveal his true identity...

When Faith meets Tom in the office kitchenette, she can't stand him. No matter, she's fallen for the mysterious man she met in the cupboard and can't wait to meet him again. Oh, and she's got a new rule: one lie and he's out. She's not getting duped again!

But everyone loves Tom. Her best friend, her chronically ill sister—who's on the lookout for a man herself. Even gay neighbours Luke and Gavin—who've fallen out over Luke wanting a baby. They urge Faith to give Tom a chance. But how can she have strong feelings for two men?

Even worse, how will she react when she discovers that Tom is the man in the cupboard—and, heaven forbid, a Catholic priest?

Readers' Favorite International Book Awards 2023 – Silver Medal – Fiction – Humor/Comedy
The Wishing Shelf Book Awards 2023 – Bronze Medal - Fiction

Paperback: ISBN-13: 979-8373616942
Paperback: ISBN-10: 8373616942
eBook: ASIN: B08772BTFZ
Buy it from Amazon: https://shorturl.at/vlPQk